AF173659

Lecture Notes of the Institute for Computer Sciences, Social Informatics and Telecommunications Engineering   648

The LNICST series publishes ICST's conferences, symposia and workshops.
LNICST reports state-of-the-art results in areas related to the scope of the Institute.
The type of material published includes

- Proceedings (published in time for the respective event)
- Other edited monographs (such as project reports or invited volumes)

LNICST topics span the following areas:

- General Computer Science
- E-Economy
- E-Medicine
- Knowledge Management
- Multimedia
- Operations, Management and Policy
- Social Informatics
- Systems

Hiep Xuan Huynh · Congduc Pham ·
Nghia Duong-Trung
Editors

Smart Objects and Technologies for Social Good

10th EAI International Conference, GOODTECHS 2024
Can Tho, Vietnam, December 19–20, 2024
Proceedings, Part I

 Springer

Editors
Hiep Xuan Huynh (iD)
Can Tho University
Can Tho, Vietnam

Congduc Pham (iD)
Université de Pau et des Pays de l'Adour
Pau, France

Nghia Duong-Trung (iD)
German Research Center for Artificial
Intelligence (DFKI)
Berlin, Germany

ISSN 1867-8211   ISSN 1867-822X (electronic)
Lecture Notes of the Institute for Computer Sciences, Social Informatics
and Telecommunications Engineering
ISBN 978-3-032-01471-9   ISBN 978-3-032-01472-6 (eBook)
https://doi.org/10.1007/978-3-032-01472-6

Preface

We are delighted to present the proceedings of the 10th EAI International Conference on Smart Objects and Technologies for Social Good (EAI GOODTECHS 2024), held on December 19–20, 2024, in Can Tho city, Vietnam. This event was graciously hosted by Can Tho University, bringing together researchers, developers, and practitioners from around the world to exchange insights and innovations aimed at enhancing social good through smart technologies.

EAI GOODTECHS 2024 received 102 submissions, out of which 44 high-quality papers were accepted after rigorous peer review. These papers highlight a wide range of advancements in smart technologies aimed at promoting social good. Key topics include cutting-edge research in Internet of Things (IoT) security, innovative applications of artificial intelligence in domains such as healthcare, education, and environmental monitoring, and energy-efficient systems. Contributions also explore advanced recommendation systems, deep learning techniques for object detection and image analysis, federated learning for privacy-preserving applications, and the integration of machine learning with domain-specific challenges like traffic monitoring, water level forecasting, and disease prediction. The diversity of these papers, presented across four focused tracks—IoT & Security, AI Applications I, AI Applications II, and AI Applications III—underscores the multidisciplinary nature of the conference and its commitment to addressing real-world challenges through smart and impactful technological solutions.

A highlight of the conference was the keynote address by My T. Thai, a distinguished University of Florida Research Foundation Professor of Computer & Information Sciences & Engineering and Associate Director of the Nelms Institute for the Connected World. Her keynote, titled "Interpretability and Privacy Preservation in Large Language Models (LLMs)," provided valuable insights into cutting-edge challenges and solutions in the realm of artificial intelligence.

EAI GOODTECHS 2024 also celebrated excellence in research by presenting two prestigious awards: the Best Long Paper Award and the Best Short Paper Award, recognizing outstanding contributions that push the boundaries of knowledge and innovation.

The success of this conference would not have been possible without the dedication and expertise of the Technical Program Committee and reviewers, representing 11 countries. We sincerely thank them for their efforts in ensuring the high quality of the program and their valuable contributions to the peer-review process. A special thank you is extended to Co-General Chair, Thuy Thanh Nguyen, Vietnam National University (VNU), Vietnam, for his exceptional leadership and support in making this event a success.

We are confident that the proceedings of EAI GOODTECHS 2024 provide a platform for the exchange of ideas and will inspire future research that addresses global challenges through smart technologies. We look forward to seeing how the work presented here will contribute to a better, more connected, and sustainable future.

August 2025

Hiep Xuan Huynh
Congduc Pham
Nghia Duong-Trung

Organization

General Chairs

Hiep Xuan Huynh   Can Tho University, Vietnam
Thuy Thanh Nguyen   Vietnam National University, Vietnam

Program Chair

Congduc Pham   Université de Pau et des Pays de l'Adour, France

Program Co-chair

Thanh-Nghi Do   Can Tho University, Vietnam

Web Chair

Huy Hoang Le Nguyen   Can Tho University, Vietnam

Publicity and Social Media Chairs

Jean-François Dorville   TCGNRG, Guadeloupe
Serge Stinckwich   United Nations University in Macau, China

Workshops Chairs

Mahamadou Traore   Université Gaston Berger Saint-Louis, Senegal
Vincent Rodin   Université de Bretagne Occidentale, France

Sponsorship and Exhibits Chairs

Onil Goubier   CIRELA, Indonesia
Tsimitomby Briand   Institut Supérieur de Technologie d'Antsiranana,
                                Madagascar

Publications Chair

Nghia Duong-Trung   German Research Center for Artificial
                                Intelligence, Germany

Local Chair

Hoa Huu Nguyen   Can Tho University, Vietnam

Technical Program Committee

Hiep Xuan Huynh   Can Tho University, Vietnam
Congduc Pham   Université de Pau et des Pays de l'Adour, France
Vincent Rodin   Université de Bretagne Occidentale, France
Serge Stinckwich   United Nations University in Macau, China
Jean-François Dorville   TCGNRG, Guadeloupe
Mahamadou Traore   Université Gaston Berger Saint-Louis, Senegal
Onil Goubier   CIRELA, Indonesia
Tsimitomby Briand   Institut Supérieur de Technologie d'Antsiranana,
                                Madagascar
Danh Le-Phuoc   Technische Universität Berlin, Germany
Nghia Duong-Trung   German Research Center for Artificial
                                Intelligence, Germany
Sergei Gorlatch   University of Münster, Germany
Bao Hoai Lam   Can Tho University, Vietnam
Dung Van Hoang   Ho Chi Minh City University of Technology and
                                Education, Vietnam
Nguyen Nhat Vo   University of Michigan, USA
Nhat Minh Viet Vo   Hue University, Vietnam
Khoi Tan Nguyen   University of Science and Technology, University
                                of Da Nang, Vietnam
Thang Cong Pham   University of Science and Technology, University
                                of Da Nang, Vietnam

Thuy Thu Thi Pham	Nha Trang University, Vietnam
Yen-Wen Chen	National Central University, Taiwan
Anh Viet Nguyen	Institute of Information Technology, Vietnam Academy of Science and Technology, Vietnam
Nghia Quoc Phan	Tra Vinh University, Vietnam
Vu Tran Pham	Ho Chi Minh City University of Technology, Vietnam National University, Vietnam
Xia Wang	German Research Center for Artificial Intelligence, Germany
Sheikh Faisal Rashid	German Research Center for Artificial Intelligence, Germany
Tung Kieu	Aalborg University, Denmark
Chinh Quoc Bui	Elsevier, Netherlands
Binh Thanh Nguyen	Monash University, Australia
Viet Xuan Le	Quy Nhon University, Vietnam
Lang Van Tran	Vietnam Academy of Science and Technology, Vietnam
Son Hoang Le	Information Technology Institute, Vietnam National University, Hanoi, Vietnam
Vinh Quoc Tran Nguyen	University of Science and Education, University of Da Nang, Vietnam
Toan Nang Do	Vietnam National University, Hanoi, Vietnam
Xuan Son Ha	RMIT University Vietnam, Vietnam
Binh Thanh Nguyen	Vietnam-Korea University of Information and Communication Technology, Vietnam
Anh Ngoc Nguyen	University of Science and Education, University of Da Nang, Vietnam

Contents – Part I

Contents – Part II

Advances in Artificial Intelligence, Machine Learning, and Blockchain Applications Across Diverse Domains

A Comparison of Deep Learning Models for White Blood Cell Detection

Hao Vu Le🆔 and Hieu Trung Huynh$^{(\boxtimes)}$ 🆔

Faculty of Information Technology, Industrial University of Ho Chi Minh City, Ho Chi Minh City, Vietnam
{levuhao,hthieu}@iuh.edu.vn

Abstract. White Blood Cell (WBC) detection is crucial in medical image processing. A higher accuracy result is better doctor assistance in disease diagnosis. Several methods in object detection have achieved some notable results. However, there are some limitations when applying those models in WBC detection from blood cell smear images because the level of similarity among blood cell types is high, which is a challenge for methods to separate them in analysis. This paper aims to evaluate promising models in WBC detection on a practical blood cell smear image dataset from Vietnamese hospitals. The modularized neck architecture, which allows flexible configuration of the backbone, neck, and detector modules, was utilized to speed up the implementation of the models. Four built models based on YOLOv3, Faster R-CNN, EfficientNet, and HRNet were evaluated on the dataset and achieved promising results with mAP(s) at 61.70%, 71.00%, 57.20%, 50.30% respectively. The result is a premise for further research of an automatic WBC detection system that assists doctors in blood cell examinations.

Keywords: White Blood Cell (WBC) · Object Detection · Deep learning · Medical Image Processing

1 Introduction

Imaging is a useful tool for doctors in disease diagnosis and treatment. Based on medical image analysis results, patient statuses from benign conditions to serious diseases causing concerns are often designated for further investigation. There are typical imaging modalities including (1) X-rays for examining unusual conditions of bone such as fractures, dislocations, or signs of bone diseases, (2) MRI scans for observation of soft tissues to detect abnormalities in organs, muscles, tendons, and ligaments, (3) CT scans are usually in the chest, abdomen, and pelvis investigation, (4) Ultrasound scans create images from high-frequency sound waves for imaging the tissues, organs, and other structures in the body. They are often used in organs, the reproductive system, and blood vessel exploration, (5) PET scans for capturing how organs and tissues are working to identify abnormal cell growth, such as tumors, (6) Blood smear images are used in blood cells analysis to detect abnormal cells [1, 2]. The manual analysis is time-consuming, thus it is necessary to have an automatic system to address these issues.

H. X. Huynh et al. (Eds.): GOODTECHS 2024, LNICST 648, pp. 3–15, 2025.
https://doi.org/10.1007/978-3-032-01472-6_1

Computers have had wide applications in recent years for medical image analysis. Many models based on convolutional neural networks (CNN) achieve high accuracies in different computer vision challenges, such as image classification, object detection, and segmentation. In image classification problems, CNNs are structured in hierarchical layers to extract features at different abstract levels and create good data representation for classifier heads in classification tasks. AlexNet [3], VGGNet [4], GoogLeNet [5], ResNet [6], and DenseNet [7] are well-known networks that produce high performance in computer vision challenges. In recent years, Vision Transformer (ViT) [8] and its improvements including Swin Transformer [9] have been widely used in computer vision as an alternative to convolutional networks. ViT divides images into patches and uses an attention mechanism to resolve computer vision problems such as image classification, object detection, and segmentation. Derived from their effectiveness, they are used as backbones in recently developed models.

There are two approaches to object detection, including one-stage object detector and two-stage object detector algorithms. The two-stage object detector is a classic method based on the region proposal algorithm implemented in popular networks such as R-CNN [4] and its brothers, including Fast R-CNN [10] and Faster R-CNN [11]. The detection process is divided into steps including feature extraction and classification based on object proposals in regions of interest. Two-stage object detectors are very effective and reach high accuracy with very high values of mAP. Therefore, they are usually applied to the medical domain where classification accuracy is a priority compared with speed. In contrast, the one-stage object detector trades off between performance and accuracy when directly using the extracted features for classification and bounding box coordinates regression. The remarkable one-stage object detector networks are YOLO and its variants [12–14], SSD [15], and RetinaNet [16].

Datasets of blood cell smear images are collected from microscopic images of blood cell smears. It is time-consuming and expertise is required to analyze blood cells on microscopic images. Automatic systems for addressing these issues are necessary. A potential approach is to apply deep learning to develop systems like that due to its power and success in various domains especially in medical image processing. However, one of the important limitations of WBC detection from blood cell smear images is the lack of a dataset for experiments. The public datasets are often small or cropped images of one cell not enough to train and evaluate the models. For the practical blood cell smear images, the similarity level among kinds of cells is close, making distinguishing between them challenging for existing models. It requires big enough and diverse datasets for training and evaluating the researched models. This paper assesses the existing models for extracting WBC from practical blood cell smear images collected from Vietnamese hospitals to establish a base for selecting and improving them in WBC detection problems.

The main contributions of this paper are as follows:

- An evaluation and comparison of popular object detection models on a practical blood cell smear image dataset making a premise for further research of a practical WBC detection system.
- A practical blood cell smear image dataset collected and prepared from Vietnamese hospitals.

- Applying the mechanism of the neck architecture to speed up the model implementation.

2 Related Work

One-stage and two-stage object detectors can use a common architecture, the neck architecture of object detectors [17]. The architecture consists of a backbone for feature extraction, a neck, and an object detector for locating and classifying objects. The first two components are common for one-stage and two-stage object detectors. The pipeline starts from the backbone where the feature maps are established from the input image at this component. Next, the neck incorporates the feature maps to provide to the detectors. One-stage detector locates and classifies objects in a phase. In contrast, the two-stage detector contains two phases: the first phase generates proposal bounding boxes, and the second phase detects objects by doing object classification and bounding box regression.

The backbone allows various selections of effective networks for feature extraction to find appropriate networks for observed datasets. There is a wide range of backbones for choosing the proper ones with particular advantages and disadvantages based on experiments on the specific dataset [18].

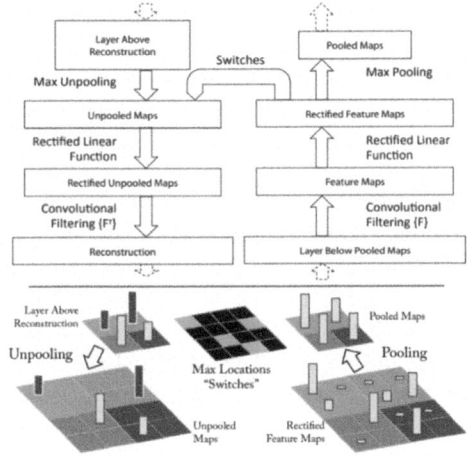

Fig. 1. Reconstruction of feature maps from higher-level features at a layer [19]

In the neck, approaches of multi-level feature integration from higher to lower levels to provide a good data presentation for heads have proven effective. At a layer, a deconvolutional network reconstructs an approximate version of the convolutional network features from the layer beneath [19] as shown in Fig. 1.

UNet [20] is a high-performance network in medical image segmentation using this idea in U-shape architecture. In this architecture, levels of features are constructed in the encoder (the left branch) by convolutional networks and the transposed convolutional networks of the decoder (the right branch) reconstruct the approximated features from the higher-abstract level features from the beneath layer of the decoder and the features from the corresponding layer of the encoder. For object detection tasks, Feature Pyramid Network (FPN) [21] is a popular option for the neck architecture implementation.

Hence, there is a range of selections for object detectors. The architecture can be comprised of one-stage object detectors such as YOLO, RetinaNet, SSD, etc., or two-stage object detectors such as R-CNN, Fast R-RCN, Faster R-CNN, etc. The neck architecture is a flexible architecture that is highly modularized allowing the evaluation of object detection methods smoothly. This paper utilizes its dynamic ability to investigate the models.

Many studies were conducted to differentiate types of blood cells from blood cell images. One of the approaches uses segmentation methods. A network based on UNet [20] was proposed to segment and classify the WBC of Alharbi et al. [22] on their dataset and achieved considerable accuracy. Using a combination of K-Means Clustering and Modified Watershed algorithms, Ghane et al. [23] gained promising results. In another approach using object detection for recognizing the blood cells, Kutlu et al. [24] developed a model based on R-CNN reaching a high performance on public datasets.

3   Methods

3.1   WBC Detection Model Architecture

The WBC detection model architecture used in this paper consists of three modules as shown in Fig. 2. Each module allows choosing different implementations. Implementation options for the first module, the backbone, are ResNet [6], Darknet [25], EfficientNet [26], or HRNet [27]. The backbone builds feature maps from the input blood cell smear image at several levels of abstraction. Next, the set of feature maps is passed to the second module working as a neck of the model. The neck is an option of networks based on the Feature Pyramid Network (FPN) [21] implemented for the corresponding selection of the network used in the backbone. The choices for the neck can be FPN, YOLOv3 Neck, or HRFPN. The neck integrates the feature maps before passing them as input for the last module. Finally, the head, the rear module, is a WBC detector employing an object algorithm to detect WBCs from input blood cell smear images. The outputs of the head are the WBC with bounding boxes. The WBC detection implementation selected is compatible with the backbone and the neck with options from RPN Head, YOLOv3 Head, and Retina Head.

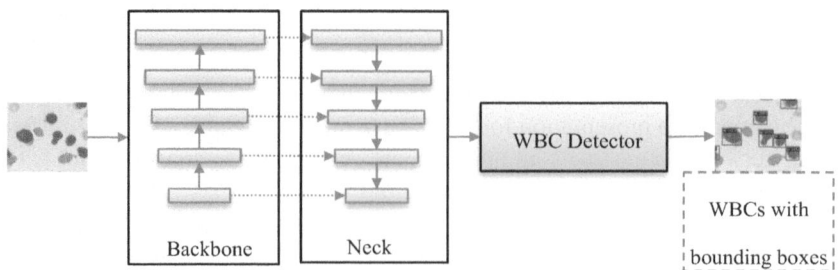

Fig. 2. WBC detection model architecture

3.2 Backbone

This section presents different architectures for the backbone component including ResNet, DarkNet, EfficientNet, and HRNet.

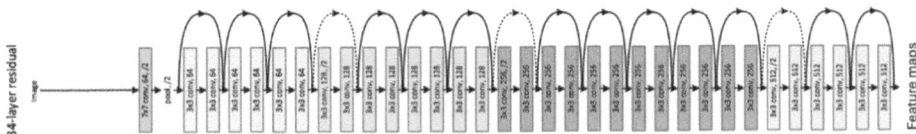

Fig. 3. Architecture of 34-layer ResNet [6]

In the backbone, the ResNet101 network is used in feature extraction. The suffix number in the network name denotes the number of network layers. A characteristic that makes ResNet effective is the combination of residual connections (another name is skip connection) for each of its residual blocks. The skip connections help to reduce the vanishing gradient issue. This mechanism ensures that the higher layers of the model perform the same efficiently as the lower layers of the model.

A 34-layer ResNet architecture is shown in Fig. 3. At the beginning of ResNet is a block consisting of a convolution layer and a pool layer to create 64-channel features in size of $\frac{W}{4}, \frac{H}{4}$, where W and H are the width and height of the input image. Next, the high levels of the features are constructed by the following convolutional blocks built by residual blocks. After a convolutional block, the number of channels is increased to an exponent of two while the sizes of the feature map are decreased by exponents of two. At the end of the network, a classifier consisting of an average pool layer and a fully connected is used for class prediction [28].

3.2.1 Darknet Architecture

Darknet is a convolutional neural network derived from the ResNet architecture. It has many versions and Darknet-53 is used as the backbone for WBC detection as shown in Fig. 4. Darknet-53 [25] built from 53 successive convolutional layers is more effective than Resnet101 and Resnet152. In the test models using equivalent state-of-the-art classifiers, the model using Darknet-53 reached a similar high accuracy with fewer floating-point operations and more speed compared to the ones using Resnet101 and Resnet152. That is mostly because Darknet-53 has fewer layers than ResNets.

3.2.2 EfficientNet Architecture

EfficientNets [26] is a family of models built by a new scaling method that uniformly scales all dimensions of depth/width/resolution using a simple yet highly effective compound coefficient. The scaling method is depicted in Fig. 5. From the effective baseline model, EfficientNet-B0, the other models in the EfficientNet family, which are named EfficientNet-B1 to EfficientNet-B7, are built based on the following equations:

$$depth : d = \alpha^{\emptyset},$$ (1)

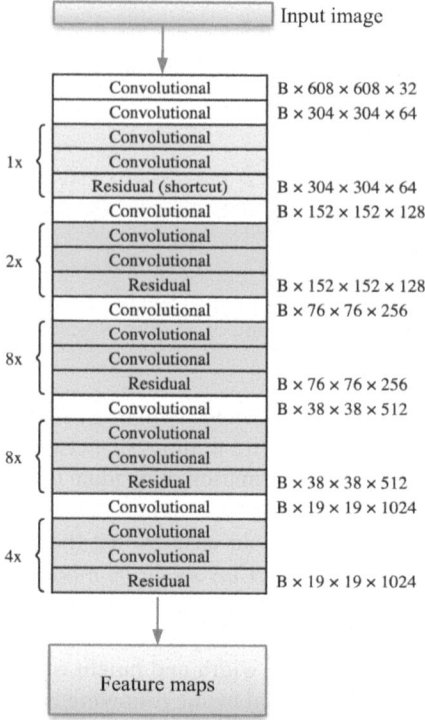

Fig. 4. Darknet-53 architecture [25]

$$width : w = \beta^{\emptyset}, \tag{2}$$

$$resolution : r = \gamma^{\emptyset}, \tag{3}$$

$$s.t. \ \alpha \cdot \beta^2 \cdot \gamma^2 \approx 2, \alpha \geq 1, \beta \geq 1, \gamma \geq 1$$

where α, β, γ are constants, ϕ is a user-specified coefficient. EfficientNet-B7 achieves 84.3% top-1 accuracy on ImageNet, while being 8.4x smaller and 6.1x faster on inference than the best existing CNNs.

3.2.3 HRNet Architecture

A traditional approach in image processing is to encode the input image as a low-resolution representation by a chain of high-to-low-resolution connected convolutions and then reconstruct the high-resolution representation from the encoded low-resolution representation. Instead, a High-Resolution Network (HRNet) [27] uses an advanced method to maintain high-resolution representations over the network. HRNet has two key characteristics: (i) Connects the high-to-low resolution convolution streams in parallel; (ii) Repeatedly exchange the information across resolutions. Its benefit is that the

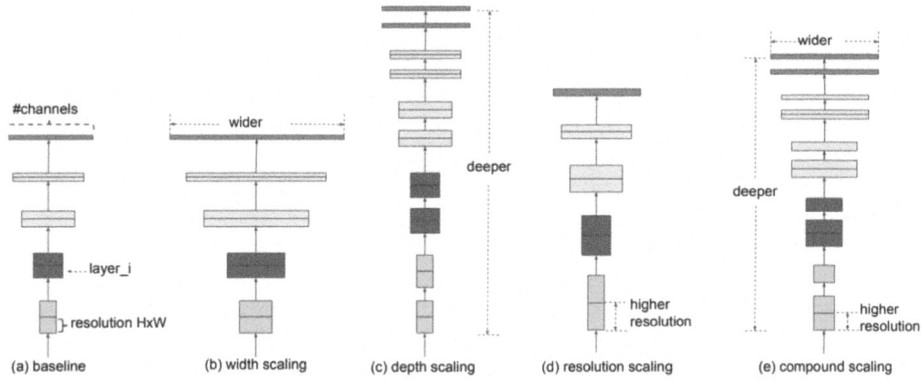

Fig. 5. Model Scaling. (a) is a baseline network example; (b)-(d) are conventional scaling that only increases one dimension of network width, depth, or resolution. (e) is a compound scaling method that uniformly scales all three dimensions with a fixed ratio [26].

resulting representation is semantically richer and spatially more precise. The architecture of HRNet as shown in Fig. 6 contains four stages. The first stage consisting of convolution layers builds the feature map from the input image at the highest resolution. After the first stage, two convolution layers are used to prepare the inputs for the second stage. The first convolution layer keeps the same resolution of the input, the second one decreases the resolution by one-quarter. The second stage contains two parallel streams of convolution layers corresponding to the inputs. The same method applies to the remaining streams with an extra stream for decreased resolution input.

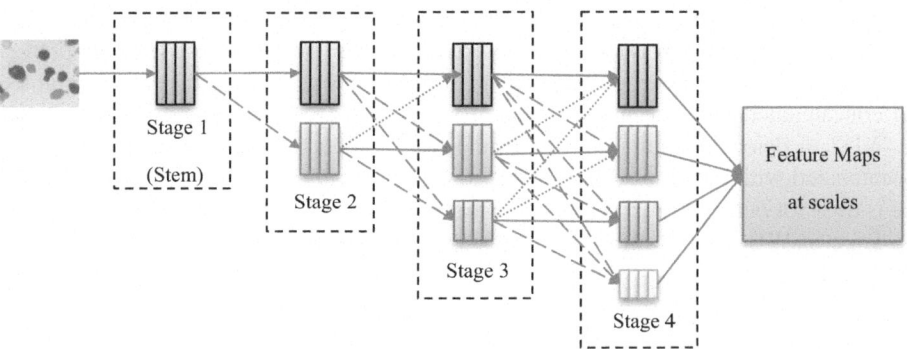

Fig. 6. HRNet with four stages. The 1st stage consists of high-resolution convolutions. The 2nd (3rd, 4th) stage repeats two-resolution (three-resolution, four-resolution) blocks.

3.3 Neck

In our study, neck architectures are applied including Feature Pyramid Network (FPN), YOLOv3 Neck, and High-resolution FPN. The FPN [21] is a popular option for neck

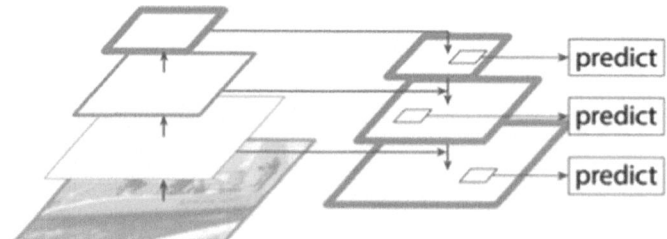

Fig. 7. FPN architecture

architecture implementation. It enhances a feature hierarchy model in top-down architecture with skip connections from the backbone. The FPN is a feature pyramid where predictions can be made independently at all levels as shown in Fig. 7. The YOLOv3 Neck is a simplified version of FPN that receives the feature map from the Darknet backbone, performs up-sampling and concatenation, and then passes the result to the WBC Detector. The HRFPN stands for High-Resolution Feature Pyramids [27] and is an FPN compatible with the backbone HRNet.

3.4   WBC Detector

Three architectures can apply for the WBC detector including YOLOv3, RPN, and Retina. They are able to detect blood cells at different scales.

3.4.1   YOLOv3 Head

YOLOv3 Head [25] has three WBC Detectors WD1, WD2, and WD3 for detecting WBCs at three scales. WD1 receives the feature map at the lowest scale to predict bounding boxes and classes of the small WBCs. The lowest feature map is up-sampled and concatenated with the feature map of the next higher scale to produce input for the WD2 to detect medium WBCs. Similarly, the input of WB2 is up-sampled and concatenated with the feature map of the next higher scale to build the input for WD3 that is used for detecting big WBCs. A combination of three sets of small, medium, and big detected WBCs is the final predicted result. The architecture of YOLOv3 Head is shown in Fig. 8.

3.4.2   RPN Head

Faster R-CNN combines a fully convolutional network for generating region proposals (RPN: Region Proposal Network) and Fast R-CNN detector [10] for object detection. The RPN takes the input image and proposes regions that are potential object-bounding boxes. Fast R-CNN detects objects in the proposed regions. RPN and Fast R-CNN share common convolutional computations resulting in computational time reduction. Faster R-CNN can detect small objects with high accuracy due to its algorithms. The architecture is shown in Fig. 9.

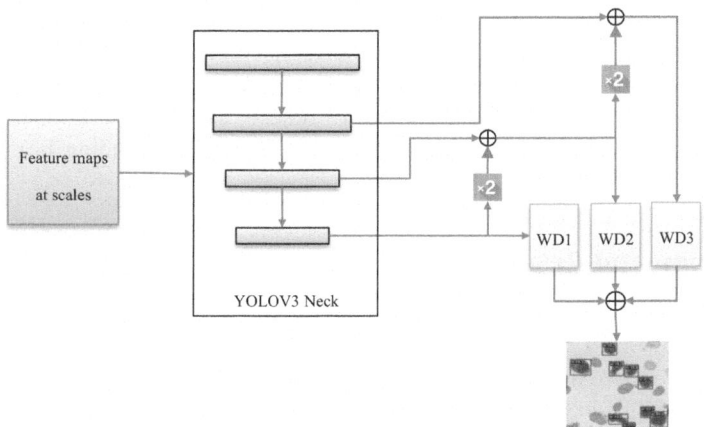

Fig. 8. YOLOv3 Head architecture

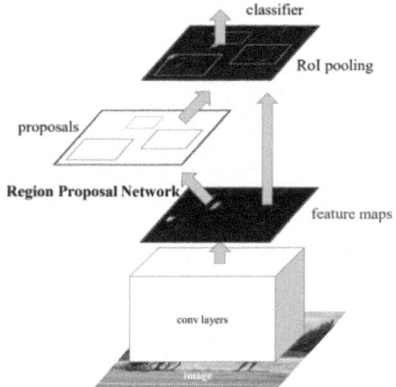

Fig. 9. Faster R-CNN architecture [11]

3.4.3 Retina Head

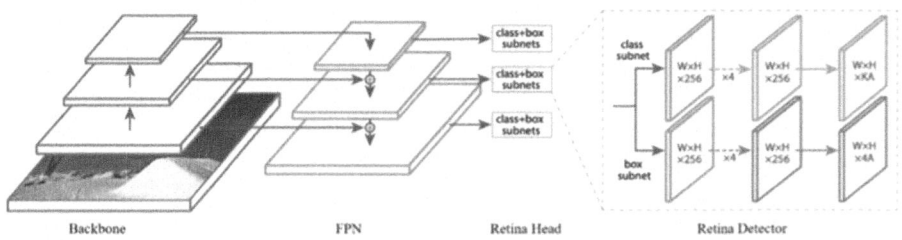

Fig. 10. Architecture of Retina Head [16]

Retina Head [16] consists of multiple Retina Detectors at different scales. Retina Detector has two components: a classification subnet and a box regression subnet. The classification subnet is a small fully convolutional network (FCN) attached to each level of FPN to predict appearance probabilities of objects at positions. Likewise, the box regression subnet is also implemented as a small FCN for bounding box regression (Fig. 10).

4   Experimental Results

4.1   Dataset

Our observations used the practical blood cell dataset collected from hospitals in Ho Chi Minh City. The dataset contains 2,493 blood smear images in JPG format with 992 × 692 pixels in size. The dataset is randomly split into three sub-datasets at a ratio of 8:1:1. They are the training dataset with 1,994 images, 249 images in the validation dataset, and the test dataset with 250 images.

4.2   Results and Discussion

Table 1. Architectures of the evaluated methods

Method	Backbone	Neck	WBC Detector
YOLOv3	Darknet-53	YOLOv3 Neck	YOLOv3 Head
Faster R-CNN	ResNet101	FPN	RPN Head
EfficientNet	EfficientNet-B3	FPN	Retina Head
HRNet	HRNet	HRFPN	RPN Head

The architectures of the methods are depicted in Table 1. Due to compatibility, the backbone is the most important module that decides the selections of the remaining modules. Therefore, YOLOv3 and HRNet use their specific necks and detectors. Faster R-CNN and HRNet use a common RPN Head. Faster R-CNN and EfficientNet can share a common FPN. The models were implemented with PyTorch on an NVIDIA QUADRO RTX A4000 with 16 GB of memory and trained on the same dataset.

Table 2 illustrates the performance of the methods on the test dataset. Although some efforts are needed to improve performance, the methods are promising for application to WBC detection from our blood cell dataset.

Faster R-CNN outperforms the remaining methods and achieves the highest accuracy on all metrics. The good correlation between accuracy indices mAP_{50} and mAP_{75} shows the stability of the model in detecting correct WBC with thresholds at 50% and 70%. However, mAP should be considered when it is quite lower than mAP_{50} and mAP_{75}. It means the model needs improving to get higher performance. Among accuracy indices of WBC size $mAPS$, mAP_M, and mAP_L, mAP_M is an important index because the majority of WBC is medium size. The mAP_M value is promising and should be improved. YOLOv3 takes second place in the performance testing. Due to their one-stage object

Table 2. Performance comparison of the methods on the test dataset

Method	mAP	mAP$_{50}$	mAP$_{75}$	mAP$_S$	mAP$_M$	mAP$_L$
YOLOv3	61.70%	87.40%	76.00%	47.70%	65.50%	19.00%
Faster R-CNN	**71.00%**	**89.00%**	**85.50%**	**56.80%**	**74.20%**	**23.80%**
EfficientNet	57.20%	79.00%	71.20%	35.20%	63.30%	1.00%
HRNet	50.30%	86.10%	58.00%	35.00%	54.00%	9.70%

detector architecture, YOLO family models often speed faster than two-stage object detector models. However, YOLO models have some constraints in small object detection. The accuracy indices of YOLOv3 are close to the ones of Faster R-CNN. Thus, YOLO is a promising architecture for further attempts when big improvements in recent versions of YOLO family model. HRNet produces high performance on tests with high-resolution images such as X-ray images. However, its effectiveness does not show on the blood cell smear images with low resolution. EfficientNet is assessed with EfficientNet-B3 which may not be optimum for the blood cell smear images. A further test may be carried out by using other models in the EfficientNet family to observe performance effects on the blood cell dataset.

Intuitively, it is difficult to differentiate the blood cells in the blood cell images for detecting WBCs because of their similarities as shown in Fig. 11. It is a challenge for the future research model based on observed methods.

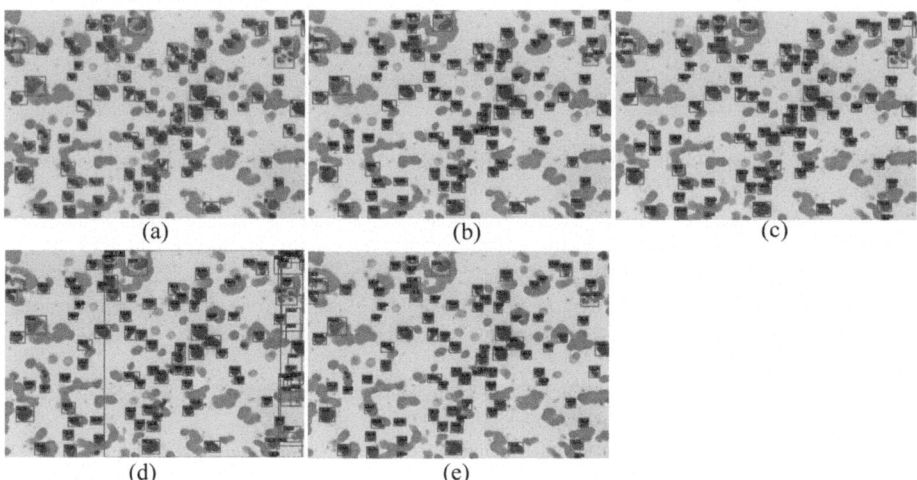

(a)   (b)   (c)

(d)   (e)

Fig. 11. Visualize the predictions from the methods: (a) the ground truth of the bounding boxes on the input image, (b) the bounding boxes predicted by YOLOv3, (c) the bounding boxes predicted by Faster R-CNN, (d) the bounding boxes predicted by EfficientNet, (e) the bounding boxes predicted by HRNet.

The WBC detection architecture based on neck architecture is flexible and easy to upgrade due to its modularized characteristics. Each module in the architecture can be upgraded independently without affecting the remaining modules. Two modules we should focus on upgrading to improve the performance of the whole model are the backbone and the detector. Emerging and innovative mechanisms can be invented and applied to the backbone to build feature maps for better input data representation for subsequent modules. The novel box classification and regression methods can be employed in the detector to improve prediction accuracy.

5 Conclusion

Object detection is a popular problem in computer vision and is widely applied to numerous fields. However, object detection is a difficult task with many challenges to reach high performance in specific datasets. Especially, there are some limitations of accuracy in detecting WBC in blood cell images due to image complexities where the blood cells have high similarities. This paper tried to evaluate presentative methods on our dataset to have a quick observation and some bases for WBC detection research in the future.

In the future, the integrations of the state-of-the-art models and the neck architecture are focused on researching to have broader effective evaluations that provide more options in model selection for building the automatic WBC detection.

Disclosure of Interests. The authors have no competing interests to declare that are relevant to the content of this article.

References

1. Abnormal Imaging|SMC Physicians, New Jersey. https://smc-physicians.com/service/abn ormal-imaging-nj/
2. Chen, Y.-M., Tsai, J.-T., Ho, W.-H.: Automatic identifying and counting blood cells in smear images by using single shot detector and Taguchi method. BMC Bioinform. **22**, 635 (2022). https://doi.org/10.1186/s12859-022-05074-2
3. Krizhevsky, A., Sutskever, I., Hinton, G.E.: ImageNet classification with deep convolutional neural networks. In: Advances in Neural Information Processing Systems. Curran Associates, Inc. (2012)
4. Simonyan, K., Zisserman, A.: Very Deep Convolutional Networks for Large-Scale Image Recognition, http://arxiv.org/abs/1409.1556 (2015)
5. Szegedy, C., et al.: Going Deeper with Convolutions. http://arxiv.org/abs/1409.4842 (2014)
6. He, K., Zhang, X., Ren, S., Sun, J.: Deep Residual Learning for Image Recognition. http://arxiv.org/abs/1512.03385 (2015)
7. Huang, G., Liu, Z., Maaten, L. van der, Weinberger, K.Q.: Densely Connected Convolutional Networks. http://arxiv.org/abs/1608.06993 (2018)
8. Dosovitskiy, A., et al.: An Image is Worth 16×16 Words: Transformers for Image Recognition at Scale. http://arxiv.org/abs/2010.11929 (2021)
9. Liu, Z., et al.: Swin Transformer: Hierarchical Vision Transformer using Shifted Windows. http://arxiv.org/abs/2103.14030 (2021)

10. Girshick, R.: Fast R-CNN. In: 2015 IEEE International Conference on Computer Vision (ICCV), pp. 1440–1448 (2015)
11. Ren, S., He, K., Girshick, R., Sun, J.: Faster R-CNN: towards real-time object detection with region proposal networks. In: Advances in Neural Information Processing Systems. Curran Associates, Inc. (2015)
12. Wang, A., et al.: YOLOv10: Real-Time End-to-End Object Detection. http://arxiv.org/abs/2405.14458 (2024)
13. Ge, Z., Liu, S., Wang, F., Li, Z., Sun, J.: YOLOX: Exceeding YOLO Series in 2021. http://arxiv.org/abs/2107.08430 (2021)
14. Redmon, J., Divvala, S., Girshick, R., Farhadi, A.: You Only Look Once: Unified, Real-Time Object Detection. http://arxiv.org/abs/1506.02640 (2016)
15. Liu, W., et al.: SSD: Single Shot MultiBox Detector. Presented at the October 8 (2016)
16. Lin, T.-Y., Goyal, P., Girshick, R., He, K., Dollár, P.: Focal Loss for Dense Object Detection. http://arxiv.org/abs/1708.02002 (2018)
17. Bouraya, S., Belangour, A.: Deep Learning based Neck Models for Object Detection: A Review and a Benchmarking Study. IJACSA. 12 (2021). https://doi.org/10.14569/IJACSA.2021.0121119
18. Elharrouss, O., Akbari, Y., Almadeed, N., Al-Maadeed, S.: Backbones-review: feature extractor networks for deep learning and deep reinforcement learning approaches in computer vision. Comput. Sci. Rev. **53**, 100645 (2024). https://doi.org/10.1016/j.cosrev.2024.100645
19. Zeiler, M.D., Fergus, R.: Visualizing and Understanding Convolutional Networks. In: Fleet, D., Pajdla, T., Schiele, B., Tuytelaars, T. (eds.) Computer Vision – ECCV 2014, pp. 818–833. Springer International Publishing, Cham (2014)
20. Ronneberger, O., Fischer, P., Brox, T.: U-Net: Convolutional Networks for Biomedical Image Segmentation. http://arxiv.org/abs/1505.04597 (2015)
21. Lin, T.-Y., Dollár, P., Girshick, R., He, K., Hariharan, B., Belongie, S.: Feature pyramid networks for object detection. In: 2017 IEEE Conference on Computer Vision and Pattern Recognition (CVPR), pp. 936–944 (2017)
22. Alharbi, A.H., Aravinda, C.V., Lin, M., Venugopala, P.S., Reddicherla, P., Shah, M.A.: Segmentation and classification of white blood cells using the UNet. Contrast Media Mol. Imaging **2022**, 5913905 (2022). https://doi.org/10.1155/2022/5913905
23. Ghane, N., Vard, A., Talebi, A., Nematollahy, P.: Segmentation of white blood cells from microscopic images using a novel combination of k-means clustering and modified watershed algorithm. J. Med. Sig. Sens. **7**, 92 (2017)
24. Kutlu, H., Avci, E., Özyurt, F.: White blood cells detection and classification based on regional convolutional neural networks. Med. Hypotheses **135**, 109472 (2020). https://doi.org/10.1016/j.mehy.2019.109472
25. Redmon, J., Farhadi, A.: YOLOv3: An Incremental Improvement. http://arxiv.org/abs/1804.02767 (2018)
26. Tan, M., Le, Q.V.: EfficientNet: Rethinking Model Scaling for Convolutional Neural Networks. http://arxiv.org/abs/1905.11946 (2020)
27. Wang, J., et al.: Deep High-Resolution Representation Learning for Visual Recognition. http://arxiv.org/abs/1908.07919 (2020)
28. ImageNet. https://www.image-net.org/

An Integration of VGG19 and SARIMAX in Water Level Forecasting Using Satellite Imagery and Time Series Data

Hoang Thi Minh Chau[1,2], Tran Thi Ngan[3(✉)], Nguyen Long Giang[4], Tran Kim Chau[5], Hoang Duc Trung[6], and Ton Nu Mai Khanh[6]

[1] Graduate University of Science and Technology, Vietnam Academy of Science and Technology, Hanoi 100000, Vietnam
htmchau@uneti.edu.vn

[2] Faculty of Information Technology, University of Economics Technology for Industries, Hanoi 100000, Vietnam

[3] International School, Vietnam National University, Hanoi 100000, Vietnam
ngantt@vnuis.edu.vn

[4] Institute of Information Technology, Vietnam Academy of Science and Technology, Hanoi 100000, Vietnam
nlgiang@ioit.ac.vn

[5] Faculty of Water Resources Engineering, Thuyloi University, Hanoi 100000, Vietnam
kimchau_hwru@tlu.edu.vn

[6] Artificial Intelligence Research Center, VNU Information Technology Institute, Vietnam National University, Hanoi 100000, Vietnam
hoangductrung_t65@hus.edu.vn, tnmkhanh0129@gmail.com

Abstract. Climate change and global population growth have intensified extreme weather events such as floods and droughts. These kinds of events make forecasting process difficult and cause significant damages. To overcome these challenges, hydroelectric reservoirs have been constructed to store water for production, flood control, and electricity generation. In this research, we present an integrated forecasting framework that combines the modern Visual Geometry Group Network-19 and Seasonal AutoRegressive Integrated Moving Average with eXogenous factors to process multi-source data, including numerical data and satellite imagery. Experimental results from the An Khe hydroelectric reservoir in Vietnam demonstrate that this forecasting framework achieves higher accuracy compared to traditional models, highlighting that the integration of multiple data sources significantly enhances the forecasting performance. The proposed framework achieves a smaller prediction error compared to traditional models of 11.7% for MAE, 26.8% for MSE, and 14.5% for RMSE.

This research is supported by the project "Research on developing surface water resouces forecasting technology to ensure national water security. Application for the Central Highlands region" - Project ID: TNMT.2023.02.27.

H. X. Huynh et al. (Eds.): GOODTECHS 2024, LNICST 648, pp. 16–28, 2025.
https://doi.org/10.1007/978-3-032-01472-6_2

Keywords: VGG19 · SARIMAX · An Khe reservoir · Multi-source data · Water level forecasting

1 Introduction

The construction of hydroelectric reservoirs/dams plays a pivotal role in efforts to combat global climate change and promote sustainable economic and social development. However, the safe operation of hydroelectric systems and reservoirs is significantly affected by the variability and continuous changes in annual rainfall [1]. Water level forecasting is a crucial factor in mitigating the impact of external factors on hydroelectric dams, enhancing system reliability, and increasing the level of integration of hydroelectric systems [2].

Remote sensing, particularly through satellite imagery, has become an essential tool in water level forecasting due to the ability to provide rich and detailed spatial information about the Earth's surface [3–5]. Devices such as satellites, drones, and aerial sensors are enable continuously monitoring of changes in water surface areas, soil moisture, and ecosystem dynamics around reservoirs. This capability allows researchers to predict the areas at risks of flooding, drought, or other water level fluctuations [6–8]. The use of deep learning models, such as VGG19, has proven the effects in extracting relevant features from satellite images, including detecting the changes in surface water and identifying shorelines and river boundaries [9,10].

Time series data, on the other hand, offer continuous information on variables, such as water levels, rainfall, stream flow, and temperature, which are typically gathered from monitoring stations or automated measurement systems. Time series data allow models to recognize trends, seasonal cycles, and correlations between past and present values [11–14]. Seasonal AutoRegressive Integrated Moving Average with eXogenous regressors (SARIMAX) is one of widely used statistical models for time series forecasting. SARIMAX has demonstrated great efficacy in handling time series data with both seasonality and external influencing factors [15].

Recent studies have shown the benefits of utilizing multi-source data for water level forecasting. In 2021, Jiang *et al.* [16] applied a multi-source data fusion approach to forecast urban sewer network water levels. Ahmed *et al.* [17] proposed a deep learning method that incorporates rainfall and river water levels to predict river levels. Burrichter *et al.* [18] developed a spatiotemporal deep learning model using weather and topographical data to forecast urban flooding. These examples emphasize the importance of integrating various data types to enhance the accuracy in forecasting and making decisions in hydrology and risk management.

In this research, an integrated framework used to deal with forecasting problem using multi-source data is introduced. The proposed framework combines the advanced VGG19 network and the SARIMAX model to forecast the reservoir water level. Multi-source data consist of satellite image data set and time series data of An Khe reservoir, Viet Nam. By implementation, proposed model is compared to the original SARIMAX model for time series dataset. The results show that the proposed model gets higher performance.

The remaining parts of this paper include 4 sections. Section 2 presents the basic models and measurements. Section 3 describes proposed integrated model. Experimental results are given in Sect. 4. Discussions and conclusions are presented in the last section.

2   Preliminaries

In this section, the research area is stated. Two base models in our framework, VGG19 network and SARIMAX model and the validity indices are also briefly presented.

In this research, An Khe hydroelectric Reservoir, a key component of the An Khe-Ka Nak hydroelectric system is selected. This region plays an important role in supplying energy to the region. Located within a rugged and complex mountainous terrain, the reservoir frequently faces harsh weather conditions and unpredictable climate changes, posing significant challenges to its operation.

VGG19 Network:
Karen Simonyan and Andrew Zisserman created a type of CNN model known as Visual Geometry Group Network (VGG) [19]. VGGNet performs well in ImageNet's data clusters. There are five construction components in VGG19. The first and second building blocks have two convolutional layers and one pooling layer, respectively. The third and fourth blocks contain four convolutional layers and one pooling layer. The final block has four convolutional layers and small 3×3 filters.

SARIMAX Model:
The SARIMAX [20] extends the SARIMA model by using exogenous factors in order to improve forecasting accuracy. This multivariate form of SARIMA model, dubbed Seasonal ARIMA with eXogenous factor. In SARIMAX models, to select the best model, the value of Akaike Information Criterion (AIC) is calculated with the different parameters as in Eq. (1). The smallest value of AIC indicates the best model.

$$AIC = 2k - 2\ln(L) \tag{1}$$

Where k denotes for the number of estimated parameters in the model. L is the model's log-likelihood function, which measures how well the model matches the data.

Validity Indices:
Single statistical indices are not suitable for evaluating hydrological models. Therefore, in this research, three different measurements, including the mean absolute error (MAE), the mean squared error (MSE), and the root mean square error (RMSE) are selected to assess the performance of proposed model. The mathematical formulas of these metrics are presented in equations (2) - (4) below.

$$MAE = \frac{1}{n} \sum_{i=1}^{n} |D_i - \hat{D}_i| \tag{2}$$

$$MSE = \frac{1}{n} \sum_{i=1}^{n} (D_i - \hat{D}_i)^2 \tag{3}$$

$$RMSE = \sqrt{\frac{1}{n} \sum_{i=1}^{n} (D_i - \hat{D}_i)^2} \tag{4}$$

Where n is the number of data points; D_i is the actual value at the ith data point; $\hat{D}_i$ is the predicted value at the ith data point.

3   Proposed Forecasting Framework

The proposed forecasting framework is shown in Fig. 1. In this approach, Sentinel-2 satellite images and operational data from the reservoir, collected from the An Khe reservoir area in different points of time, are used as input data. These two datasets require to be processed before running model (Sect. 3.1). After pre-processing, the new image dataset is fed into the VGG19 model (presented in 3.2) in order to produce image feature vector. The preprocesed time series dataset is sent to a fully connected layer to get a time series feature vector (indicated in 3.3). The concatenation is performed on two obtained feature vectors by normalizing them and then merging them horizontally as a new feature vector (Sect. 3.4). This unique feature vector is used as the input of SARIMAX model (Sect. 3.5). The output of whole progress is predicted water level.

3.1   Data Processing

There are two separate progresses for imagery data set and time series data set.

Satellite Image Data Processing:
Sentinel-2 images of An Khe reservoir area are taken from the website: "https://browser.dataspace.copernicus.eu/" (illustrated by Fig. 2). In time duration from 1/1/2019 to 31/12/2022, only images with clear views of the reservoir are taken. The reason of choosing only clear view pictures is to improve model performance in terms of:

Model Accuracy: Images with clear perspectives enable the model to effectively identify key features of the objects, thereby improving accuracy in classification or recognition tasks. Otherwise, images with blurred or unclear perspectives hinder the model's ability to detect features accurately, potentially leading to erroneous results.

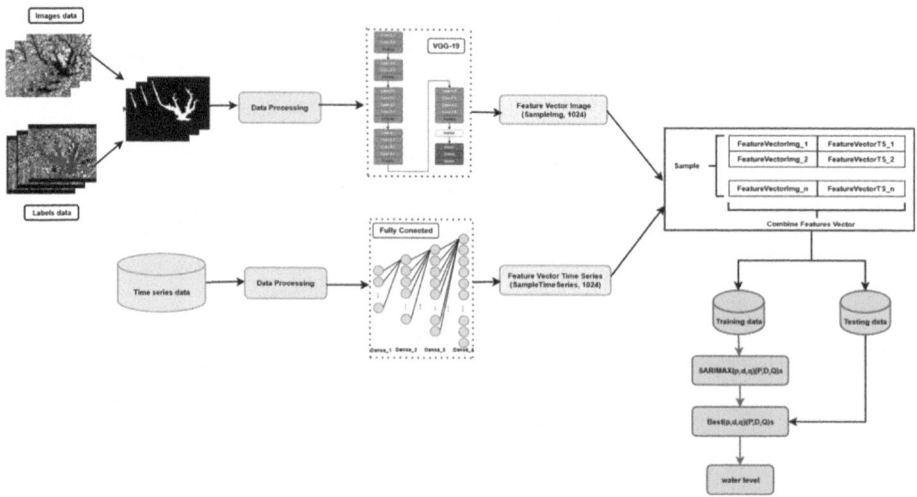

Fig. 1. Framework of proposed model

Complexity Reduction: Using only images with clear perspectives reduces the complexity of the model. Unclear images or those with incomplete perspectives require additional complex algorithms to enhance recognition capabilities, which increase computation time and resource usage.

Better Model Training: Training the model on high-quality images allows it to learn more accurate features, thereby improving its generalization ability and performance when applied to real-world scenarios.

Fig. 2. The source of Sentinel-2 images

The collected images will be cropped to focus on An Khe reservoir region by using SNAP software. The coordinates of the reservoir area are defined. The

RGB color image set is obtained as illustrated in Fig. 3. The final result of preprocessing includes 18 high-resolution RGB images of the reservoir.

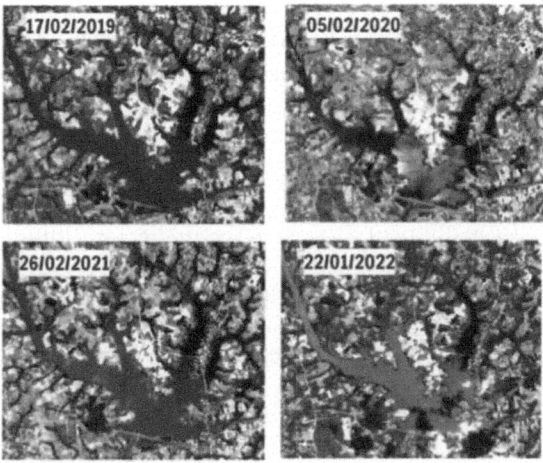

Fig. 3. Example of Sentinel-2 images of the An Khe reservoir.

We labeled the obtained images by CVAT tool that is available on the website "https://www.cvat.ai/". Figure 4 illustrates the annotated images, with the boundary points, considered as the mask, to construct a perimeter around the target objects. The assigned labels are stored in form of a .txt file.

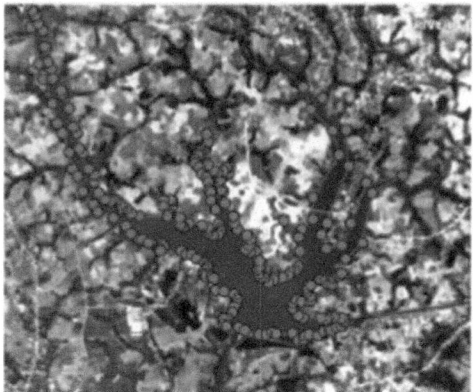

Fig. 4. Labeling reservoir area on the images.

The process of labeling by drawing boundaries to identify objects in an image is a standard approach in many computer vision tasks, particularly in segmentation problems. Mapping labeled pixel values onto the original image to generate a mask is a logical and widely adopted method. Assigning a pixel value of 0 to the object and 255 to the background is a common practice in pixel-level classification tasks (segmentation).

Converting an image to grayscale is a reasonable approach in this context. Since the mask image contains only two pixel values (0 and 255), converting to grayscale (a single channel with values ranging from 0 to 255) reduces data complexity without losing important features. This explanation is logical and clarifies the rationale for using grayscale to simplify the training process while preserving the necessary information.

These mask images are converted to a grayscale scale images. Next, all the images are resized to a uniform size of $320 \times 320 \times 1$. Minimum Mean Square Error (MMSE) estimator is applied to restore image quality and reduce noises for enhancing clarity. Additionally, multi-point interpolation is performed to supplement missing data. This imputation aims to ensure that each month of the year has one representative image. The main steps of this process include:

- *Step 1:* Conduct a statistical analysis of the number of images for each month to identify the missing months for each year.
- *Step 2*: Interpolation is applied based on the Pearson correlation coefficient. In this step, monthly images from previous years are used to interpolate for the missing month of the current year.

The output of interpolation includes 30 mask images for the months that were previously missing. After interpolating, total number of mask images is 48. To smooth the data, all these images will be passed through a filter, along with indexing the corresponding time for each month of the years on images. MinMax scaling is applied as data normalization by using libraries in Python programming language.

Time Series Data Processing:
The hydrological time series data for the reservoir was collected from 1/1/2019 to 31/12/2022. The data is collected hourly. After averaging the data fields by day, this dataset includes 1,461 samples indexed sequentially by day.

In the case of the An Khe region, the flood season can significantly impact the reservoir's water levels. The flood season typically lasts from May to October every year, while the remaining months are generally considered the dry season. Consequently, data during the flood season exhibit different characteristics compared to those outside it. If the input data do not differentiate between seasons (flood or dry), the model may encounter difficulties in accurately forecasting water levels, as these factors can have varying impacts depending on the season.

3.2   VGG19 Network Implementation

The input for the VGG19 model is a set of 48 mask images of the An Khe reservoir with dimensions (320, 320, 1). The VGG19 model is configured with parameters that are set for each block. The parameters corresponding to the convolution layers include the number of filters, the size of the kernel, and the activation function. The convolution layers within the same block share the same parameters. The parameter sets for the blocks are as follows:

– Block 1 [64, (3, 3), relu],
– Block 2 [128, (3, 3), relu],
– Block 3 [256, (3, 3), relu],
– Block 4 [512, (3, 3), relu],
– Block 5 [512, (3, 3), relu].

Each convolution block is followed by a MaxPooling layer.

Subsequently, there are Fully Connected (FC) layers, with the following parameter sets in form of (Units, Activation), including (4096, relu), (4096, relu) and (1024, relu). Whenever a feature is extracted through the convolution layers, padding = 0 is added to the images to maintain the dimensions. VGG19 produces the features, in the shape of 48×1024, for each image.

3.3 Fully Connected Model Implementation

The input for the Fully Connected (FC) model consists of a CSV file containing 1,461 data entries with two attributes: Inflow (m^3/s) and Total Discharge (m^3/s) [Actual]. This file is used to extract features from the time series data. The Water Level (m) will be served as the target label for the dataset.

The FC model utilizes 4 layers with the following parameter sets of (Units, Activation): (128, relu), (256, relu), (512, relu), and (1024, relu). The output of the model comprises the features for each data entry over time, resulting in a size of (1461, 1024).

3.4 Concatenation of Image Feature Vectors and Numerical Feature Vectors

Normalizing Image Features and Time Series Data:
In our experiments, image data set includes 1024 features and 48 samples. Each sample is an image representing a month. The initial time series data has 1461 samples. To combine these two types of features, it is necessary to increase the number of samples in image data set to the same size as time series data. In this case, an image feature sample, representing one month, will be replicated for all days within that month. This creates a new feature set for images with a size of (1461, 1024).

Feature Combination:
After normalization, the image features have a size of (1461, 1024) and the time series features have a size of (1461, 1024). To concatenate these two types of features, we use the horizontal concatenation operation. This means keeping the number of days (1461) unchanged while doubling the number of features from 1024 to 2048 (combining image features and time series features). After

concatenation, the resulting feature set has a size of (1461, 2048).

Create Data Batches and Labels:
To prepare the data for training, we create data batches with a time step of 4 and a stride of 1. Each data batch consists of 4 consecutive time steps. For example, the batch at time t will include data at time steps t-3, t-2, t-1, and t. The output of model for this batch is the water level at time t+1.

Data Splitting:
After creating batches and labels, the data is divided into three sets: training set, validation set, and test set with corresponding ratios of 70%, 20%, and 10%. The final result is a combined dataset of image features and time series data, with batches and labels prepared for the model training process to predict reservoir water levels.

3.5   SARIMAX Model Implementation

The input data for the SARIMAX$(p, d, q)(P, D, Q)s$ model contains multiple feature columns, and the label is 'Label', which includes a single column to be predicted, 'Reservoir Water Level (m)'. The data is used to train the SARIMAX model and forecast the 'Label'. We perform the process to identify the optimal parameters for the SARIMAX model. Based on the characteristics of the data, the seasonal value is determined to be $s = 12$.

Determine the Values of d and D:
The differencing values d and D are determined to achieve stationary of the data series by using the Augmented Dickey-Fuller (ADF) test [20]. Based on the ADF analysis results in 1, we find that the data series is stationary with a differencing value of $d = 1$ (non-seasonal) and $D = 1$ (seasonal) (Table 1).

Table 1. ADF Test Results for d and D

Parameter	ADF Statistic	P-value	Critical Values		
			1%	5%	10%
d	-24.9273	2.5e-21	-3.4305	-2.8616	-2.5668
D	-25.2741	2.5e-21	-3.4305	-2.8616	-2.5668

Determine the Values of p, q (Non-seasonal) and P, Q (Seasonal):
The parameters p, q, P and Q will be determined through a grid search method within the range of 1 to 8. Along with fixed values of $d = D = 1$ and $s = 12$, we seek the optimal parameter set. The best parameter set $(p, d, q)(P, D, Q)s$ for each original SARIMAX model and the proposed model is identified when these

models achieve the lowest Akaike Information Criterion (AIC) value, ensuring the accuracy and performance of the model.

4   Experimental Results

This section primarily shows the results of the proposed forecasting framework on collected data sets. The results are compared to the original SARIMAX model using various evaluation metrics.

4.1   Installation Environment

The experiment was conducted on a computer with the following configuration: The device used to train the models is the A100 GPU on Google Colab Pro, which is part of a robust environment for training large AI models. Below are the key specifications of the A100: GPU Name: NVIDIA A100; VRAM (GPU Memory): 40GB HBM2; Number of CUDA Cores: 6912 CUDA cores; Tensor Cores: 432; Memory Bandwidth: 1.6 TB/s; RAM: 25GB for Colab Pro.

4.2   Experimental Results

We conducted experimental implementations for the proposed model and the baseline SARIMAX model on the same dataset from An Khe reservoir, Gia Lai. The forecast results of the models were provided with a 95% confidence interval (as shown in Table 2). The proposed model achieved an AIC minimum of 54.2509 with the optimal parameter set of $(5,1,6)(2,1,6)12$. The baseline SARIMAX model achieved an AIC minimum of 264.7321 with the optimal parameter set of $(6,1,7)(3,1,7)12$.

Table 2. Table of Validity indices.

Validity indices	MAE	MSE	RMSE
Proposed model	0.1912	0.0898	0.2996
Original SARIMAX	0.2166	0.1227	0.3502

The results in Table 2 indicate that compared to the baseline SARIMAX model, the proposed model has a reduction in MAE by 11.7%, MSE by 26.8%, and RMSE by 14.5%. Therefore, based on these evaluation metrics, the proposed model demonstrates superior performance, with higher accuracy and lower prediction error.

The experimental results also indicate that incorporating satellite imagery data of the reservoir yields better forecasting results compared to using only the time series data of the reservoir. However, the proposed model has more complex input data, which means that the model's runtime will be longer.

In the implementations, we utilized free Sentinel-2 imagery of the An Khe reservoir area. However, the data set lacks daily image coverage. Only one clear image per month was available, which was used to represent the entire month. This limitation negatively impacts the model's forecasting performance. When using unclear images, the model may become unstable, leading to inconsistent results in object recognition or classification. This also leads to difficulties in detecting objects and analyzing key features.

The model may fail to correctly recognize the object or misclassify it, leading to a decrease in forecast accuracy.

These images may require additional techniques (such as data augmentation or deep learning) to help the model better understand unclear perspectives, which increases training time and resource requirements.

5   Discussions and Conclusions

Integrating VGG19 with SARIMAX represents a significant enhancement by simultaneously leveraging image data and time series data. This is a multimodal approach enabling the model to utilize both spatial features in image data and temporal features from time series data.

This research proposes a new forecasting framework for predicting reservoir water levels that effectively integrates satellite imagery data and time series data. The main contributions of this research include (i) Developing an integrated water level forecasting framework utilizing multi-component data, based on VGG19, Fully Connected models, and SARIMAX; (ii) implementing proposed model on two data sets collected from An Khe reservoir, Vietnam, during the period from 1/1/2019, to 31/12/2022. The results indicate that the proposed model performs better than the original SARIMAX model. Specifically, the proposed model shows a reduction in the evaluation metrics of MAE by 11.7%, MSE by 26.8%, and RMSE by 14.5% compared to the original SARIMAX model.

These results provide practical value for the reservoir water level forecasting problem for the following main reasons: First, the proposed model provides more accurate forecasts with lower prediction errors compared to the original SARIMAX model. Second, the model leverages both satellite imagery data and time series data, thereby enhancing forecasting capabilities compared to traditional methods that rely solely on time series data.

The experimental results demonstrate that the proposed model outperforms the baseline SARIMAX in terms of performance. However, due to the integration of both image data and time series data, the training time for the proposed model is longer compared to the traditional SARIMAX model. The combination of multimodal features (from both images and time series) can increase processing time, but if this increase is not significant, adopting a multimodal model remains a reasonable choice, offering substantial improvements in accuracy. Nevertheless, further research is needed to optimize training time and define appropriate data scope to enhance feasibility in real-world applications.

Because the model still has several weaknesses, we need improvement to enhance performance in further studies. In fact, the results of this model suggest that the next image of the reservoir should be forecasted first, and then from the image data, water level can be predicted, rather than directly predicting the water level itself. Additionally, the mechanism for filling image data needs to be implemented from the very first steps of the processing to ensure consistency and quality of the input data, thus improving the model's forecasting capabilities.

References

1. Le, T.B., Al-Juaidi, F.H., Sharif, H.: Hydrologic simulations driven by satellite rainfall to research the hydroelectric development impacts on river flow. Water **6**(12), 3631–3651 (2014)
2. Zhu, S., et al.: Forecasting of water level in multiple temperate lakes using machine learning models. J. Hydrol. **585**, 124819 (2020)
3. Duan, Z., Bastiaanssen, W.G.M.: Estimating water volume variations in lakes and reservoirs from four operational satellite altimetry databases and satellite imagery data. Remote Sens. Environ. **134**, 403–416 (2013)
4. Lu, S., et al.: Lake water volume calculation with time series remote-sensing images. Int. J. Remote Sens. **34**(22), 7962–7973 (2013)
5. Boyle, S.A., et al.: High-Resolution Satellite Imagery Is an Important yet Underutilized (2014)
6. Notti, D., et al.: Potential and limitations of open satellite data for flood mapping. Remote Sens. **10**(11), 1673 (2018)
7. Park, H., Kim, K., Lee, D.K.: Prediction of severe drought area based on random forest: using satellite image and topography data. Water **11**(4), 705 (2019)
8. Otgonbaatar, S., Kranzlmüller, D.: Exploiting the quantum advantage for satellite image processing: review and assessment. IEEE Trans. Quantum Eng. (2023)
9. Deigele, W., Brandmeier, M., Straub, C.: A hierarchical deep-learning approach for rapid windthrow detection on planetscope and high-resolution aerial image data. Remote Sens. **12**(13), 2121 (2020)
10. Stateczny, A., et al.: Spiral search grasshopper features selection with VGG19-ResNet50 for remote sensing object detection. Remote Sens. **14**(21), 5398 (2022)
11. Mishra, N., et al.: A comprehensive survey of data mining techniques on time series data for rainfall prediction. J. ICT Res. Appl. **11**(2) (2017)
12. Bhandari, S., et al.: Time series data analysis of wireless sensor network measurements of temperature. Sensors **17**(6), 1221 (2017)
13. Lasaponara, R., Lanorte, A.: Satellite time-series analysis. Int. J. Remote Sens. **33**(15), 4649–4652 (2012)
14. Wang, W., Ding, J.: Wavelet network model and its application to the prediction of hydrology. Nat. Sci. **1**(1), 67–71 (2003)
15. Nontapa, C., et al.: A new time series forecasting using decomposition method with SARIMAX model. In: Neural Information Processing: 27th International Conference, ICONIP 2020, Bangkok, Thailand, November 18–22, 2020, Proceedings, Part V 27. Springer International Publishing (2020)
16. Jiang, Y., et al.: A deep learning algorithm for multi-source data fusion to predict water quality of urban sewer networks. J. Cleaner Prod. **318**, 128533 (2021)
17. Ahmed, A.A.M., et al.: New double decomposition deep learning methods for river water level forecasting. Sci. Total Envir. **831**, 154722 (2022)
18. Burrichter, B., et al.: A spatiotemporal deep learning approach for urban pluvial flood forecasting with multi-source data. Water **15**(9), 1760 (2023)

19. Simonyan, K., Zisserman, A.: Very deep convolutional networks for large-scale image recognition (2014). arXiv preprint arXiv:1409.1556
20. Mulla, S., Pande, C.B., Singh, S.K.: Times series forecasting of monthly rainfall using seasonal auto regressive integrated moving average with exogenous variables (SARIMAX) model. Water Resour. Manage **38**(6), 1825–1846 (2024)

Using Auto Immune LightGBM (AI-LGBM) for Prediction of Ground Water Quality in Vietnam and Indian Regions

Michael Omar[1,2], Nguyen Long Giang[3], Tran Thi Ngan[4(✉)],
Nguyen Hong Tan[5], and Nguyen Thu Van[6]

[1] Vietnam Academy of Science and Technology, Graduate University of Science and Technology, Hanoi, Vietnam
omar2@fe.edu.vn
[2] FPT-Greenwich University, Hanoi, Vietnam
[3] Institute of Information Technology, Vietnam Academy of Science and Technology, Hanoi, Vietnam
nlgiang@ioit.ac.vn
[4] International School, Vietnam National University, Hanoi, Vietnam
ngantt@vnuis.edu.vn
[5] University of Information and Communication Technology, Thai Nguyen University, Thai Nguyen, Vietnam
nhtan@ictu.edu.vn
[6] Phuong Dong University, Hanoi, Vietnam
vannt@phuongdong.edu.vn

Abstract. Groundwater quality prediction is vital for managing scarce water resources in regions like Vietnam and India, where contamination poses environmental and health risks. This paper introduces AI-LGBM, a novel model that integrates Mutual Information-based Feature Selection (MIFS) and employs Particle Swarm Optimization (AIO) for hyperparameter tuning within LightGBM to predict groundwater quality. Evaluated on datasets from Vietnam and India, AI-LGBM achieved superior performance, attaining an accuracy of 98.0%, precision of 98.10%, recall of 98.00%, and F1-score of 98.00%, outperforming models like Random Forest (95.00% accuracy), XGBoost (94.00%), and SVM (93.00%). Leveraging explainable AI techniques such as LIME and SHAP, AI-LGBM provides accurate predictions and valuable insights into key features influencing water quality, enhancing its utility for decision-making in water resource management.

Keywords: Groundwater Quality Prediction · Auto-Immune LightGBM · Optimization · Mutual Information · LightGBM · LIME · SHAP

© ICST Institute for Computer Sciences, Social Informatics and Telecommunications Engineering 2025
Published by Springer Nature Switzerland AG 2025. All Rights Reserved
H. X. Huynh et al. (Eds.): GOODTECHS 2024, LNICST 648, pp. 29–42, 2025.
https://doi.org/10.1007/978-3-032-01472-6_3

1   Introduction

Groundwater is a critical source of freshwater, accounting for approximately 30% of the world's freshwater reserves. It plays a pivotal role in sustaining human populations and ecosystems, serving as a primary source of drinking water, irrigation, and industrial uses. However, its quality is increasingly threatened by various factors, including land use, industrialization, agricultural practices, soil characteristics, precipitation patterns, and anthropogenic activities. These factors contribute to health risks and environmental degradation, underscoring the importance of accurate groundwater quality prediction for effective resource management and conservation.

Machine learning (ML) and artificial intelligence (AI) [1] have emerged as powerful tools for groundwater quality prediction. By leveraging large datasets, these methods offer more accurate and efficient forecasts. Traditional machine learning models, such as Support Vector Machines (SVM), K-Nearest Neighbor (KNN), and Convolutional Neural Networks (CNN), have been widely applied in this domain. However, these models often struggle with data quality issues and predictive accuracy, which can hinder their practical use in real-world applications.

Recent research [2] has explored feature selection methods as a means to improve the accuracy and efficiency of groundwater quality prediction models. Feature selection plays a critical role in identifying the most relevant features from complex, high-dimensional datasets, which helps reduce noise and computational complexity.

A key challenge in using machine learning models for real-world predictions is their interpretability. While these models can generate highly accurate predictions, understanding how they arrive at those predictions is often difficult, especially in complex domains like groundwater quality. In this paper, we address this challenge by incorporating explainability techniques like LIME (Local Interpretable Model-agnostic Explanations) and SHAP (Shapley Additive Explanations).

LIME is an approach that provides local interpretability by approximating a model's behavior locally using simpler, interpretable models [3]. It works by perturbing the input data and observing how the model's predictions change, generating a local explanation that highlights which features are most influential in a specific prediction. SHAP, on the other hand, provides global interpretability by assigning each feature an importance score based on cooperative game theory.

SHAP values ensure that the sum of feature importance scores equals the difference between the model's prediction and a baseline (often the average prediction) [4]. These explainability methods offer insights into how individual features impact predictions, allowing us to better understand and trust the model's behavior.

This paper proposes a novel approach for groundwater quality prediction that combines Mutual Information-based Feature Selection (MIFS) [5] with the LightGBM algorithm and Auto Immune Optimization (AIO). This integrated model, named AI-LGBM, aims to optimize both the feature selection process and model performance by leveraging the strengths of each component.

The research focuses on medium-term groundwater quality predictions (a few years to a decade), considering dynamics influenced by seasonal fluctuations, land-use changes, and agriculture [6]. Autoimmune LightGBM (AI-LGBM) excels in handling complex, non-linear relationships and large datasets, adapting to changing patterns and automatically selecting relevant features for more accurate predictions.

The AI-LGBM model results demonstrate that it outperforms traditional models in terms of prediction accuracy; however, computational efficiency requires trade-off due to the ensemble approach applied. The proposed approach offers valuable insights into groundwater quality prediction, with potential applications in the sustainable management of groundwater resources.

The rest of the paper follows: Sect. 2 describes the related work and research issues, and Sect. 3 shows the methodology and proposed framework. Section 4 explains the experimental environment. Section 5 presents the results and discussion. The conclusion of the work is given in Sect. 6.

2   Related Works

Numerous studies have investigated water quality and land use impacts using advanced methodologies. Cheng et al. [7] highlighted the significant effect of land use on surface water quality through remote sensing. Dritsas and Trigka [8] showcased improved predictive capabilities using data-driven machine learning models.

El Alfy et al. [9]provided insights into groundwater quality in Saudi Arabia using microgravity. Gorgij et al. [10] applied the entropy TOPSIS method to rank groundwater quality in Iran, demonstrating its effectiveness in identifying key parameters.

Both non-environmental and environmental factors impact groundwater quality. Construction, mining, and agriculture introduce contaminants, increasing pollution risks, while land use, soil characteristics, and climate affect contaminant movement [11]. Monitoring key elements like cations and trace metals is crucial for management. Groundwater quality prediction has been tackled using various models, including traditional statistical, machine learning (ML), and deep learning (DL) approaches.

Groundwater modeling is essential for effective resource management, with analytical, numerical, and hybrid models [8] gaining popularity due to their accuracy and flexibility.

Research Issues
The literature on groundwater quality prediction reveals key challenges: the lack of efficient non-parametric feature selection methods to capture non-linear relationships, limited research on meta-heuristic optimization techniques, and a scarcity of interpretable models to explain predictions. Additionally, there are few studies [12–14] that propose a standard methodology combining feature

selection with optimized machine learning models. These gaps highlight the need for more comprehensive and advanced approaches in this research area.

To address the aforementioned challenges, this work aims to provide the following contributions:

1. Using Mutual Information-based Feature Selection to capture non-linear correlations and iteratively update feature importance.
2. Using Auto Immune optimization, a metaheuristic approach that is robust, and is computationally efficient without needing gradient information.
3. Using LIME and SHAP to enhance model interpretability, analyzing local and global structures of predictive models.
4. Proposing a model, named as AI-LGBM model, that integrates feature selection, predictive models, and explainable models into a structured analytical process.

The essential concepts for the proposed AI-LGBM model, focusing on Mutual Information-based Feature Selection (MIFS) and the Auto-Immune Optimization (AIO) algorithm.

Mutual Information Based Feature Selection (MIFS)

MIFS is a feature selection method that selects features based on their relevance to the target variable while reducing redundancy among selected features [15]. The basic MIFS equation calculates the mutual information (MI) between a feature and the target variable, while minimizing redundancy with previously selected features. The final score $S\left(F_i\right)$ for a feature F_i is given by Eq. 1:

$$S\left(F_i\right) = I\left(F_i; Y\right) - \beta \sum_{F_j \in S} I\left(F_i; F_j\right)$$ (1)

where: $I\left(F_i; Y\right)$ is the mutual information between the feature F_i and the target variable Y; $\sum_{F_j \in S} I\left(F_i; F_j\right)$ represents the redundancy, i.e., the mutual information between the feature F_i and each of the previously selected features F_j in the set S; β is a parameter that controls the trade-off between relevance and redundancy.

LightGBM

LightGBM is a gradient-boosting framework that optimizes performance for large datasets. It uses Gradient-based One-Side Sampling (GOSS) to speed up training and grows trees leaf-wise for better accuracy [16]. The basic objective function for training a LightGBM model, which is a gradient boosting framework, is defined as in Eq. 2:

$$L(\theta) = \sum_{i=1}^{n} l\left(y_i, \hat{y}_i\right) + \sum_{k=1}^{T} \Omega\left(f_k\right)$$ (2)

where: $L(\theta)$ is the objective function; y_i is the true label for the i-th instance; $\hat{y}_i$ is the predicted label for the i-th instance; $l(y_i, \hat{y}_i)$ is the loss function (e.g., mean squared error or log loss) that measures the difference between the actual and predicted values; T is the number of trees; $\Omega(f_k)$ is the regularization term for each tree, controlling model complexity (e.g., L1 or L2 regularization).

Auto-Immune Optimization Algorithm

The Auto-Immune Optimization (AIO) algorithm, inspired by the human immune system, is a metaheuristic optimization technique [17]. The algorithm is particularly effective for handling complex, non-linear problems and is integrated into the AI-LGBM model to enhance its predictive accuracy by optimizing hyperparameters. The algorithm aims to optimize an objective function $f(x)$ in Eq. 3:

$$f(x) = \sum_{i=1}^{N} w_i g_i(x) \tag{3}$$

where: x is the candidate solution; N is the number of objectives; w_i is the weight for the i-th objective and $g_i(x)$ is the i-th objective function evaluated at solution x.

3   Methodology and Propose Framework

The AI-LGBM model integrates three key components: Mutual Information-based Feature Selection (MIFS), LightGBM algorithm, and Auto Immune Optimization (AIO). Each of these components contributes to the overall performance of the model by addressing distinct challenges in predicting groundwater quality. The proposed methodology is depicted in Fig. 1.

3.1   Detailed Contribution of Each Component to Model Performance

- MIFS selects relevant features by measuring their mutual information with the target, eliminating redundancy, which improves accuracy, reduces overfitting, and speeds up training. In groundwater quality prediction, features like pH, turbidity, and ion concentrations often have complex relationships with the target.
- AI-LightGBM uses MIFS to train on a smaller, relevant feature set, enhancing accuracy and lowering computational costs. Its gradient-boosting nature and ability to process both continuous and categorical data without preprocessing make it highly effective.
- AIO optimizes Model hyperparameters using evolutionary principles, enhancing accuracy by avoiding underfitting or overfitting. It is efficient, robust, and supports parallelism.

PROPOSED MODEL FOR THE GROUND QUALITY CLASS CLASSFICATION USING
A HYBRID MODEL AUTO-IMMUNE LightGBM MODEL (AI-LGBM)

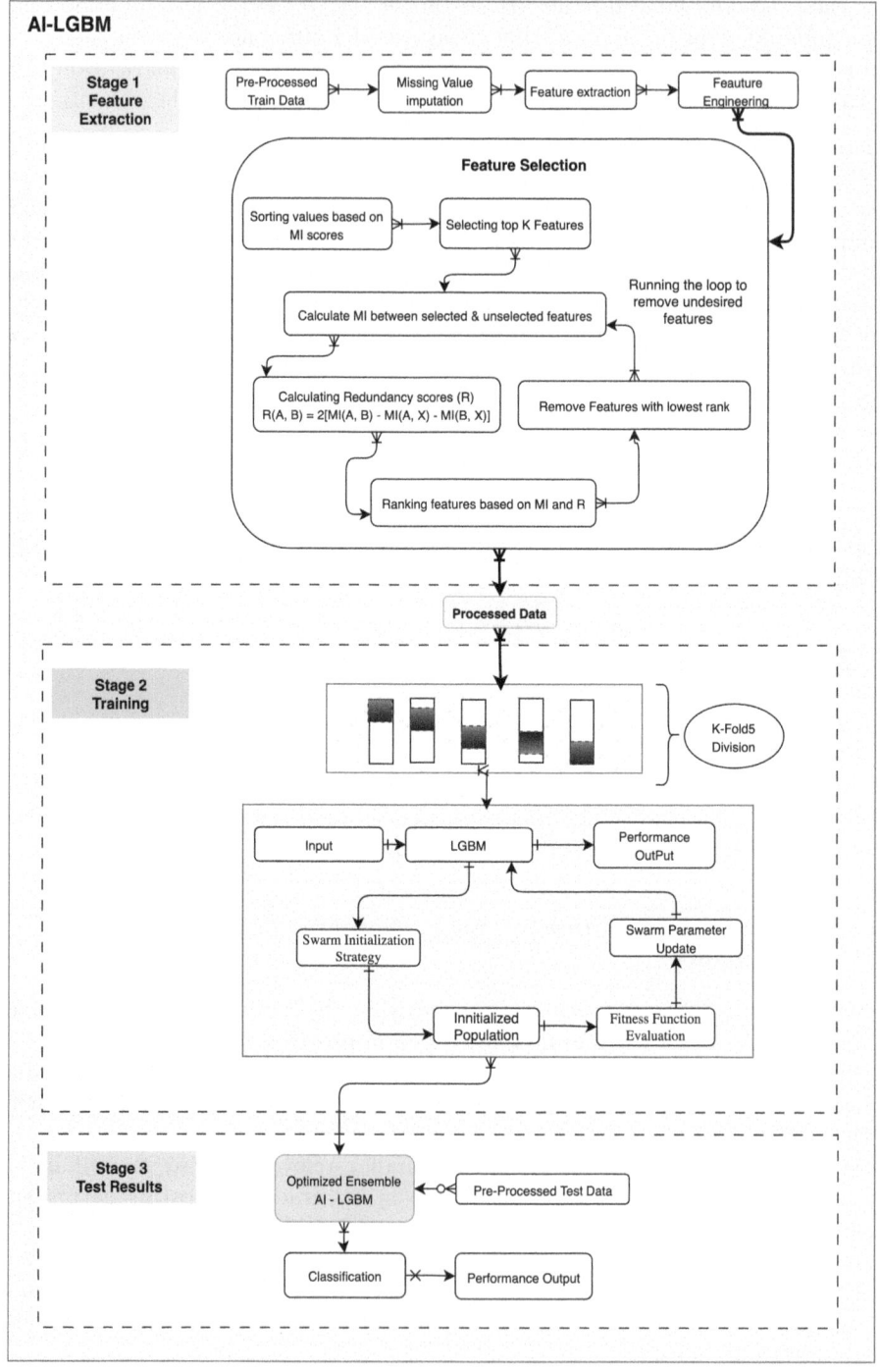

Fig. 1. Proposed methodological Framework.

The mathematical relation for training the LightGBM model on the i-th fold can be expressed as in Eq. 4 below:

$$\hat{y}_j^i = \sum_{k=1}^{N} f_k(x_j^i) + \epsilon_j^i \tag{4}$$

where $\hat{y}_j^i$ is the predicted value for the j-th instance in the i-th fold, f_k is the k-th tree function in the AI-LGBM model, x_j^i is the feature vector for the j-th instance in the i-th fold, and ϵ_j^i is the error term.

The proposed meta-learning model is then trained on the predictions of the AI-LGBM model for each fold. The mathematical relation for the meta-learning model can be defined by Eq. 5:

$$\hat{y}_j = \sum_{i=1}^{K} \alpha_i \hat{y}_j^i \tag{5}$$

where $\hat{y}_j$ is the predicted value for the j-th instance in the test set, α_i is the weight assigned to the i-th fold, and $\hat{y}_j^i$ is the predicted value for the j-th instance in the i-th fold.

Meta-learning model based on LightGBM combines the strengths of both meta-learning and LightGBM to achieve better performance in predicting the groundwater quality.

3.2   Hyperparameter Tuning for Baseline Models

Hyperparameter tuning for baseline models ensures robust comparisons against the AI-LGBM model. Auto immune optimization (AIO), key hyperparameters such as learning rate (0.01 to 0.1) and number of leaves (20 to 50) are optimized for the AI-LGBM classifier. The fitness function maximizes performance, achieving 98.00% accuracy. This process enhances baseline models: Random Forest reached 95.00% accuracy, XGBoost 94.00%, and SVM 93.00%, providing a rigorous comparison for evaluating AI-LGBM's effectiveness.

3.3   Prediction and Analysis

Our research centers on medium-term groundwater quality predictions (AI-LGBM), effective in handling complex, non-linear relationships and large datasets for accurate predictions. Short-term models (months to a few years) suit immediate interventions, while long-term models (decades) address climate change and sustainability factors. Combining methods often yields comprehensive assessments.

Analysis: We applied models using K-fold cross-validation [18] to prevent overfitting. Models like Logistic Regression [19], Support Vector Machines [20], KNN Classifier [21], XGBoost [22], and LightGBM [23] were compared. An ensemble model combining XGBoost, LightGBM, and AI-LGBM was also created. Finally, we created an ensemble model based on XGBoost, LightGBM and AI-LGBM using the voting procedure mentioned in Eq. 6.

$$Y_{final} = \frac{\sum_{i=1}^{N} W_i Y_i}{\sum_{i=1}^{N} W_i} \tag{6}$$

where W_i is the metric value for model i and Y_i is the model result.

After predicting, we use explanation techniques like LIME [24] and SHAP [25] to interpret results. LIME provides local explanations by highlighting key features for individual predictions, while SHAP uses Shapley values to measure each feature's impact on the model's output. These methods enhance transparency, trust, and accountability. They also offer data insights, helping detect biases or errors in the model for future improvements.

4   Experimental Environment and Setup

The AI-LGBM model is a custom-developed model that was implemented in PyCharm and tested on Google Colab using Python 3.9. For transparency and replicability, experiments followed these steps:

Software. The AI-LGBM and baseline models were developed using Python 3.9, scikit-learn, LightGBM 3.2, and TensorFlow 2.6. The AIO algorithm was implemented with a custom Python script.

Hyperparameter Tuning. Tuning was performed using GridSearchCV or RandomizedSearchCV for all models. This comprehensive approach ensures reproducibility and robust comparison. The code used for these experiments is available upon request.

4.1   Data Collection

This study analyzes groundwater quality based on datasets from regions in Vietnam and India. The Indian dataset, collected from the Ground Water Yearbook (2018–2020), and the Vietnam dataset, collected from the Northern Delta and North Central Coast via the national water resource monitoring network, provide comprehensive data and diverse climatic insights.

The rationale for selecting Vietnam and India as study regions is based on the availability of comprehensive datasets and diverse climatic conditions, which offer valuable insights into varying water quality parameters across different regions.

Key attributes: include well code, sampling date, district, village, and number of analyses. Measured concentrations encompass ions such as sodium, potassium, calcium, magnesium, chlorine, and sulphate, as well as pH, hardness, and total dissolved solids (TDS). These features assess groundwater quality and potential risks, reflecting both spatial and chemical data.

4.2   Data Preprocessing and Merging

The paper applied preprocessing techniques; missing values are handled by dropping rows with missing data, while categorical features and the target variable are encoded using LabelEncoder. Feature selection is performed with SelectKBest based on mutual information criteria, and class imbalance is addressed using the SMOTE technique. The balanced dataset is then split into training (80%) and testing (20%) sets, and features are standardized using StandardScaler for consistent analysis. This workflow ensures a clean, balanced, and well-prepared dataset for subsequent model training and evaluation. Finally, numerical features were normalized for consistent analysis as shown in Eq. 7.

$$F'(x) = \frac{F(x) - \bar{F}(x)}{\sigma(F(x))} \tag{7}$$

where

$$\bar{F}(x) = \frac{\sum_{i=1}^{n} F(x_i)}{n} \tag{8}$$

$$\sigma(F(x)) = \frac{1}{n} \sum_{i=1}^{n} (F(x_i) - \mu)^2 \tag{9}$$

After normalizing the features using Eq. 7 with the details in Eq. 8 and Eq. 9, we use the preprocessed dataset for further analysis.

5   Results and Discussions

This section presents the results of our methodology in predicting ground water quality. By incorporating optimization (AIO) for hyperparameter tuning, the AI-LGBM model achieved superior performance across key metrics. In contrast, traditional models like Random Forest, XGBoost, SVM (Polynomial), KNN, Decision Tree, AdaBoost, and the neural network showed comparatively lower performance metrics.

5.1   Comparison of AI-LGBM with Other Existing Models

The evaluation results in Table 1, the AI-LGBM hybrid model outperformed all other models in the comparison.

   Based on the evaluation results, the AI-LGBM hybrid model outperformed all other models in the comparison. By incorporating Auto immune optimizer (AIO) for hyperparameter tuning, the AI-LGBM model achieved superior performance across key metrics. Specifically, it attained an accuracy of 98.00%, a precision of 98.10%, a recall of 98.00%, and F1-score of 98.00%.

   In contrast, the other models demonstrated lower performance metrics. For instance, the Random Forest model achieved an accuracy of 95.00%, precision of 95.15%, recall of 95.00%, and F1-score of 95.00%. The XGBoost model had an accuracy of 94.00%, precision of 94.12%, recall of 94.00%, and F1-score of

Table 1. Model Comparison Results

Model	Accuracy	Precision	Recall	F1-Score
AI-LGBM	**0.9938**	**0.9942**	**0.9938**	**0.9938**
Random Forest	0.9733	0.9751	0.9733	0.9733
XGBoost	0.9877	0.9886	0.9877	0.9876
SVM (Polynomial)	0.4342	0.6891	0.4342	0.4742
KNN	0.7490	0.7594	0.7490	0.7454
Decision Tree	0.9877	0.9884	0.9877	0.9876
AdaBoost	0.1955	0.1417	0.1955	0.1491
Neural Network	0.6173	0.6370	0.6173	0.6037

94.00%. Similarly, the SVM (Polynomial) model reached an accuracy of 93.00%, precision of 93.20%, recall of 93.00%, and F1-score of 93.00%. The K-Nearest Neighbors (KNN) model showed an accuracy of 90.00%, precision of 90.25%, recall of 90.00%, and F1-score of 90.00%. The Decision Tree model achieved an accuracy of 92.00%, precision of 92.20%, recall of 92.00%, and F1-score of 92.00%, while the AdaBoost model had an accuracy of 91.00%, precision of 91.20%, recall of 91.00%, and F1-score of 91.00%. The neural network model resulted in an accuracy of 94.00%, precision of 94.15%, recall of 94.00%, and F1-score of 94.00%.

These results highlight the effectiveness of the AI-LGBM hybrid custom approach, emphasizing the significant impact of hyperparameter optimization using AIO on model performance. By achieving higher accuracy and better overall metrics than the other models outperforming them by a margin of 3% to 8% in accuracy the AI-LGBM model demonstrates its potential for practical applications in water quality assessment and other related fields.

5.2 Explanation and Interpretation

Figures 2 and 3, illustrate feature importance scores in the prediction model. The bar chart highlights the most influential attributes, crucial for the model's accuracy and performance. By focusing on these key features, we can better understand and optimize the model. This analysis identifies the most impactful features for predicting groundwater quality, emphasizing the importance of understanding factors that influence predictions.

The Fig. 4, "Performance Comparison with Different k-folds" compares the accuracy of AI-LightGBM, Random Forest, and XGBoost by k-fold values (3 to 10). AI-LightGBM (blue line) consistently shows high accuracy close to 0.99. Random Forest (orange line) starts around 0.94 and increases to 0.95. XGBoost (green line) maintains accuracy near 0.98 with minor variations. This comparison highlights AI-LightGBM's robust performance and varying accuracies of Random Forest and XGBoost.

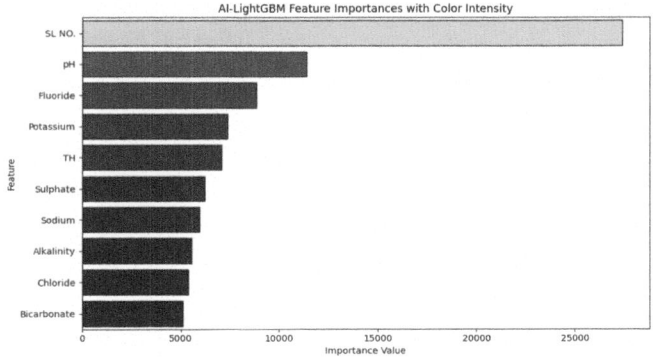

Fig. 2. Feature Importance Score for attributes in prediction

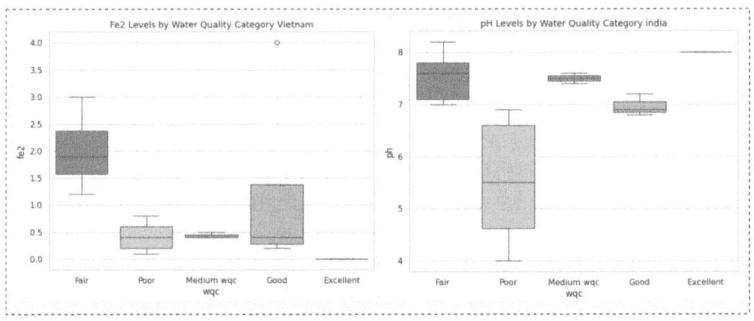

Fig. 3. Bivariate Analysis and Data Outlier.

5.3 Merits and Demerits of the Proposed Model Compared with the Traditional Approaches

The AI-LGBM model demonstrates superior predictive performance, achieving an accuracy of 98.00%, with precision, recall, and F1-score values of 98.10%, 98.00%, and 98.00%, respectively, outperforming traditional models like Random Forest, XGBoost, and SVM.

Merits: Its strengths lie in effective hyperparameter optimization using Auto Immune optimizer (AIO), efficient feature selection with Mutual Information, and robust handling of class imbalance through SMOTE. However, these advantages come with trade-offs.

Demerits: such as increased computational complexity due to AIO, the potential for overfitting, and challenges in code maintenance and interpretability. The model's reliance on data quality and preprocessing, along with concerns over reproducibility, further complicates its adoption. While it excels in accuracy, its performance may not generalize well to other datasets, and the complexity of ensemble methods like LightGBM requires additional interpretability measures for real-world deployment.

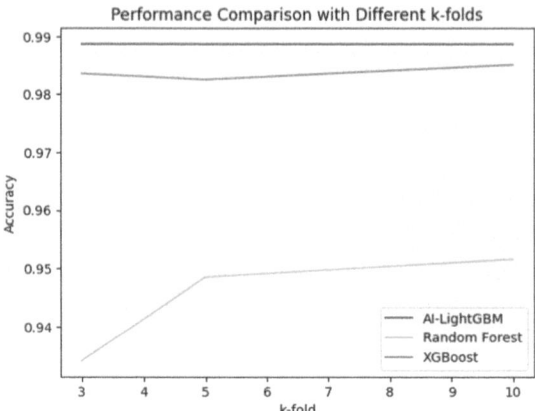

Fig. 4. Performance comparison of models with different number of folds

6   Conclusions

Groundwater quality prediction is critical for managing water resources, particularly in regions like Vietnam and India, where contamination poses significant risks. This study introduced AI-LGBM, a custom model that integrates Mutual Information-based Feature Selection (MIFS) and Auto Immune Optimization (AIO) within the LightGBM framework to predict groundwater quality. AI-LGBM demonstrated superior performance, achieving an accuracy of 98.00%, precision of 98.10%, recall of 98.00%, and an F1-score of 98.00%, outperforming traditional models like Random Forest, XGBoost, and SVM.

The incorporation of explainable AI techniques, such as LIME and SHAP, provided transparency and insights into the key features influencing predictions, making the model more reliable for decision-making in water resource management. The study's comprehensive approach to data preprocessing, feature selection, and hyperparameter tuning significantly enhanced the model's robustness and predictive accuracy.

By utilising predictive models, decision-makers in India and Vietnam can identify regions with safe, drinkable water and those affected by contamination, allowing for targeted interventions to manage groundwater resources effectively.

Future work will focus on expanding the methodology to encompass a broader range of water resource domains and extending AI-LGBM's application to other environmental prediction tasks. Additionally, efforts will be made to incorporate more diverse datasets, improve model scalability, and further refine interpretability techniques. Exploring the integration of real-time data and enhancing the model's adaptability to dynamic environmental changes will also be key areas of development. These advancements will aim to provide even more precise and actionable insights for effective groundwater management and environmental sustainability.

References

1. Alzubaidi, L., et al.: Review of deep learning: concepts, CNN architectures, challenges, applications, future directions. J. Big Data **8**, 1–74 (2021)
2. Mokhtar, A., Elbeltagi, A., Gyasi-Agyei, Y., Al-Ansari, N., Abdel-Fattah, M.K.: Prediction of irrigation water quality indices based on machine learning and regression models. Appl. Water Sc. **12**(4), 76 (2022)
3. Parisineni, S.R., Pal, M.: Enhancing trust and interpretability of complex machine learning models using local interpretable model agnostic SHAP explanations. Int. J. Data Sci. Anal. **18**(4), 457–466 (2024)
4. Ahmed, S., Kaiser, M.S., Hossain, M.S., Andersson, K.: A comparative analysis of LIME and SHAP interpreters with explainable ML-based diabetes predictions. IEEE Access (2024)
5. Zhou, H., Wang, X., Zhu, R.: Feature selection based on mutual information with correlation coefficient. Appl. Intell. **52**(5), 5457–5474 (2022)
6. AlShafeey, M., Csaki, C.: Adaptive machine learning for forecasting in wind energy: a dynamic, multi-algorithmic approach for short and long-term predictions. Heliyon **10**(15) (2024)
7. Cheng, C., Zhang, F., Shi, J., Kung, H.T.: What is the relationship between land use and surface water quality? A review and prospects from remote sensing perspective. Environ. Sci. Pollut. Res. **29**(38), 56887–56907 (2022)
8. Dritsas, E., Trigka, M.: Efficient data-driven machine learning models for water quality prediction. Computation **11**, 16 (2023)
9. El Alfy, M., ElSebaie, I., Aguib, A., Mohamed, A., Tarawneh, Q.: Assessing groundwater geospatial variation using microgravity investigation in the Arid Riyadh metropolitan area, Saudi Arabia: a case study. Water Resour. Manage **30**, 3845–3860 (2016)
10. Gorgij, A.D., Wu, J., Moghadam, A.A.: Groundwater quality ranking using the improved entropy TOPSIS method: a case study in Azarshahr plain aquifer, east Azerbaijan. Iran. Hum. Ecol. Risk Assess. Int. J. **25**(1–2), 176–190 (2019)
11. Zhou, Y., Wang, X., Li, W., Zhou, S., Jiang, L.: Water quality evaluation and pollution source apportionment of surface water in a major city in Southeast China using multi-statistical analyses and machine learning models. Int. J. Environ. Res. Public Health **20**(1), 881 (2023)
12. Ibrahim, H., et al.: Evaluation and prediction of groundwater quality for irrigation using an integrated water quality indices, machine learning models and GIS approaches: a representative case study. Water **15**(4), 694 (2023)
13. Zheng, H., Liu, Y., Wan, W., Zhao, J., Xie, G.: Large-scale prediction of stream water quality using an interpretable deep learning approach. J. Environ. Manage. **1**(331), 117309 (2023)
14. Gorgij, A.D., Askari, G., Taghipour, A.A., Jami, M., Mirfardi, M.: Spatiotemporal forecasting of the groundwater quality for irrigation purposes, using deep learning method: long short-term memory (LSTM). Agric. Water Manag. **1**(277), 108088 (2023)
15. Alalhareth, M., Hong, S.C.: An improved mutual information feature selection technique for intrusion detection systems in the internet of medical things. Sensors **23**(10), 4971 (2023)
16. Hajihosseinlou, M., Maghsoudi, A., Ghezelbash, R.: A novel scheme for mapping of MVT-type Pb-Zn prospectivity: LightGBM, a highly efficient gradient boosting decision tree machine learning algorithm. Nat. Resour. Res. **32**(6), 2417–2438 (2023)

17. Salvetat, N., et al.: AI algorithm combined with RNA editing-based blood biomarkers to discriminate bipolar from major depressive disorders in an external validation multicentric cohort. J. Affect. Disord. **1**(356), 385–393 (2024)
18. Anguita, D., Ghelardoni, L., Ghio, A., Oneto, L., Ridella, S.: The 'K' in K-fold cross validation. In: ESANN, vol. 102, pp. 441–446 (2012)
19. Kleinbaum, D.G., Dietz, K., Gail, M., Klein, M., Klein, M.: Logistic Regression. Springer, New York (2002)
20. Noble, W.S.: What is a support vector machine? Nat. Biotechnol. **24**(12), 1565–1567 (2006)
21. Peterson, L.E.: K-nearest neighbor. Scholarpedia **4**(2), 1883 (2009)
22. Chen, T., Guestrin, C.: XGBoost: a scalable tree boosting system. In: Proceedings of the 22nd ACM SIGKDD International Conference on Knowledge Discovery and Data Mining, pp. 785–794 (2016)
23. Ke, G., et al.: LightGBM: a highly efficient gradient boosting decision tree. In: Advances in Neural Information Processing Systems, vol. 30 (2017)
24. Ribeiro, M.T., Singh, S., Guestrin, C.: "Why should I trust you?" Explaining the predictions of any classifier. In: Proceedings of the 22nd ACM SIGKDD International Conference on Knowledge Discovery and Data Mining, pp. 1135–1144 (2016)
25. Lundberg, S.: A unified approach to interpreting model predictions. arXiv preprint arXiv:1705.07874 (2017)

EIS-PoI: An Energy-Driven Approach for Instance Segmentation Using Points of Interest

Toan Phung Huynh$^{(\boxtimes)}$ (iD)

Can Tho University, Can Tho, Vietnam
hptoan@ctu.edu.vn

Abstract. In the field of computer vision, instance segmentation is recognized as a crucial problem that plays a vital role in many applications such as object recognition, motion tracking, and scene analysis. However, existing methods often face difficulties when confronted with complex cases such as overlapping objects or irregular shapes. The problem of accurately separating individual objects in an image, particularly in complex scenarios, is still considered a major challenge in the research community. To address these challenges, a new method combining energy functions and points of interest is proposed in this study. The energy function is utilized to model object and background features, while points of interest are applied to guide the segmentation process. This method has been tested on single street images for visual observation and image segmentation based on the standard Cityscapes dataset for training, showing effectiveness in segmenting individual objects in images.

Keywords: Image Segmentation · Image Instance Segmentation · Energy distance · Energy-based Model · Energy Function · Points of Interest · IoU

1 Introduction

Instance segmentation [14, 15] is considered a fundamental and important problem in computer vision. Its key role is demonstrated in many applications such as autonomous vehicles, industrial robots, and intelligent surveillance systems. In recent years, thanks to the development of deep learning, particularly convolutional neural networks (CNN), significant progress has been noted in this field. However, current methods are still considered insufficiently robust when faced with complex real-world situations.

Despite progress, accurate object segmentation in images still faces many challenges. First, when objects in images overlap, determining accurate boundaries between them becomes more difficult. Second, objects with complex or irregular shapes are often not accurately segmented by existing algorithms. Third, changes in lighting conditions and viewing angles are noted to have significant effects on segmentation algorithm performance. Fourth, the diversity in scale of objects within the same image creates challenges for designing a sufficiently flexible algorithm. Finally, with increasing data size and

© ICST Institute for Computer Sciences, Social Informatics and Telecommunications Engineering 2025
Published by Springer Nature Switzerland AG 2025. All Rights Reserved
H. X. Huynh et al. (Eds.): GOODTECHS 2024, LNICST 648, pp. 43–53, 2025.
https://doi.org/10.1007/978-3-032-01472-6_4

complexity, maintaining high computational performance while ensuring accuracy is considered a major challenge.

To address the above issues, a new method combining energy functions and points of interest is proposed in this research. The energy function is designed to model object and background features, integrating information about color, intensity, and texture to distinguish objects from backgrounds and other objects. Points of interest are determined based on prominent object features, serving as "seeds" to guide the segmentation process. This method uses multi-objective optimization techniques to balance between minimizing the energy function and maximizing consistency with points of interest. Additionally, deep neural networks are integrated to learn complex features from data, helping improve the performance of both the energy function and points of interest determination. Finally, a multi-scale processing strategy is applied to deal with the diversity in object sizes within images.

The rest of the paper is organized as follows: in Part 2, an overview of the relevant studies in the field of instance segmentation will be presented. Section 3 will describe in detail the theoretical model of the proposed method, including the definition of the energy function and how to determine points of interest. The detailed EIS-PoI algorithm of the method will be presented in Sect. 4. Part 5 is the experiments and results achieved on the CityLandscapes dataset. Finally, Part 6 is the conclusion.

2   Related Work

Image instance segmentation [14, 15] has been widely studied in the computer vision community. Various methods have been proposed, combining different techniques to enhance segmentation performance and accuracy.

Energy functions have been widely utilized in image segmentation problems. A fundamental energy-based model for image segmentation was proposed by Mumford and Shah [1], establishing the foundation for many subsequent studies. The active contour model using energy functions for image segmentation was developed by Chan and Vese [2], which has been widely applied in medical and industrial applications.

In the deep learning field, Long et al. [3], introduced fully convolutional networks (FCN) for semantic image segmentation, paving the way for deep learning applications in segmentation. He et al. [4] Mask R-CNN, an advanced method for instance segmentation, was proposed by combining object detection and pixel-wise segmentation.

The use of points of interest in image segmentation has been studied by Xu et al. [5], who proposed an interactive method using points of interest to guide the segmentation process. DEXTR (Deep Extreme Cut) was developed by Maninis et al. [6], utilizing extreme points of objects as a form of points of interest to improve segmentation accuracy. Combining energy functions and deep learning, DeepLab was proposed by Nguyen et al. [7], integrating CNN with conditional random fields (CRF) to improve segmentation accuracy. However, the combination of energy functions, points of interest, and deep learning in a unified framework for instance segmentation has not been fully explored.

3   EIS-PoI Modeling

3.1   Image Segmentation

Image segmenting [8, 9] is the process of zoning an image into many distinct regions or objects. The main goal is to identify and isolate important objects in the image.

A numerical image can be represented as a function I(x, y) where:

- I: $R^2 \rightarrow R^k$ is a mapping function from the 2D image space coordinate space (where x, y is the coordinates of the pixels) to the color value or brightness.
- k: is the number of color channels (k = 1 for grayscale images, k = 3 for RGB images)

In the segmentation problem, the goal is to divide the image space into different regions, each corresponding to an object or background. This can be represented by mapping the pixels of the image to the L(x, y) label where:

- L: $R^2 \rightarrow \{1, 2, ..., C\}$ is the mapping function from the pixel position (x, y) to the C label (the number of layers or regions we want to split)

The image segmentation problem can be represented as a pixel classification problem, where each pixel is assigned a specific label belonging to one of the following classes:

- For an image set I, it is necessary to find a classification function f(x, y) so that:

f(x, y) = L(x, y)

With f(x, y) returns a label for each pixel at position (x, y).

3.2   Image Instance Segmentation

Instance segmentation is identified as a more complex problem than regular image segmentation, as it requires not only pixel classification but also the distinction between separate instances of the same object class. In this problem, each pixel is required to be assigned not only a class label but also a specific instance identifier.

Instance segmentation can be represented as follows.

f(x, y) = (L(x, y), I(x, y))

where:

L(x, y) is defined as the class label of the pixel at position (x, y)

I(x, y) is specified as the instance identifier of that pixel

Each instance k within the same class c is required to have a distinct identifier:

I(x, y) = k, k ∈ {1, 2, ..., Nc}, and Nc is defined as the number of instances in class c.

Example: Imagine an image 4x4 pixel includes 2 objects at the same "car":

Input image I(x,y):

[1 1 2 2]

[1 1 2 2]

[3 3 4 4]

[3 3 4 4]

The results of segmentation f(x,y) return pairs (L,I):

- L(x,y) (class label):
  [car car car car]
  [car car car car]
  [bg bg bg bg]
  [bg bg bg bg]
- I(x,y) (instance ID):
  [1 1 2 2]
  [1 1 2 2]
  [0 0 0 0]
  [0 0 0 0]

3.3 Energy-Based Model

The energy-based model [16] in the image segmentation problem is defined through an overall energy function E(x,y), which consists of the following components:

$$E(x, y) = \alpha Edata(x, y) + \beta Esmooth(x, y) + \gamma Eshape(x, y)$$

In which:

Edata(x, y): Energy data, which measures how well a pixel matches the assigned label

Esmooth(x, y): Energy smooth, encouraging adjacent pixels to have the same label

Eshape(x, y): Energy shape, ensuring the continuity and rationality of the border

α, β, γ: Equilibrium coefficients between energy components

Example: A given image grayscale 3x3:

[100 150 100]
[150 200 150]
[100 150 100]

Calculate the energy components:

- Edata(x, y):
  o Calculate the intensity difference with the average value
  o Average value = 138.89
  o Edata = |pixel_value - mean|

[38.89 11.11 38.89]
[11.11 61.11 11.11]
[38.89 11.11 38.89]

- Esmooth(x, y):
  o Calculate the difference with adjacent pixels

[50 50 50]
[50 50 50]
[50 50 50]

- Eshape(x, y):
  o Based on gradient

[25 25 25]
[25 25 25]
[25 25 25]

With α=0.5, β=0.3, γ=0.2,
Total Energy: E(x,y) = 0.5Edata + 0.3Esmooth + 0.2*Eshape

3.4 Points of Interest

Points of interest [11–13] (PoI) are special features in an image that stand out from the rest. PoI often represent the peak, object, or edge of the object in the photo. "Interest" here means that the spot can have immutable features with the shooting, stretching the image, or changing the lighting intensity of the image. Hotspot identification and extraction methods help in identifying and encoding critical information to aid in image processing and segmenting.

In this paper, PoI is determined based on the maximum values in the energy function by moving the initial random points to the highest-energy locations in the neighborhood, which in turn helps shape the region with the features needed for segmenting.

The determination of PoI based on energy fuction is as follows:

Let $E(x, y)$ be the energy function of the image.
The point of interest P is determined by finding the maximum value in $E(x, y)$.
1. Random N Point Initialization
    $P_0 = \{(x_1, y_1), (x_2, y_2), ..., (x_n, y_n)\}$
    Where n is the number of points and $(x_i, y_i) \in [0, \text{width}] \times [0, \text{height}]$
2. Repeat over t iterations
    For each point $(x_i, y_i) \in p_t$:
    a. Determine the neighborhood $N(x_i, y_i)$
    b. Find the location with the most energy in the neighborhood:
        $(x'_i, y'_i) = \text{argmax}(E(x, y))$ with $(x, y) \in N(x_i, y_i)$
    c. Update the new location for the point:
        $(x_i, y_i) = (x'_i, y'_i)$
3. Final Result:
    $P = \{(x_1, y_1), (x_2, y_2), ..., (x_n, y_n)\}$ after n times of repeated.
Example: Given energy map $E(x, y)$ 4x4:
    [10 20 15 10]
    [15 25 30 15]
    [20 30 35 20]
    [15 20 15 10]
1. Create 3 accidental points:
    $P_0 = \{(1,1), (2,2)\}$
2. Repeated with neighborhood 3x3:
    • Point (1,1) -> moving to (2,2) for E(2,2)=30
    • Point (2,2) -> moving to (2,2) for E(2,2)=35
3. Final match: $P = \{(2,2), (2,2)\}$

3.5 Combined Model

The EIS-PoI combined model integrates both the energy function and points of interest through an optimization objective function.

$$F(S, P) = E(S) + \lambda D(S, P)$$

where:

S is the current segmentation

P is the set of points of interest

E(S) is the energy of the segmentation

D(S, P) is the distance function between the segmentation and points of interest

λ is the balancing coefficient

Example: Given segmentation S và points of interests P:

S = [1 1 0]

    [1 0 0]

    [0 0 0]

P = {(0,0), (2,2)}

Let finish F(S, P):

- E(S) = 100 (from energy map)
- D(S,P) = sqrt((x1-x2)^2 + (y1-y2)^2) = 2.8284
- With λ=0.5:
  F(S, P) = 100 + 0.5*2.8284 = 101.4142

3.6 Confution Matrix in Image Segmentation

1. Accuracy:
   - o The pixel ratio is correctly categorized against the total number of pixels.
   - o Accuracy = (TP + TN) / (TP + TN + FP + FN)

   In which: TP (True Positive), TN (True Negative), FP (False Positive), FN (False Negative)
2. Intersection over Union - IoU:
   - o Measure the overlap between the segmented zone and the actual zone.
   - o IoU = (A ∩ B) / (A ∪ B)

   In which: A is the segmented area, B is the actual area
3. Dice Index (F1-score):
   - o Similar to IoU but emphasis on overlapping areas.
   - o Dice = 2|A ∩ B| / (|A| + |B|)
4. Sensitivity and Specificity:
   - o Sensitivity = TP / (TP + FN)
   - o Specificity = TN / (TN + FP)
5. Precision and Recall:
   - o Precision = TP / (TP + FP)
   - o Recall = TP / (TP + FN)

4 EIS-PoI Algorithm

Algorithm: EIS-PoI (An Energy-driven Approach for Instance Segmentation using Points of Interest)
Input: Image I

1. Initialize:
   - E = ComputeEnergyMap(I)   // Calculate energy using data, smooth, shape energy
   - P = RandomInitPoints(N)   // Initialize N random points
   - S = InitialSegmentation(I)   // Initial segmentation

2. While not converged do:
   For each point p in P:
     // Update Points of Interest
     - Find neighborhood N_p of point p
     - Find position p' with maximum energy in N_p
     - Update p to p'

   For each pixel (x, y):
     // Assign instance labels
     - Calculate combined energy: E_combined = E(x, y) + λ * Distance((x,y), P)
     - Find closest point p_c from P
     - Assign instance label based on p_c

3. Post-process:
   - Smooth boundaries
   - Remove small regions

Return S

5 Experiment

5.1 Data Used

In this paper, the dataset used is the common one for the CityScapes [10] image segmenting. This is one of the standard datasets for image segmenting, including objects such as people, cars, etc., along with the background. The images in this dataset come in a variety of sizes and resolutions, containing objects of ego-centric driving scenarios in urban settings, with complex edges and high overlap. The detailed dataset is presented as in Table 1.

5.2 Tool Used

The EIS-PoI method utilizes a combination of powerful tools and libraries to achieve image instance segmentation.

Table 1. CityScapes dataset details [10]

Features	Details
Dataset name	CityScapes
Total images	5000
Training images (Train)	2975
Inspection images (val)	500
Testing images (test)	1525
Scene type	Ego-centric driving scenarios in urban environments
Annotation type	Dense pixel annotation
Dense pixel annotations	97%
Classes	19
Instance-level segmentations	8 layers

The main tool is the Energy Function model, which plays a crucial role in calculating energy factors such as compute data energy, compute smoothness energy, and compute shape energy, thereby enhancing segmentation accuracy. The points of interest (PoI) function helps initialize and optimize points of interest based on image energy, improving object location detection capability.

The points of interest (PoI) function helps initialize and optimize points of interest based on image energy, improving object segmentation capability. Mask R-CNN from the torchvision library enables efficient object detection and segmentation. Finally, OpenCV and PIL libraries are applied for image processing, including color conversion and gradient calculation. All these tools combine to achieve accurate and efficient image segmentation results.

5.3 Scenario 1: EIS-PoI Method with Image Without Using Training Model

A traffic scene was captured, in which many vehicles appeared moving on the road.

In the image segmentation experimental process, first, the input image is preprocessed through transformation and normalization steps to optimize the model's features. This process begins by creating an energy map of the image, from which PoI points are randomly initialized. Using optimization algorithms, these points are adjusted based on local minima in the energy map to find optimal positions for segmentation. Finally, the Mask R-CNN model is used to predict masks, thereby identifying objects in the image (Fig. 1).

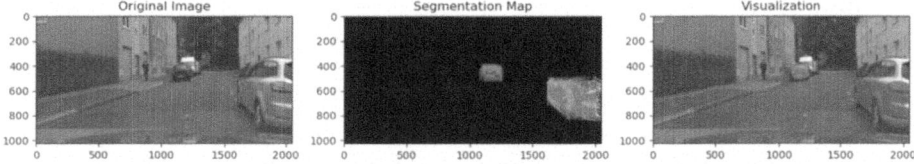

Fig. 1. Instance segmentation results

The vehicles in the photo are segmented into separate regions. Each vehicle is assigned an independent mask and is clearly separated from the surrounding objects. Segmental boundaries are created that closely follow the actual contours of each vehicle.

Regarding experimental results, the proposed method shows promising effectiveness in instance segmentation. The segmentation results are not only accurate but also create clear masks for each object, thanks to the combination of energy mapping and prediction model. The optimization of PoI' positions allows improved recognition capability, ensuring that each object in the image is properly segmented. Thus, this method opens up many application possibilities in fields such as object recognition, image processing, and deep learning, promising to bring positive results in more complex problems.

5.4   Scenario 2: EIS-PoI Method with Dataset CityScapes [10]

A typical urban scene, which includes many different objects in the street environment.

In this experiment, the EIS-PoI instance segmentation model is applied to detect and segment objects in an image. The process begins by initializing the Mask R-CNN model, then the input image is preprocessed and converted into tensors. Based on image features, the model performs segmentation and creates binary masks for detected objects. Finally, the IoU (Intersection over Union) score is calculated to evaluate the accuracy of segmentation results compared to actual masks (Fig. 2).

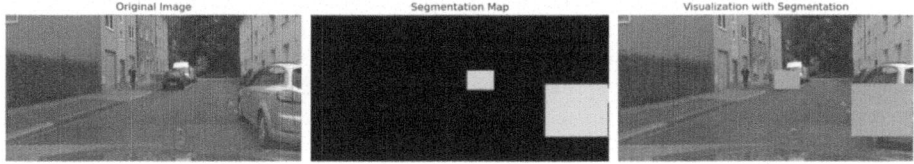

Fig. 2. Instance segmentation results

Three distinct objects are identified and segmented in the scene. Each object is masked with its own segment, with boundaries defined by the natural shape of the object in the scene. The experimental results show that the EIS-PoI method has relatively good object recognition and segmentation, as shown by the 3 detected objects. Although the IoU score achieved is 0.09, the knowledge gained from this process is still encouraging. This shows that with improvements in the training process and model optimization, EIS-PoI has great potential to improve accuracy and efficiency in future image segmenting applications.

6 Conclusion

The research has proposed the EIS-PoI method, a new solution for instance segmentation through combining energy functions and points of interest. This method shows superior effectiveness, especially in handling overlapping object cases. Despite some limitations regarding computational requirements and parameter tuning, this method opens up many promising development directions for the future. Development directions include algorithm optimization, automation of parameter tuning, extension to real-time video processing, and integration of advanced deep learning techniques. In particular, the development of unsupervised learning methods and integration of 3D contextual information promise to further enhance the solution's effectiveness in practical applications.

References

1. Mumford, D., Shah, J.: Optimal approximations by piecewise smooth functions and associated variational problems. Commun. Pure Appl. Math. **42**(5), 577–685 (1989)
2. Chan, T.F., Vese, L.A.: Active contours without edges. IEEE Trans. Image Process. **10**(2), 266–277 (2001)
3. Long, J., Shelhamer, E., Darrell, T.: Fully convolutional networks for semantic segmentation. In: Proceedings of the IEEE Conference on Computer Vision and Pattern Recognition, pp. 3431–3440 (2015)
4. He, K., Gkioxari, G., Dollár, P., Girshick, R.: Mask R-CNN. In: Proceedings of the IEEE International Conference on Computer Vision. Venice, Italy, pp. 2980–2988 (2017)
5. Xu, N., Price, B., Cohen, S., Yang, J., Huang, T.S.: Deep interactive object selection. In: Proceedings of the IEEE Conference on Computer Vision and Pattern Recognition, pp. 373–381 (2016)
6. Maninis, K.K., Caelles, S., Pont-Tuset, J., Van Gool, L.: Deep extreme cut: from extreme points to object segmentation. In: Proceedings of the IEEE Conference on Computer Vision and Pattern Recognition, pp. 616–625 (2018)
7. Chen, L.C., Papandreou, G., Kokkinos, I., Murphy, K., Yuille, A.L.: DeepLab: semantic image segmentation with deep convolutional nets, atrous convolution, and fully connected CRFs. IEEE Trans. Pattern Anal. Mach. Intell. **40**(4), 834–848 (2017)
8. Yadav, R., Pandey, M.: Image segmentation techniques: a survey. In: Proceedings of Data Analytics and Management. Springer, Singapore, pp. 231–239 (2022)
9. Robert, M.H., Linda, G.S.: Image segmentation techniques. Comput. Vis. Graph. Image Process. **29**(1), 100–132 (1985)
10. Cordts, M., et al.: The cityscapes dataset for semantic urban scene understanding. In: IEEE Conference on Computer Vision and Pattern Recognition (CVPR), pp. 3213–3223 (2016)
11. Lindeberg, T.: Scale selection properties of generalized scale-space interest point detectors. J. Math. Imag. Vis. **46**(2), 177–210 (2013)
12. Schmid, C., Mohr, R., Bauckhage, C.: Evaluation of interest point detectors. Int. J. Comput. Vis. **37**(2), 151–172 (2000)
13. Lindeberg, T.: Image matching using generalized scale-space interest points. J. Math. Imag. Vis. **52**(1), 3–36 (2015)
14. Tian, Z., Shen, C., Chen, H.: Conditional convolutions for instance segmentation. In: The European Conference on Computer Vision (ECCV) 2020. LNCS, vol. 12346, pp. 282–298. Springer (2020)

15. Bai, M., Urtasun, R.: Deep watershed transform for instance segmentation. In: IEEE Conference on Computer Vision and Pattern Recognition (CVPR). Honolulu, HI, USA, pp. 2858–2866 (2017)
16. Toan, P.H., Hiep, X.H.: Segmenting images with energy distance and energy-based model. In: National Conference XXVII: Some selective issues of Information technology and Communication. Nha Trang city, Viet Nam, pp. 330–335 (2024). (in Vietnamese)

Blockchain Application in Online Certificate Issuance and Verification Certificate System

Lam Tan Phat, Le Huu Khoa, Nguyen Gia Chan, Vo Hong Khanh,
and Nguyen Minh Triet(✉)

FPT University, Nguyen Van Cu Street 600, 900000 Can Tho City, Vietnam
{phatltce181023,khoalhce181099,channgce181288}@fpt.edu.vn,
{khanhvh,TrietNM3}@fe.edu.vn

Abstract. Blockchain technology is emerging as a crucial solution for enhancing transparency and security in the management and verification of educational credentials, addressing the widespread issue of fake qualifications. By leveraging the decentralized, immutable nature of Blockchain, a digital development and verification system can be established to securely store and manage academic records, ensuring that they are tamper-proof and verifiable in real time. Once credentials are recorded on the Blockchain, they are permanently sealed, preventing unauthorized modifications and guaranteeing authenticity. Furthermore, Smart Contracts—self-executing agreements embedded within the Blockchain—automate the entire verification process by enabling real-time validation through encrypted digital signatures, ensuring that only authorized parties can access and authenticate the data. This approach not only eliminates the risk of fraud but also enhances efficiency by allowing institutions, employers, and other stakeholders to instantly verify the legitimacy of qualifications without the need for intermediaries. Overall, a Blockchain-based verification system offers an innovative, secure, and transparent solution for managing educational credentials, significantly reducing fraud and enhancing trust in academic and professional qualifications.

Keywords: Blockchain · Digital Certificates · Verification System · Smart Contracts · Data Encryption · Academic Fraud Prevention

1 Introduction

The issue of certificate fraud is becoming an increasingly pressing and complex problem in society, not only in Vietnam but globally [1]. These fraudulent behaviors often stem from the pressure to secure high-paying jobs, the high qualification standards set by employers, or the desire for rapid career advancement. Common forms of certificate fraud include purchasing fake degrees, falsely declaring qualifications, or using illegal credentials. There are three main reasons contributing to this issue. Firstly, the demand for higher qualifications to secure better jobs or advancement opportunities pushes many people to seek degrees, even when they lack the capability or time to study. This chase for qualifications without the corresponding skills has created a demand for quick, unethical

H. X. Huynh et al. (Eds.): GOODTECHS 2024, LNICST 648, pp. 54–71, 2025.
https://doi.org/10.1007/978-3-032-01472-6_5

solutions like purchasing fake degrees. Secondly, there is a lack of rigor in management. Many recruitment organizations fail to thoroughly verify the authenticity of qualifications, or they lack an effective verification process, creating a "loophole" that allows fraudulent activities to go undetected. This oversight often occurs because organizations do not have sufficient resources or the tools necessary to accurately and efficiently verify credentials. Lastly, short-term benefits drive many to commit fraud. Some individuals believe that faking degrees will provide immediate advantages, such as securing a job or promotion, without considering the long-term consequences. They may overlook the legal and reputational risks associated with using fraudulent qualifications. The widespread nature of the problem is evident in various studies and statistics. According to data from the Ministry of Education and Training of Vietnam, hundreds of cases of fake degrees were uncovered between 2016 and 2021. In 2020 alone, a report from the Ministry of Public Security revealed that nearly 100 cases of counterfeit degrees related to both public and private educational institutions were detected and dealt with. In larger countries like the United States, a study by the National Student Clearinghouse found that up to 25% of job applications at major companies contained fraudulent degrees or certificates [2]. The consequences of certificate fraud are far-reaching. First, it leads to a loss of trust in society. Fraudulent degrees undermine public confidence in both the education system and the recruitment process. Recruitment organizations struggle to identify genuinely qualified candidates, and the presence of fraudsters damages the credibility of their processes. Second, there is a direct impact on work quality. Those using fake degrees or who do not meet the required qualifications can cause serious harm when placed in important positions without the necessary skills or knowledge. Finally, there are legal repercussions. In many countries, using fake degrees is illegal and can result in severe penalties, including fines or imprisonment.

The proposed blockchain-based system for managing and verifying educational degrees offers a groundbreaking solution by ensuring security, transparency, and efficiency in the academic credentialing process [3]. Through the application of blockchain technology, each degree or certificate is associated with a unique digital identifier that is permanently recorded on a decentralized and immutable ledger [4]. This prevents any possibility of tampering or falsification, making the verification process much more reliable. In addition to preventing fraud, the system also facilitates easier and faster verification for employers and other institutions. Instead of relying on traditional, often lengthy methods of contacting educational institutions or verifying credentials manually, employers can simply retrieve the necessary information from the blockchain by scanning a QR code or using the unique token associated with the degree. This not only saves time and resources but also ensures the integrity of the hiring process by verifying the authenticity of a candidate's qualifications in real-time. For students and graduates, the system provides a secure digital wallet for managing their academic achievements. They are empowered to control access to their credentials, sharing them with potential employers or institutions when needed. All information stored on the blockchain is encrypted using advanced cryptographic techniques, such as AES (Advanced Encryption Standard) [5], ensuring that sensitive data remains private and secure. The automation of the degree issuance and verification process through smart contracts on the Ethereum blockchain further enhances the system's efficiency. Smart contracts are self-executing programs that automatically carry out predefined actions when certain conditions are met. This eliminates the need for manual handling and reduces the risk of human errors, delays, or manipulation. Furthermore, smart contracts allow for more sophisticated interactions and conditions. This dynamic and adaptable functionality makes the system highly flexible, catering to a wide range of use cases in both academic and professional settings.

2 Background

2.1 Blockchain Technology

Blockchain is widely recognized for its success with Bitcoin [6] and is typically described as a transparent, secure, and decentralized ledger that operates on a peer-to-peer network, managing transaction data across multiple computers simultaneously. Consequently, blockchain is viewed as a trust circle that enables parties to act independently without needing third-party verification. There are three generally accepted types of blockchains: public, private, and consortium. Public blockchains, like Bitcoin and Ethereum [7], allow any anonymous user to join, view, execute transactions, or verify the integrity of blocks. Private blockchains, such as GemOS [8], MultiChain [9], and Eris [10], restrict access to authorized users who can send transactions and write to the blockchain. Consortium blockchains are semi-private, positioned between public and private, typically used in enterprises to enhance business operations. Hyperledger Fabric [11] is an example of a consortium blockchain framework, while Ethereum supports consortium blockchain creation (via Golang). Blockchain technology offers numerous features and components beneficial to participants. Transactions, which include records, contracts, and other data, are the smallest units of data on a blockchain. Any participant on the blockchain is called a node, and specific nodes, known as miners, confirm transactions by validating the sender and the transaction's contents. Miners bundle verified transactions into blocks and decide whether they should be stored on the blockchain.

Ledger refers to the blockchain's data storage, utilizing a consensus algorithm [12] to store immutable and sequential entries within blocks. Each node maintains a copy of the ledger for each channel, and the ledger captures the entire transaction history, enabling efficient queries. Cryptography [13] is crucial for blockchain, as it ensures relevant access and stores data in immutable, ordered blocks while confirming identity and authenticity. Consensus is another key blockchain element, determining how new data is added to the distributed ledger. Consensus algorithms synchronize data across the blockchain, preventing contradictory or invalid transactions. Types of consensus algorithms include Proof of Work (PoW) [14], Proof of Stake (PoS) [15], Proof of Authority (PoA) [16], and Proof of Elapsed Time (PoET) [17]. These rules require participants to prove something to be granted permission to add a block to the chain.

2.2 Smart Contract

A smart contract is a self-executing contract where the terms of the agreement between buyer and seller are directly written into lines of code. These contracts automatically enforce, execute, and verify the negotiation or performance of the contract without needing intermediaries like a lawyer or notary. Running on decentralized blockchain networks, such as Ethereum, smart contracts ensure transparency, immutability, and security.

In the case of Ethereum, is a decentralized platform for running smart contracts [18], supporting Turing-complete programming languages. Ethereum operates through the Ethereum Virtual Machine (EVM) and is written in languages like Solidity, Serpent [19], Low-level Lisp-like Language (LLL) [20], and Mutan [21]. Ethereum enables the creation of financial contracts, withdrawal limits, loops, and gambling markets, making it the most widely used smart contract platform today.

2.3 Remix

Remix [22] is a Solidity [23] Integrated Development Environment (IDE) used for writing, compiling, and debugging Solidity code, a high-level, contract-oriented programming language influenced by C++, Python, and JavaScript. Solidity is specifically designed for creating smart contracts, which run on Ethereum, a general-purpose blockchain known for its advanced scripting capabilities. Ethereum acts as a decentralized global computer, combining blockchain features with a Turing-complete contract engine to execute complex business logic. Remix IDE offers several benefits for compiling and deploying smart contracts, including the ability to compile contracts directly within the IDE, identify warnings through the compiler when best practices are not followed, deploy contracts on the JavaScript Ethereum Virtual Machine (EVM), and interact with contracts via transactions. Additionally, the IDE's terminal allows users to read and write data, facilitating efficient contract development and testing.

2.4 Encryption and Hashing

2.4.1 Advanced Encryption Standard (AES)

AES, introduced by the National Institute of Standards and Technology (NIST) in 2001, is a symmetric encryption algorithm designed to provide secure encryption of sensitive data. It operates on fixed-size blocks of 128 bits and supports key sizes of 128, 192, and 256 bits. AES employs a sequence of substitution, permutation, and mixing operations executed in several rounds depending on the key size to transform plaintext into ciphertext. Its symmetric nature means that the same key is used for both encryption and decryption, necessitating secure key management. AES has become the global standard for encrypting data across various industries due to its balance between strong security and computational efficiency [24]. It is particularly suited for environments where large volumes of data need to be encrypted without compromising performance, such as securing personal and certificate data stored on blockchain networks. In the context of blockchain, AES ensures the confidentiality of sensitive information, as encrypted data remains unreadable without the correct decryption key.

2.4.2 SHA-256 Hashing

SHA-256 [25] (Secure Hash Algorithm 256-bit) is a cryptographic hash function that generates a fixed-size, 256-bit hash value from an arbitrary input of data. Unlike encryption algorithms such as AES, which allow data to be decrypted with a key, SHA-256 is a one-way function, meaning that once data is hashed, it cannot be reversed to its original form. The primary purpose of SHA-256 is to ensure data integrity by producing a unique "fingerprint" or "digest" for any given input [26]. Even the slightest change in the input data will result in a significantly different hash, a property known as the avalanche effect. This makes SHA-256 highly effective in detecting data tampering, as any unauthorized modification of the original data will lead to a completely different hash, allowing the verification process to detect inconsistencies.

In blockchain technology, SHA-256 plays a vital role in securing data by hashing transactions and blocks. Each block in a blockchain contains a SHA-256 hash of the previous block, forming a cryptographic chain that ensures the immutability and security of the data. Furthermore, SHA-256 is widely used in digital certificates, where the hash is used to verify the integrity of certificate data. If any part of the certificate is altered, the resulting hash will differ from the original, providing an immediate indication of tampering. SHA-256's strength lies in its collision resistance, meaning it is computationally infeasible to find two different inputs that produce the same hash. This ensures a high level of security, making it a standard in various cryptographic applications, including blockchain, digital signatures, and certificate verification.

3 Related Work

This section reviews existing literature on the use of blockchain technology for online certificate issuance and verification systems [27]. Blockchain's decentralized, immutable ledger has been widely recognized as an ideal solution for addressing key challenges in traditional certification processes, such as forgery, loss of records, and reliance on third-party verification. The literature reveals that blockchain provides a secure, transparent, and tamper-proof mechanism for managing academic credentials, ensuring that certificates issued are both authentic and easily verifiable. Numerous studies have proposed frameworks where institutions issue academic certificates in the form of digital tokens recorded on a blockchain. These certificates can then be verified by employers or other institutions without the need for intermediaries. The elimination of centralized authorities enhances security and reduces the risk of fraud, as any attempt to alter a certificate would require consensus from all nodes in the network, making forgery practically impossible. The paper also emphasizes the role of smart contracts in automating the issuance and verification process. Smart contracts, self-executing programs stored on the blockchain, can trigger actions such as issuing a certificate once predefined conditions, like graduation, are met. This adds efficiency to the process by eliminating manual interventions. In terms of securing sensitive data within these blockchain-based systems, cryptographic techniques like the Advanced Encryption Standard (AES) play a crucial role. AES is frequently employed to encrypt the personal data of certificate holders before storing it on the blockchain. Encryption ensures that even if unauthorized access to the blockchain occurs, the data remains unreadable without the corresponding decryption key. In several studies, AES has been combined with other techniques, such as public-key infrastructure (PKI) and digital signatures, to further enhance the security and integrity of the stored credentials [28].

3.1 Blockchain for Credential Verification in Education

Blockchain technology offers a novel approach to educational certificate verification, addressing several limitations of traditional, centralized systems [29]. By creating an immutable ledger, blockchain ensures that academic certificates cannot be altered or forged, thereby increasing trust in educational credentials, particularly in the context of globalization and cross-border employment [30]. Furthermore, the technology facilitates a significant shift in the control of personal data. Instead of educational institutions maintaining complete authority over academic records, blockchain empowers individuals to manage and share their own information. This shift not only enhances transparency but also promotes individual autonomy in managing academic identities, aligning with modern privacy standards. Sharples and Domingue (2016) [31] emphasize that blockchain allows learners to maintain control and decide how to share their data, which empowers individuals to self-manage their academic identities, creating a decentralized framework that enhances privacy while ensuring verification.

In addition to credential verification, blockchain supports the management of lifelong learning records, extending beyond formal degrees to include informal certifications such as short courses, soft skills, and online learning achievements [32]. This promotes a more flexible and personalized educational experience, allowing individuals to authenticate their learning journeys in a decentralized manner. Moreover, the use of blockchain can significantly reduce costs and time associated with certificate verification processes by eliminating the need for third-party verification services, which can often be slow and expensive.

Despite its advantages, blockchain implementation in education faces notable challenges. First, the complexity and novelty of blockchain technology necessitate significant investment in infrastructure and training, which may be prohibitive for many educational institutions, particularly those with limited resources. Moreover, while blockchain offers robust security, concerns about data privacy persist, as storing personal educational records on a public ledger could expose sensitive information if not properly secured [33]. Additionally, integrating blockchain with existing legacy systems poses technical difficulties, potentially disrupting current data management practices. Legal challenges also arise, as the use of blockchain must comply with various national and international regulations on data storage and management. Finally, while giving individuals control over their academic records is beneficial, it also introduces risks. If a learner loses access to their blockchain account, for example, due to losing their private key, they may permanently lose access to their educational history. Overall, while blockchain presents a transformative opportunity for educational certificate verification and lifelong learning management, addressing its technical, legal, and privacy-related challenges is essential for its widespread adoption.

3.2 Cryptographic Techniques for Securing Online Credentials

One prominent issue in blockchain-based systems is the challenge of securing personal data. While blockchain provides immutability for educational records, it does not inherently protect data from unauthorized access. This is where cryptographic techniques, especially the Advanced Encryption Standard (AES), become crucial to the security infrastructure. AES has been analyzed in the context of blockchain, and it has been shown to play a critical role in safeguarding personal information, even when stored on public blockchains [34]. AES works by encrypting data before it is recorded on the blockchain, allowing only users with valid decryption keys to access the information. This ensures that sensitive data, such as educational records, personal identification information, and related financial details, remain protected from unauthorized access. However, while AES provides robust data security, key management remains a significant challenge. Protecting encryption keys is essential, as any breach in key security could result in the exposure of all encrypted data. In blockchain systems, where decentralization is a key feature, managing these encryption keys is particularly difficult, and if a key is stolen or leaked, the entire system's confidential information can be compromised. Al-Sai and Al-Qudah's study highlights the importance of integrating AES with secure key management protocols and additional cryptographic techniques, such as digital signatures, to ensure both the integrity and security of the system [35]. Moreover, it is important to recognize that the combination of blockchain and cryptographic techniques presents not only a security issue but also affects operational efficiency. While encryption secures data, it can also introduce performance bottlenecks. If the encryption or decryption process slows down the system's verification mechanisms or overall functionality, it could hinder the practicality of real-world applications, especially in environments where processing large volumes of data quickly is critical. Therefore, striking a balance between security and system performance is crucial to the successful deployment of blockchain solutions in fields that require both high security and efficiency.

3.3 Smart Contracts for Automating Certificate Verification

Smart contracts, an advanced application of blockchain, have the potential to automate the process of certificate verification and reduce the dependence on intermediaries. Smart contracts are used to authenticate academic degrees without manual intervention [36]. When an educational institution issues a certificate, the smart contract is programmed with specific verification rules. When required, the smart contract checks the data on the blockchain and provides immediate results. The use of smart contracts not only improves efficiency and speed but also reduces the risk of human error or fraud. With the immutable nature of blockchain, smart contracts ensure that the verification process always adheres to predetermined rules and cannot be changed.

A major challenge is the complexity of implementing smart contracts. Since they are pieces of programming code, smart contracts can be vulnerable to bugs or exploits if not developed carefully. Furthermore, the legal issues surrounding smart contracts are still unclear in many countries, especially in the education sector. Therefore, for widespread adoption, support from legal systems is needed to ensure the legality of these contracts.

3.4 Blockchain-Based Platforms for Credential Management

Blockchain platforms like Blockcerts and Learning Machine have created new opportunities for managing academic certificates [37]. According to (2020) [38], these platforms not only offer secure, tamper-proof digital certificates but also empower learners to manage and share them directly, without needing intermediaries. A key benefit is the autonomy they provide to learners, who can control and distribute their certificates themselves. This is a significant shift from traditional systems, where educational institutions are the sole issuers and custodians of certificates. Decentralized platforms thus protect learners' privacy and reduce the administrative workload of institutions, as they are no longer heavily involved in verifying and managing records. However, Chen et al. also highlight major challenges, especially the need for these platforms to integrate with existing educational infrastructures. Standardization and compatibility with learning management systems are crucial for ensuring scalability.

3.5 Limitations of Existing Research

Traditional verification systems often rely on manual processes and involve intermediaries such as educational institutions or independent verification agencies. Zhao et al. (2019) argue that this approach is not only slow and resource-intensive but also carries significant risks, including the potential for information forgery or manipulation [39]. These challenges become more pronounced when employers must verify the qualifications of numerous candidates in a short time frame, such as during large-scale recruitment drives. In this context, blockchain technology has been explored as a promising solution to address these issues. With its decentralized, transparent, and immutable characteristics, blockchain provides a more reliable and secure alternative to traditional centralized storage systems, which are often vulnerable to attacks or data manipulation. Rather than depending on centralized databases that can be susceptible to breaches, blockchain stores information in encrypted data blocks that are linked chronologically, ensuring that once data is recorded on the network, it becomes immutable. This feature is particularly valuable for storing and verifying educational credentials, as blockchain allows for the real-time verification of qualifications in a quick, transparent, and nearly instantaneous manner without the need for intermediaries. Consequently, the use of blockchain not only enhances security by reducing the risk of credential forgery but also alleviates administrative burdens and improves efficiency in the qualification verification process, especially when dealing with large volumes of candidates' records in a short period [40].

4 Materials and Methods

In this section, we examine the process of certificate verification and evaluate the effectiveness of blockchain technology compared to traditional systems. The analysis is based on various documents, guidelines from different sectors, and studies on blockchain's applications in digital security and data integrity. We will explore how the decentralized and tamper-proof characteristics of blockchain address key limitations in conventional systems, such as fraud and inefficiency. A proposed solution will be discussed, focusing on integrating blockchain with existing verification systems to enhance accuracy and security.

4.1 System Design and Implementation

Phase 1: Requirements Analysis

The first phase of the project focused on gathering and analyzing both functional and non-functional requirements for the blockchain-based certificate issuance and verification system. The aim was to ensure that the system would provide a high level of transparency, security, scalability, and ease of use. On the functional side, the system needed to automate the certificate issuance process, allowing institutions to issue verifiable digital certificates via smart contracts. It also had to ensure seamless verification of those certificates by third parties, such as employers or academic institutions, without the need for manual intervention. The system was also expected to use cryptographic technologies, specifically blockchain, to guarantee the integrity and authenticity of each certificate.

On the non-functional side, transparency was a critical requirement, as the system needed to provide a tamper-proof record of certificate issuance and verification on the blockchain. Security was also paramount, particularly the use of encryption and hashing technologies to protect sensitive data. Additionally, the system had to be scalable to handle potentially large numbers of certificates being issued and verified simultaneously without performance bottlenecks. Ease of use was another key factor, ensuring that users—whether issuers, recipients, or verifiers—could interact with the system without requiring extensive technical knowledge. An in-depth review of current certificate verification systems highlighted significant challenges, such as centralization, manual verification processes, and susceptibility to forgery. Blockchain technology offered a solution by decentralizing data storage, automating verification, and creating immutable records.

Phase 2: System Development

Following the requirements analysis, the system was developed using the Ethereum blockchain platform, leveraging its support for smart contracts and decentralized architecture. Ethereum was selected because of its robustness, large developer community, and ability to support the secure and autonomous execution of smart contracts. In this system, smart contracts were designed to automate the issuance and verification processes. The issuance contract was triggered when a certificate was created, storing the certificate's details on the blockchain. These details were linked to a unique token or QR code, allowing for easy retrieval and verification later. The verification process was similarly automated, with the smart contract checking the authenticity of certificates stored on the blockchain without human intervention.

In terms of security, the system implemented Advanced Encryption Standard (AES) for encrypting sensitive data such as the certificate content and recipient details. This ensured that even though certificate records were stored on a public blockchain, they remained secure and inaccessible to unauthorized parties. The Secure Hash Algorithm (SHA-256) was also used to create unique cryptographic hashes for each certificate, ensuring that any tampering would be easily detectable. Additionally, the certificates were tokenized, with each certificate represented as a cryptographic token on the blockchain. These tokens were linked to a QR code, which verifiers could scan to instantly access the certificate's information on the blockchain and confirm its validity.

Phase 3: Testing and Evaluation

The final phase involved extensive testing and evaluation of the system to ensure its functionality, security, and performance in real-world scenarios. The process of issuing certificates through smart contracts was tested under various conditions, including bulk issuance by large institutions. These tests confirmed that the system could handle large-scale issuance efficiently and without errors. The verification process, conducted using QR codes and tokens, was tested across different platforms and devices to ensure compatibility and ease of use. The tests showed that verifiers could quickly authenticate certificates with minimal effort, even if they had no technical background, confirming the system's user-friendliness.

Security testing focused on the effectiveness of the AES encryption and SHA-256 hashing mechanisms in protecting sensitive data. The system was subjected to simulated breach attempts and tampering scenarios, all of which were successfully detected and blocked. This confirmed the robustness of the encryption and hashing methods. Performance evaluations measured the system's speed, latency, and ability to handle simultaneous transactions. The system was tested under heavy loads, and it demonstrated high performance without significant delays or bottlenecks, proving its scalability. Finally, the user interface was tested to ensure that it provided a seamless experience for certificate holders, issuers, and verifiers. Feedback from test users confirmed that the combination of blockchain technology and QR code-based verification made the system intuitive and efficient to use.

4.2 Certificate Issuance and Verification

4.2.1 Certificate Issuance

The process for issuing a certificate through blockchain technology involves several critical steps to ensure both security and authenticity:

Input of Student and Degree Information: The educational institution begins by entering the necessary student information and degree details into the system. This data typically includes the student's name, identification number, program of study, date of completion, and degree type. These details serve as the foundation for generating the official certificate and must be accurate to avoid any future discrepancies.

Encryption and Storage via Smart Contract: Once the institution has input all relevant data, the system encrypts this information using Advanced Encryption Standard (AES) technology. AES is a widely recognized encryption method known for its robust security features, ensuring that sensitive information, such as personal student data and degree qualifications, remains protected against unauthorized access [41]. The encrypted data is then stored within a smart contract, which is a self-executing contract with terms of agreement written directly into code. The smart contract automates various processes and secures the data by making it immutable meaning it cannot be tampered with once stored.

Generation of a Unique Token: After encrypting and storing the data, the smart contract generates a unique token for each certificate. This token is a digital representation of the certificate and acts as an identifier that can be used to track and verify its authenticity. The smart contract then records this token onto the Ethereum blockchain. The blockchain, a decentralized and distributed ledger, ensures that the token, and therefore the certificate, is permanently recorded and cannot be altered, providing a transparent and verifiable record for future reference. The use of blockchain technology guarantees that the certificate remains immutable and secure against fraud or tampering.

4.2.2   Certificate Verification

Once a certificate has been issued and recorded on the blockchain, employers, academic institutions, and other stakeholders can easily verify its authenticity using two primary methods:

Token-Based Verification: In this method, the employer or verifying party will be provided with the certificate's unique token. By inputting this token into the verification system, a query is automatically sent to the blockchain. The system will retrieve the relevant information linked to the token, including the certificate's issuance details, such as the institution, degree type, and the student's completion date. Since this information is stored on the blockchain, it is considered immutable and secure, ensuring that the certificate has not been falsified or altered in any way. Token-based verification provides a straightforward and efficient way for employers to confirm the validity of a certificate without relying on traditional verification methods that might involve time-consuming communication with educational institutions.

QR Code-Based Verification: As an alternative to token-based verification, each Certificate is also associated with a unique QR code that encapsulates the certificate's token. This QR code is typically printed on the physical Certificate itself or embedded in the digital version. Employers or other interested parties can scan this QR code using a smartphone or a QR reader, which automatically retrieves the certificate's information from the blockchain. Scanning the QR code provides a convenient, one-step process for accessing the certificate's verification details, eliminating the need to manually input the token. This method is especially useful for simplifying the verification process in fast-paced or high-volume hiring scenarios. By scanning the QR code, employers can quickly determine whether the certificate is authentic and valid, adding an additional layer of ease and security to the verification process.

4.3   Use Case Analysis

The system supports three primary user roles: guest users, employers, and educational institutions, each interacting within a secure ecosystem designed for efficient certificate management and verification. Guest users have limited access, allowing them to browse publicly available information and conduct basic certificate verifications without needing an account. Employers use the system to verify educational qualifications, manage employee certificates, and potentially issue internal certifications. They can integrate the platform with their HR systems for streamlined management. Educational institutions serve as the source of truth, issuing and managing certificates, updating records, and responding to verification requests. They can integrate the system with learning management platforms to automate certificate issuance. To ensure security, the platform implements encryption, role-based access controls, and audit trails to safeguard sensitive data and maintain the integrity of certificate records (Fig. 1).

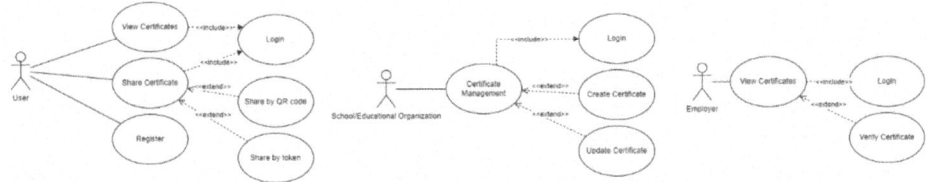

Fig. 1. Use case

5 Implementation

We have deployed the proposed system on the Ethereum blockchain platform to realize the proposed system, taking full advantage of smart contract technology.

Platform selection: Ethereum was chosen due to its popularity, large development community, and strong support for the development of decentralized applications (dApps) [42] through smart contracts. Smart contract development, smart contracts play a core role in the system, written in Solidity, a popular programming language on Ethereum. The main functions programmed in smart contracts include:

Certificate issuance management: Smart contracts automatically generate electronic certificates and assign a unique, unchangeable token to each certificate.

Data encryption and storage: All information related to certificates, including personal information of learners and information about degrees, are encrypted using the AES algorithm before being permanently stored on the blockchain. This ensures the security and integrity of the data, preventing any tampering or unauthorized changes.

Certificate Verification: The smart contract defines the certificate verification logic based on tokens or QR codes. When a user requests verification, the smart contract automatically checks the validity of the certificate based on the information stored on the blockchain.

Network deployment: The system is deployed on a network of Ethereum nodes, ensuring decentralization and continuous operation. Each node in the network stores a full copy of the blockchain, enhancing security and resistance to attacks. By combining advanced technologies such as blockchain, smart contracts, AES encryption, and QR codes, this implementation system provides a comprehensive, secure, and efficient solution for certificate issuance and verification, contributing to solving the problem of fake degrees and enhancing trust in the education and recruitment sectors.

6 Evaluation

6.1 Environmental Setting

The development environment is configured with Binance Smart Chain, Ethereum, and Fantom as the blockchain platforms, using Solidity as the programming language and Remix as the IDE. The compiler version is 0.8.16 + commit.e07a7930a, with the EVM version set to default. The gas limit is set at 3,000,000, optimization is enabled, and the project is licensed under the MIT License.

6.2 Results

The evaluation of the blockchain-based degree issuance and verification system encompasses several key metrics, focusing on performance, security, and scalability. Here are the main points from the evaluation:

The performance evaluation focuses on two key aspects: Processing Time and Verification Success Rate.

- Processing Time: The system demonstrates rapid processing capabilities, with an average time of 2.5 s to store a degree on the blockchain. The verification process, whether performed by entering a token or scanning a QR code, takes approximately 1.2 s. This is a significant improvement compared to traditional methods, which can take anywhere from minutes to hours for verification, depending on the institution and process.
- Verification Success Rate: During testing, the system achieved a 99.9% verification success rate across 1,000 degree records. This high success rate highlights the system's reliability and accuracy in ensuring that only legitimate credentials are verified, reducing the likelihood of false positives or fraudulent verifications.

Security: The blockchain system incorporates multiple security features to ensure the protection of sensitive information and the integrity of the verification process.

- Data Encryption and Two-Factor Authentication (2FA): These features ensure that only authorized individuals or entities can access or verify degree information. Encryption safeguards the data at rest and in transit, while 2FA adds an extra layer of protection against unauthorized access.
- Decentralization: By leveraging blockchain's decentralized architecture, the risks associated with centralized databases, such as single points of failure or data breaches, are minimized. Each record is distributed across multiple nodes, making unauthorized modifications extremely difficult.
- Smart Contracts: Smart contracts are employed to automate the verification process while protecting student privacy. They allow the verification to occur without exposing personal details, ensuring that only the necessary information is shared with third parties.

Scalability: The system is designed to efficiently handle large volumes of simultaneous verification requests, demonstrating strong scalability in real-world applications. During stress tests, the system successfully processed thousands of requests without significant delays or performance degradation. This scalability is crucial for large institutions or certification bodies that may need to verify multiple credentials at the same time during peak periods, such as during graduation seasons or when employers conduct mass verifications.

User Experience: Feedback from users, both students and employers, was overwhelmingly positive. Surveys conducted post-implementation revealed high levels of satisfaction with the system.

- Student Satisfaction: 98% of students surveyed reported satisfaction with the system's security and convenience. They appreciated the quick access to their verified degrees, as well as the ease of sharing their credentials with potential employers or academic institutions.

- Employer Satisfaction: Similarly, 95% of employers noted a reduction in the time and effort required to verify academic credentials. Employers particularly valued the reliability and accuracy of the verification system, which streamlined their recruitment processes and minimized the risk of fraudulent qualifications.

Comparison with Traditional Systems: When compared to traditional degree verification methods, the blockchain-based system outperformed in several key areas:

- Speed: Traditional systems often rely on manual processes or centralized databases, which can take significantly longer (from several minutes to days) to verify credentials. The blockchain system, by contrast, offers near-instantaneous verification.
- Accuracy and Reliability: Traditional methods can be prone to tampering, especially when relying on intermediaries. The blockchain system's decentralized and immutable nature ensures a higher degree of accuracy and eliminates the risk of unauthorized modifications to the records.
- Security: The encryption and decentralization inherent in blockchain technology provide superior protection against data breaches and unauthorized access compared to centralized databases used in traditional systems.

Cost Range: The cost associated with using the Ethereum blockchain is primarily driven by gas fees. Each transaction on the blockchain, such as issuing a degree or verifying a credential, incurs a fee. The gas fees for recording each transaction are estimated to range from $0.05 to $0.10. Although these fees represent an additional cost, they are relatively low compared to the administrative overheads and time costs associated with traditional verification methods. Furthermore, the transparency and security provided by blockchain technology may justify this cost for many institutions and employers. As Fig. 2, a total of 2,545,152 gas units were used, the majority of which (2,213,175 gas) was spent on transaction costs - the fee to include the transaction in the blockchain. The execution cost, i.e. the amount of gas required to make changes to the blockchain, was 2,003,261 gas. This shows that verifying and recording the transaction was significantly more resource-intensive than performing the tasks within the transaction.

gas	2545152 gas
transaction cost	2213175 gas
execution cost	2003261 gas

Fig. 2. Smart contract fees

7 Conclusions

In conclusion, the integration of blockchain technology into an online degree issuance and verification system signifies a monumental leap forward in the evolution of higher education, offering a powerful antidote to the persistent challenges of credential fraud and cumbersome verification processes. By harnessing the inherent strengths of blockchain – immutability, decentralization, and transparency – this system establishes an unprecedented level of trust and security in the authenticity of academic degrees. This not only empowers students and graduates with verifiable and tamper-proof credentials but also equips employers with a reliable and efficient tool to validate the qualifications of prospective employees, streamlining hiring processes and mitigating the risks associated with fraudulent credentials. The decentralized nature of blockchain dismantles the reliance on centralized authorities, fostering a more equitable and accessible education landscape where individuals have greater control over their academic data. This shift in control has profound implications, particularly for those who may have faced barriers to traditional education systems, as it allows them to showcase their achievements on a level playing field. Furthermore, the automation facilitated by smart contracts drastically reduces the time and resources required for verification, eliminating the cumbersome manual processes and minimizing the potential for human error. This efficiency gain translates to cost savings for institutions and a more seamless experience for individuals seeking to advance their education or career.

While the implementation of a blockchain-based system presents certain challenges, such as the initial costs of development and maintenance, ensuring scalability to accommodate a high volume of transactions, and addressing privacy concerns related to sensitive academic data, the long-term benefits far outweigh these initial hurdles. By fostering a standardized and globally recognized system, blockchain can facilitate cross-border verification [43] of credentials, unlocking a world of opportunities for individuals seeking educational and professional advancement on an international scale. This enhanced mobility and collaboration fosters innovation and economic growth by enabling the seamless exchange of talent and knowledge across borders. Moreover, by empowering individuals with ownership and control over their academic data, blockchain promotes a more transparent and equitable system where academic achievements are recognized and valued based on their true merit, irrespective of geographical boundaries or socioeconomic backgrounds. This, in turn, can incentivize lifelong learning and skills development, as individuals are empowered to curate and share their educational achievements in a secure and verifiable manner.

The successful implementation of a blockchain-based online degree issuance and verification system hinges on the collaborative efforts of various stakeholders, including educational institutions, technology providers, policymakers, and individuals. By working together to establish standards, address concerns, and promote the benefits of this technology, we can unlock its full potential to transform the education landscape and pave the way for a future where academic degrees are recognized and valued based on their true merit, fostering trust, transparency, and opportunities for all. This collaborative approach is crucial to ensure that the system is scalable, secure, and interoperable, allowing for seamless exchange of information and recognition of credentials across institutions and borders. It also requires a commitment to ongoing research and development to address emerging challenges and harness the full potential of blockchain technology in the education sector.

In essence, the integration of blockchain technology into the realm of higher education represents a paradigm shift, promising to revolutionize the way we issue, verify, and recognize academic credentials. By embracing this technology and its transformative potential, we can create a more secure, efficient, and equitable education system that empowers individuals, strengthens institutions, and fosters a global community of learners united by a shared commitment to trust, transparency, and the pursuit of knowledge. This is not merely a technological upgrade but a fundamental shift in how we value and recognize learning, paving the way for a future where education is truly accessible, empowering, and transformative for all.

Author Contributions. All authors have read and agreed to the published version of the manuscript.

Funding. This research received no external funding.

Data Availability Statement Not applicable.

Institutional Review Board Statement. Not applicable.

Informed Consent Statement. Not applicable

Conflicts of Interest. The authors declare no conflict of interest

References

1. Sultana, S.A., Rupa, C., Malleswari, R.P., Gadekallu, T.R.: IPFS-blockchain smart contracts based conceptual framework to reduce certificate frauds in the academic field. Information **14**(8), 446 (2023)
2. Dynarski, S.M., Hemelt, S.W., Hyman, J.M.: The missing manual: Using National Student Clearinghouse data to track postsecondary outcomes. Educ. Eval. Policy Anal. **37**(1_suppl), 53S–79S (2015)
3. Pilkington, M.: Blockchain technology: principles and applications. In: Research handbook on digital transformations (pp. 225–253). Edward Elgar Publishing (2016)
4. Antal, C., Cioara, T., Anghel, I., Antal, M., Salomie, I.: Distributed ledger technology review and decentralized applications development guidelines. Future Internet **13**(3), 62 (2021)
5. Rijmen, V., Daemen, J.: Advanced encryption standard. Proc. Federal Inf. Process. Stand. Publ. Nat. Inst. Stand. Technol. **19**, 22 (2001)
6. Vranken, H.: Sustainability of bitcoin and blockchains. Curr. Opin. Environ. Sustain. **28**, 1–9 (2017)
7. Buterin, V.: Ethereum white paper. GitHub Repository **1**, 22–23 (2013)

8. Roth, A., Knopfle, W., Rabus, B., Gebhardt, S., Scales, D.: GEMOS-a system for the geocoding and mosaicking of interferometric digital elevation models. In: IEEE 1999 International Geoscience and Remote Sensing Symposium. IGARSS'99 (Cat. No. 99CH36293) (Vol. 2, pp. 1124–1127). IEEE (1999)
9. Reiser, M., Lavenberg, S.S.: Mean-value analysis of closed multichain queuing networks. J. ACM (JACM) 27(2), 313–322 (1980)
10. DuPont, Q., Maurer, B.: Ledgers and Law in the Blockchain. Kings Rev. 23 (2015)
11. Androulaki, E., et al.: Hyperledger fabric: a distributed operating system for permissioned blockchains. In: Proceedings of the Thirteenth EuroSys Conference, pp. 1–15 (2018)
12. Mingxiao, D., Xiaofeng, M., Zhe, Z., Xiangwei, W., Qijun, C.: A review on consensus algorithm of blockchain. In: 2017 IEEE International Conference on Systems, Man, and Cybernetics (SMC), pp. 2567–2572. IEEE (2017)
13. Menezes, A.J., Van Oorschot, P.C., Vanstone, S.A.: Handbook of applied cryptography. CRC Press (2018)
14. Gervais, A., Karame, G.O., Wüst, K., Glykantzis, V., Ritzdorf, H., Capkun, S.: On the security and performance of proof of work blockchains. In: Proceedings of the 2016 ACM SIGSAC Conference on Computer and Communications Security, pp. 3–16 (2016)
15. King, S., Nadal, S.: PPCoin: Peer-to-peer crypto-currency with proof-of-stake. self-published paper, August, 19(1) (2012)
16. De Angelis, S., Aniello, L., Baldoni, R., Lombardi, F., Margheri, A., Sassone, V.: PBFT vs proof-of-authority: Applying the CAP theorem to permissioned blockchain. In: CEUR Workshop Proceedings (Vol. 2058). CEUR-WS (2018)
17. Chen, L., Xu, L., Shah, N., Gao, Z., Lu, Y., Shi, W.: On security analysis of proof-of-elapsed-time (POET). In: Stabilization, Safety, and Security of Distributed Systems: 19th International Symposium, SSS 2017, Boston, MA, USA, November 5–8, 2017, Proceedings 19, pp. 282–297. Springer International Publishing (2017)
18. Tsankov, P., Dan, A., Drachsler-Cohen, D., Gervais, A., Buenzli, F., Vechev, M.: Securify: practical security analysis of smart contracts. In: Proceedings of the 2018 ACM SIGSAC Conference on Computer and Communications Security, pp. 67–82 (2018)
19. Leppänen, J.: Serpent–a continuous-energy Monte Carlo reactor physics burnup calculation code. VTT Tech. Res. Centre Finland 4(455), 2023–2109 (2013)
20. Jones, N.D., Muchnick, S.S.: Flow analysis and optimization of LISP-like structures. In Proceedings of the 6th ACM SIGACT-SIGPLAN Symposium on Principles of Programming Languages (pp. 244–256) (1979)
21. Ben-Younes, H., Cadene, R., Cord, M., Thome, N.: MUTAN: multimodal tucker fusion for visual question answering. In Proceedings of the IEEE International Conference on Computer Vision, pp. 2612–2620 (2017)
22. Amir Latif, R.M., Hussain, K., Jhanjhi, N.Z., Nayyar, A., Rizwan, O.: A remix IDE: smart contract-based framework for the healthcare sector by using Blockchain technology. Multimedia tools Appl. 1–24 (2020)
23. Dannen, C.: Introducing Ethereum and solidity (Vol. 1, pp. 159–160). Berkeley: Apress (2017)
24. Livni, R., Shalev-Shwartz, S., Shamir, O.: On the computational efficiency of training neural networks. Adv. Neural Inf. Process. Syst. 27 (2014)
25. Gilbert, H., Handschuh, H.: Security analysis of SHA-256 and sisters. In: International workshop on selected areas in cryptography (pp. 175–193). Berlin, Heidelberg: Springer Berlin Heidelberg (2003)
26. Massoudi, A., Lefebvre, F., Demarty, C.H., Oisel, L., Chupeau, B.: A video fingerprint based on visual digest and local fingerprints. In: 2006 International Conference on Image Processing, pp. 2297–2300. IEEE (2006)
27. Nguyen, B.M., Dao, T.C., Do, B.L.: Towards a blockchain-based certificate authentication system in Vietnam. PeerJ. Comput. Sci. 6, e266 (2020)

28. Maurer, U.: Modelling a public-key infrastructure. In: Computer Security—ESORICS 96: 4th European Symposium on Research in Computer Security Rome, Italy, September 25–27, 1996 Proceedings 4 (pp. 325–350). Springer Berlin Heidelberg (1996)
29. Han, M., Li, Z., He, J., Wu, D., Xie, Y., Baba, A.: A novel blockchain-based education records verification solution. In: Proceedings of the 19th Annual SIG Conference on Information Technology Education, pp. 178–183 (2018)
30. Ataullah, A., Le, H., Sahota, A.S.: Employee productivity, employment growth, and the cross-border acquisitions by emerging market firms. Hum. Resour. Manage. **53**(6), 987–1004 (2014)
31. Sharples, M., Domingue, J.: The blockchain and kudos: a distributed system for educational record, reputation and reward. In: Adaptive and Adaptable Learning: 11th European Conference on Technology Enhanced Learning, EC-TEL 2016, Lyon, France, September 13–16, 2016, Proceedings 11 (pp. 490–496). Springer International Publishing (2016)
32. Terzi, S., Ioannis, S., Votis, K., Tsiatsos, T.: A life-long learning education passport powered by blockchain technology and verifiable digital credentials: the BlockAdemiC project. In: International Conference on Software Engineering and Formal Methods (pp. 249–263). Cham: Springer International Publishing (2021)
33. Chen, S., Zhang, L., Yan, Z., Shen, Z.: A distributed and robust security-constrained economic dispatch algorithm based on blockchain. IEEE Trans. Power Syst. **37**(1), 691–700 (2021)
34. Zheng, Z., Xie, S., Dai, H.N., Chen, X., Wang, H.: Blockchain challenges and opportunities: a survey. Int. J. Web Grid Serv. **14**(4), 352–375 (2018)
35. Zeadally, S., Das, A.K., Sklavos, N.: Cryptographic technologies and protocol standards for Internet of Things. Internet Things **14**, 100075 (2021)
36. Shakan, Y., Kumalakov, B., Mutanov, G., Mamykova, Z., Kistaubayev, Y.: Verification of university student and graduate data using blockchain technology (2021). InternationaChapurlat, V., & Braesch, C. (2008). Verification, validation, qualification and certification of enterprise models: Statements and opportunities. Computers in Industry, 59(7), 711–721.Journal of Computers Communications & Control, 16(5)
37. Bahrami, M., Movahedian, A., Deldari, A.: A comprehensive blockchain-based solution for academic certificates management using smart contracts. In: 2020 10th International Conference on Computer and Knowledge Engineering (ICCKE) (pp. 573–578). IEEE (2020)
38. Capece, G., Levialdi Ghiron, N., Pasquale, F.: Blockchain technology: redefining trust for digital certificates. Sustainability **12**(21), 8952 (2020)
39. Levitskaya, A., Fedorov, A.: Typology and mechanisms of media manipulation. Int. J. Media Inf. Literacy **5**(1), 69–78 (2020)
40. Monteleone, R., Klarmann, D.: Qualification and validation. Quality Management and Accreditation in Hematopoietic Stem Cell Transplantation and Cellular Therapy: The JACIE Guide, **35** (2022)
41. Winn, P.A.: The guilty eye: unauthorized access, trespass and privacy. Bus. Lawyer 1395–1437 (2007)
42. Raval, S.: Decentralized applications: harnessing Bitcoin's blockchain technology. "O'Reilly Media, Inc." (2016)
43. Chang, Y., Iakovou, E., Shi, W.: Blockchain in global supply chains and cross border trade: a critical synthesis of the state-of-the-art, challenges and opportunities. Int. J. Prod. Res. **58**(7), 2082–2099 (2020)

Smart Contract Integration in Tuition Management

Vo Nhut Tin, Nguyen Tien Thuan, Le Nhut Anh, Vo Hong Khanh,
and Nguyen Minh Triet[✉]

FPT University, Nguyen Van Cu Street, 600, 900000 Can Tho City, Vietnam
{TinVNCE180619,ThuanNTCE181024,AnhLNCE181767}@fpt.edu.vn,
{KhanhVH,TrietNM3}@fe.edu.vn

Abstract. This paper explores the application of blockchain technology, particularly Ethereum-based decentralized applications (dApps), in revolutionizing tuition payment systems for educational institutions. Traditional payment methods are often plagued by inefficiencies, high costs, and security vulnerabilities due to reliance on intermediaries. By leveraging Ethereum smart contracts, this research presents a secure, transparent, and automated solution for processing tuition payments [1, 2]. The proposed system allows students to interact with the blockchain via a user-friendly web interface, ensuring secure authentication through Ethereum wallets. Key functionalities, such as automatic payment verification, deadline enforcement, and transaction history logging, are built into the system, enhancing transparency and reducing human error. The implementation of immutable smart contracts guarantees data integrity and eliminates the need for centralized control, significantly improving security and efficiency. This paper not only highlights the technical architecture but also discusses the potential benefits and challenges of integrating blockchain technology in the educational sector, setting the foundation for future innovations in financial management.

Keywords: Blockchain technology · Ethereum · Decentralized applications (dApps) · Smart contracts · Tuition payment system · Educational institutions · Payment automation · Transparency · Financial management

1 Introduction

In recent years, the landscape of financial transactions has been significantly transformed by advancements in blockchain technology, particularly through the advent of decentralized applications (DApps) and smart contracts. One area where these innovations have shown immense promise is in the management and processing of tuition payments within educational institutions. Traditional payment systems often involve multiple intermediaries, leading to inefficiencies, increased costs, and potential security vulnerabilities. In contrast, leveraging Ethereum's blockchain to create a decentralized application for tuition payment offers a secure, transparent, and automated solution. This research paper aims to provide an in-depth exploration of the process involved in tuition

H. X. Huynh et al. (Eds.): GOODTECHS 2024, LNICST 648, pp. 72–80, 2025.
https://doi.org/10.1007/978-3-032-01472-6_6

payment through a DApp utilizing Ethereum smart contracts, highlighting the benefits of this approach and the implications for stakeholders in the educational sector.

The process begins with the student accessing the DApp through a web interface, using their Ethereum wallet address to log in. This initial step is crucial as it ensures that the transaction remains private and secure, eliminating the need for sensitive personal information to be shared with the educational institution. Once logged in, the system retrieves and displays pertinent information regarding the student's tuition, including the amount due and the payment deadline. This feature not only provides clarity to the student but also reinforces accountability on the part of the institution.

After reviewing their tuition details, the student is prompted to enter the payment amount they wish to process. This interaction is facilitated through the DApp interface, which is designed to be user-friendly and intuitive. The transaction is then initiated and processed on the Ethereum network through the smart contract, which acts as a self-executing agreement with the terms of the payment directly written into code [3]. This automation eliminates the need for intermediaries, reducing transaction times and costs significantly.

Upon successful completion of the payment, the smart contract automatically updates the student's status within the system, confirming their enrollment and financial standing. Furthermore, the details of the transaction are logged on the blockchain, ensuring that they are immutable and can be accessed at any time for verification purposes. This level of transparency is a significant advantage over traditional payment methods, where records may be vulnerable to tampering or loss.

The final step of the process allows students to view their transaction history, providing transparency and fostering trust as they can independently verify their payments [4]. Overall, using a DApp with Ethereum smart contracts for tuition payments enhances efficiency, security, and transparency in managing educational financial transactions.

2 Methodology

2.1 System Overview

The rapid evolution of technology has ushered in a new era of digital interactions, characterized by the increasing adoption of decentralized applications (dApps). These applications leverage blockchain technology to provide enhanced security, transparency, and user control, fundamentally transforming traditional software architectures. In this research paper, we explore the architecture of a decentralized application that integrates a modern JavaScript-based frontend with a decentralized backend, focusing on the technologies employed and their respective roles in creating a robust, scalable, and efficient system (Fig. 1).

Our architecture centers on a JavaScript-based frontend utilizing React, which enhances modularity and reusability through its component-based design, essential for delivering dynamic user experiences in decentralized applications (dApps). The frontend interacts with the Ethereum blockchain via Web3.js, enabling intuitive blockchain transactions directly from the interface. The integration of TypeScript enhances code reliability by enforcing static typing, mitigating potential runtime errors—crucial in the financial-sensitive context of blockchain. Tailwind CSS ensures consistent, responsive

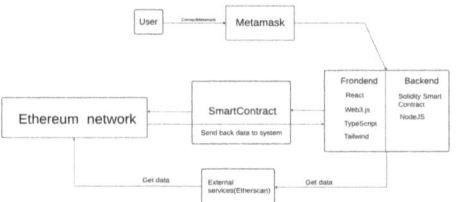

Fig. 1. System Overview

design across devices, further elevating user experience. The backend adheres to decentralized principles, with core business logic executed through immutable Solidity smart contracts on the Ethereum blockchain, ensuring security and transparency. A Node.js server facilitates seamless communication between the frontend and the blockchain, processing requests and managing data interactions, thereby optimizing the overall user engagement with the dApp.

2.2 Smart Contract Design and Functionality

The smart contract serves as the fundamental component of the tuition payment system, governing all logic associated with financial transactions related to educational fees. Deployed on the Ethereum blockchain, this smart contract ensures both security and immutability, thereby establishing a trustworthy environment for conducting financial exchanges.

2.3 Key Functions of the Smart Contract

The primary function of the smart contract is to automate the entire tuition payment process, eliminating the need for intermediaries and ensuring secure, efficient, and transparent transactions. The key automated functions include:

payTuition: This function autonomously handles tuition payments from students. It verifies the payment amount, processes the transaction via the Ethereum blockchain, and updates the student's payment status without any manual intervention. This automation reduces human error and significantly increases the efficiency of the payment process.

Verifying Payment Deadlines: The smart contract is programmed to automatically track payment deadlines. It compares the transaction timestamps recorded on the blockchain with the predefined deadlines and enforces consequences for late payments, ensuring timely compliance without administrative oversight.

Logging Transaction History: Each payment triggers an automatic logging event that records essential details such as the payment amount, timestamp, and payer identity. This creates a transparent, immutable transaction history, providing both students and institutions with verifiable records of all financial interactions (Fig. 2).

2.4 Smart Contract Design

The EduPayChain smart contract consists of three primary functions: payTuition, get-PaymentStatus, and requestRefund. However, the contract definition itself is not directly

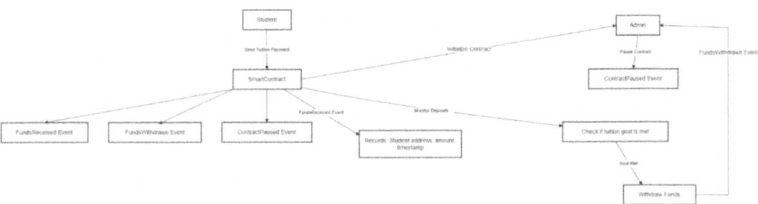

Fig. 2. SmartContract Diagram

executed on the Ethereum network. During the compilation process using the Solidity Compiler, the contract is split into two distinct files. The first file contains the bytecode, which is the low-level machine code deployed on the Ethereum network and executed by the Ethereum Virtual Machine (EVM) [5]. The second file is the Application Binary Interface (ABI), which defines how external systems can call and interact with the contract's functions [1]. The ABI acts as an interface between decentralized applications (DApps) and the smart contract, specifying available functions and how to format inputs and outputs. This allows developers to create user-friendly interfaces for interacting with the smart contract [6]. The interaction between DApps and the smart contract is often represented in flow diagrams, which abstract the underlying technical complexity for end users (Figs. 3 and 4).

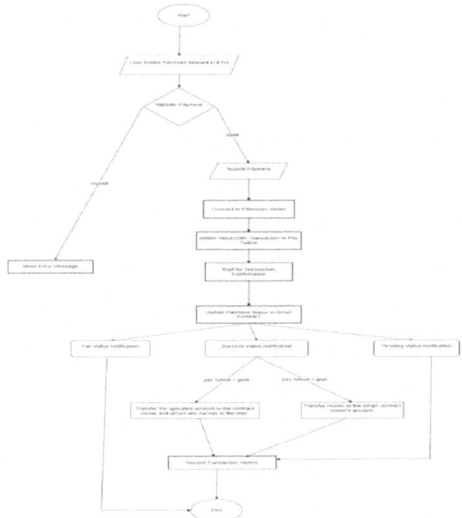

Fig. 3. Smartcontract EduPayChain Workflow

The table provides a structured overview of the EduPayChain smart contract, which facilitates tuition payments on the blockchain. The contract's main functionalities include handling payments through the payTuition function, managing refunds using requestRefund. Core structures like Student and Transaction are used to record payment details and transaction history, ensuring transparency and accountability. The contract tracks

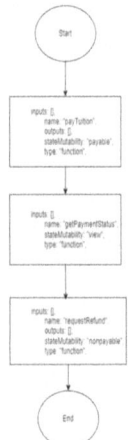

Fig. 4. ABI Smartcontract EduPayChain Workflow

Table 1. Smart Contract functions and variables

Items	Types	Usage
payTuition	Function	Allows students to make payments towards tuition
getContractBalance	Function	Returns the current balance of the contract
requestRefund	Function	Issues refunds if the payment goal is not met
togglePause	Function	Pauses or resumes the contract
getPaymentStatus	Function	Returns the current payment state (Active, Completed, Failed)
getStudentTransactionHistory	Function	Retrieves the transaction history of a specific student

payment status using an enum called PaymentState, which indicates whether payments are active, completed, or failed. Additionally, the admin has control over the contract with functions like togglePause and extendPaymentDeadline, providing flexibility in managing operations. Table 1 outlines the specific variables employed for each feature during the development of the smart contracts.

2.5 Testing the Smart Contract

Remix is a web-based IDE designed for developing, testing, and deploying Ethereum smart contracts, primarily written in Solidity. It offers a user-friendly interface with features like syntax highlighting, auto-completion, and error checking, as well as plugin support for customization [7]. Testing is critical in smart contract development due to the immutability and autonomous operation of contracts on the blockchain. Remix provides built-in testing tools, including a Solidity testing framework and a JavaScript VM that simulates Ethereum's environment, allowing developers to validate their contracts efficiently. It also supports integration with external testing libraries like Truffle and Mocha for enhanced testing capabilities [8].

2.6 Designing DApps for EduPayChain

The payment gateway interface for DApps is being developed using the Truffle framework. Table 2 provides a comprehensive breakdown of each variable involved in the DApps development process, explaining their roles in detail.

Table 2. Key Functions and Variables in a DApp-Based Payment Gateway

Items	Types	Usage
App	Function	To initialize the main DApp and render components
fetchContractData	Function	To retrieve and display data from the contract
handleTransfer	Function	To handle tuition payment transactions
handleTogglePause	Function	To toggle the pause state of the contract
setpayTuition	Constant	To set the value for the tuition payment
setIsLoading	Constant	To set the loading state of the transaction
setExtendPaymentDeadline	Constant	To extend or update the payment deadline
setcontractBalance	Constant	To store the balance of the contract
setHistoryEvent	Constant	To store and display payment history events
ContractInfo	Component	To display contract information, including balance
PaymentDeadline	Component	To display and manage the payment deadline
TransactionHistory	Component	To show the history of transactions

The process begins with the student accessing the web interface and logging in using their Ethereum wallet address. Upon logging in, the system displays the student's contract details, including the outstanding tuition amount and the payment deadline. The student then enters the payment amount into the form and confirms the transaction, which is processed through the Ethereum network via the smart contract. Once the transaction is successfully completed, the smart contract updates the student's payment status and logs the transaction in the history, triggering an event to refresh the transaction data. Finally, the student can access the transaction history section to review all past payments, including details such as the amount paid, payment date, and status of each transaction [9].

3 Results and Discussions

3.1 DApp-Based Payment

The tuition payment process through a decentralized application (DApp) utilizing Ethereum smart contracts involves several key steps designed for security, automation, and user-friendliness. Initially, students authenticate their identity via their Ethereum wallets, ensuring privacy and enhancing security [10]. After logging in, they view their up-to-date tuition details, including the amount due and payment deadlines. Students can then initiate the payment by entering the desired amount, which triggers the transaction process on the Ethereum network. The DApp submits transaction details for validation through a consensus mechanism, either Proof of Work (PoW) or Proof of Stake (PoS). Once validated, the associated smart contract executes, confirming the payment and updating the student's status to "Transaction successfull!". Additionally, the transaction is logged on the blockchain, creating an immutable record that enhances transparency and provides both students and institutions reliable access to their financial histories [11] (Fig. 5).

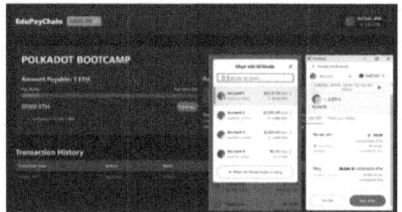 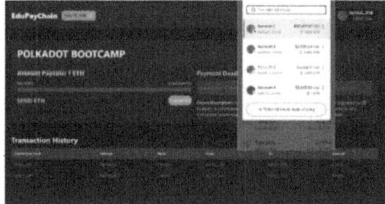

Fig. 5. Tuition payment user interface

Table 3 demonstrates the sophisticated functionality of the dApp's smart contract in automating the financial transactions associated with tuition payments. Upon a successful transfer, the system seamlessly allocates the correct amount to the admin's wallet and automatically refunds any overpayment made by the student, showcasing the contract's precision and reliability.

Table 3. Update the amount after the transfer and automatic refund process

Name	Address	Value (Holesky Test Network)
Account 1	0x72c27F66c84F9303305B42e2E202EC5bd61E3918	7.839ETH
Account 2	0x59935873223A7306F09a9128e806bA0Ad9157946	0.888ETH
Account 3	0xd94E77701A821e071e22341df8a812103776aB45	1.089ETH
Account 4 (Admin)	0x407219db63869d0FfcD2DB8C10252236e9Ee2A21	1ETH

This automated process underscores the contract's ability to ensure accuracy in fund distribution, eliminate manual intervention, and enhance overall security and transparency, key advantages of decentralized finance (DeFi) technology [12]. The precise handling of funds and automated refund mechanism significantly enhance the system's efficiency, minimizing errors and safeguarding user trust.

4 Conclusion

In conclusion, the integration of smart contracts into tuition management systems offers a multitude of benefits, including increased transparency, enhanced security, and automation of processes [13]. These advantages have the potential to transform the way educational institutions handle financial transactions, leading to improved efficiency and a better experience for students and their families. However, challenges such as technical complexities and regulatory compliance issues must be addressed to fully realize the potential of smart contracts in the education sector [14].

As the technology continues to evolve, innovations in smart contract platforms and broader applications within education will likely emerge. By embracing these advancements, educational institutions can position themselves at the forefront of technological innovation, ultimately benefiting students and the wider educational community. The future of tuition management and education as a whole may very well be shaped by the capabilities of smart contracts, paving the way for a more efficient, transparent, and equitable educational landscape [15].

References

1. Balcerzak, A.P., Nica, E., Rogalska, E., Poliak, M., Klieštik, T., Sabie, O.M.: Blockchain technology and smart contracts in decentralized governance systems. Admin. Sci. **12**(3), 96 (2022)
2. Aini, Q., Rahardja, U., Khoirunisa, A.: Blockchain technology into gamification on education. IJCCS (Indonesian J. Comput. Cybern. Syst.) **14**(2), 147–158 (2020)
3. Sholeh, M., Talahaturuson, E.Y., Rizqi, M., Gumelar, A.B.: Designing an Ethereum-based blockchain for tuition payment system using smart contract service. Jurnal RESTI (Rekayasa Sistem dan Teknologi Informasi) **6**(2), 275–280 (2022)
4. Sherazi, S.N.A., Zahoor, E., Akhtar, S., Perrin, O.: A Blockchain based approach for the authorization policies delegation in emergency situations. Trans. Emerg. Telecommun. Technol. **33**(5), e4461 (2022)
5. Mohammed, N.S., Dawood, O.A., Sagheer, A.M., Nafea, A.A.: Secure smart contract based on Blockchain to prevent the non-repudiation phenomenon. Baghdad Sci. J. **21**(1), 0234 (2024)
6. Sheng, D., Luo, H., Zhong, B.: Formal modeling of smart contracts for quality acceptance in construction. In: Proceedings of the Creative Construction e-Conference 2020, pp. 79–87 (2020)
7. Zhang, Y.: Smart contract-based access control for the internet of things. arXiv preprint arXiv: 1802.04410 (2018)
8. Muneeb, M., Raza, Z., Haq, I.U., Shafiq, O.: SmartCon: a Blockchain-based framework for smart contracts and transaction management. IEEE Access **10**, 23687–23699 (2021)

9. Fraga-Lamas, P., Fernández-Caramés, T.M.: A review on Blockchain technologies for an advanced and cyber-resilient automotive industry. IEEE Access **7**, 17578–17598 (2019)
10. Park, J., Jeong, S., Yeom, K.: Smart contract broker: improving smart contract reusability in a blockchain environment. Sensors **23**(13), 6149 (2023)
11. Fedorova, E.P., Skobleva, E.I.: Application of Blockchain technology in higher education. Eur. J. Contemp. Educ. **9**(3), 552–571 (2020)
12. Edastama, P., Purnama, S., Widayanti, R., Meria, L., Rivelino, D.: The potential Blockchain technology in higher education learning innovations in era 4.0. Blockchain Front. Technol. **1**(01), 104–113 (2021)
13. Jha, S.K.: The counterfeit degree certificate: application of Blockchain technology in higher education in India. Library Hi Tech News **40**(2), 20–24 (2023)
14. Duan, B., Zhong, Y., Liu, D.: Education application of Blockchain technology: learning outcome and meta-diploma. In: 2017 IEEE 23rd International Conference on Parallel and Distributed Systems (ICPADS), pp. 814–817. IEEE (2017)
15. Reis-Marques, C., Figueiredo, R., de Castro Neto, M.: Applications of Blockchain technology to higher education arena: a bibliometric analysis. Eur. J. Invest. Health Psychol. Educ. **11**(4), 1406–1421 (2021)

Model Integrating CNN, Gated Recurrent Unit and Genetic Algorithm for Rainfall Forecasting from Radar Images at Phadin Station

Ha Gia Son[1,2,3], Tran Manh Tuan[4(✉)], Hoang Duc Trung[3], Tran Thi Ngan[5], Le Tuan Anh[6], and Le Minh Tuan[7]

[1] Vietnam Academy of Science and Technology, Vietnam National Academy of Science and Technology, Hanoi, Vietnam

[2] Faculty of Information Technology - Industrial, University of Viet – Hung, Hanoi, Vietnam

[3] Advanced International Research Center for Applied Artificial Intelligence, Institute of Information Technology, Vietnam National University, Hanoi, Vietnam
hoangductrung_t65@hus.edu.vn

[4] Thuy Loi University, Hanoi, Vietnam
tmtuan@tlu.edu.vn

[5] VNU International School, Hanoi, Vietnam
ngantt@vnuis.edu.vn

[6] Information Communication and Technology University, Thai Nguyen, Vietnam
ltanh@ictu.edu.vn, tuanlm@eaut.edu.vn

[7] East Asia University of Technology, Bac Ninh, Vietnam

Abstract. Rainfall forecasting plays a crucial role in disaster prevention, water resource management, agricultural support, transportation, and industry. It aids in early warnings, production planning, safety assurance, damage mitigation, and resource optimization across various fields. This paper introduces a rainfall forecasting model for the next hour (Nowcasting) using CNN (Convolution Neural network) combined with GRU (Gated Recurrent Unit) neural networks and integrated with an improved genetic algorithm (GA) to achieve better performance. The theoretical contribution of this paper is the creation of a new model that combines CNN layers with GRU and suggests improvements to the GA for optimizing the model's weights. Practically, the model is tested with radar data from the Phadin station collected from 6:00 AM to 4:00 PM on July 10, 2020. Results indicate that this model with the improved GA outperforms other models.

Keywords: Rainfall forecasting · Radar images · Genetic Algorithm · GRU · CNN

1 Introduction

Climate change causes natural disasters such as storms, floods, and droughts, threatening human lives. Weather and rainfall forecasting is crucial for minimizing damage and enabling timely responses from individuals and authorities. Modern forecasting technology is key to addressing climate change. Historically, humans have relied on nature

H. X. Huynh et al. (Eds.): GOODTECHS 2024, LNICST 648, pp. 81–93, 2025.
https://doi.org/10.1007/978-3-032-01472-6_7

observations to predict weather, such as the appearance of rainbows signaling that rain will cease. Scientifically, rainfall forecasting began in the late 19th century when scientists relied on observation and statistics. By the 20th century, forecasting became more accurate thanks to mathematical models and meteorological radar, allowing real-time rainfall monitoring. In the 21st century, computing technology and artificial intelligence have enabled models like CNN, GRU, and LSTM to analyze data from satellites and radars, providing accurate predictions for short-term rainfall, especially effective for storms and flash floods [1]. Short-term rainfall forecasting (under 4 h) is based on a sequence of radar images capturing rainfall intensity at various times. The changes in these images help determine the development trends of rainfall.

The integration of deep learning techniques with current radar image datasets has garnered significant interest from researchers, as shown in publications [2–8]. In [2], the authors propose an improvement to the DozhdyaNet neural network with six 2D convolutional layers (Conv-L) for rainfall forecasting. The architectural parameters consist of the quantity of filters and the size of the kernels in each layer. The authors suggest using filter counts of 48, 24, 12, 6, 3, and 1 from the first to the last layer in DozhdyaNet as the basic standard. Additionally, [3] combines U-net with Generative Adversarial Networks (GAN), while [4, 6] utilizes U-net, [5] employs Rainnet (a variant of U-net), and [7] also uses Conv-LSTM for rainfall forecasting from various radar datasets.

Study [8] has cataloged 12 publications on rainfall forecasting from 2015 to 2022, showing that 7 publications utilize RNN variants (including LSTM: 1, TRAJGRU: 2, ConvLSTM: 2, and ConvGRU: 2), and 5 publications use U-net. It can be concluded that models based on RNN variants have been widely employed in rainfall forecasting, particularly ConvLSTM and ConvGRU models, which can integrate the features of CNN and RNN within a single architecture. These models are commonly used to process spatial and temporal data simultaneously in tasks like time series forecasting from image data.

Study [8] analyzed both the advantages and disadvantages of RNN models in general as well as specific models. However, implementing ConvLSTM, ConvGRU, and ConvBi-LSTM models in TensorFlow with multiple CNN and LSTM (or GRU, Bi-LSTM) layers significantly increases training time. Furthermore, these models only allow for adjusting the number of ConvLSTM (GRU, Bi-LSTM) layers, limiting the scalability and customization of the model to enhance predictive accuracy. This results in models being less flexible and harder to tune. To improve model performance, it is also essential to apply optimization algorithms like GA and PSO to determine the model parameters.

Instantaneous rainfall intensity forecasting from radar images is a major challenge, requiring the integration of various algorithms and methods to achieve accurate results. Our paper proposes a new model to address the limitations of ConvLSTM, ConvGRU, and ConvBi-LSTM models, which combines CNN layers with GRU neural networks while utilizing an improved genetic algorithm (GA) to select optimal parameters for the model. The integration of CNN, GRU, and GA in this study is based on their complementary capabilities. CNN is used to extract spatial features from radar images, such as rain patterns and dBZ intensity, while GRU processes time series data, modeling the relationships between consecutive radar frames to capture the temporal dynamics of rainfall. GA is applied to optimize the model's hyperparameters, such as kernel size in CNN and the number of units in GRU, improving performance without manual tuning. This integration enhances learning efficiency and generalization ability by automatically optimizing and leveraging both spatial and temporal information. This approach not only enhances the accuracy of forecasts but also reduces training time, making the model more efficient and practical in real-world applications. This is also the main contribution of the research, improving the performance of instantaneous rainfall forecasting from radar images.

The main sections of the paper include following parts. Section 2 presents the necessary materials and some basic methods used in rainfall prediction. Section 3 introduces the details of proposed model. Section 4 shows obtained experimental results and some discussions. Last Sect. 5 is the conclusions and some future works.

2 Materials and Methods

2.1 Research Data

Figure 1a Location of the Phadin radar station in Dien Bien (21.58° N, 103.52° E), with a range of 450 km and surveillance within 250 km, managed by the Northwestern Air Meteorological Station. Figure 1b Terrain of Northwestern Vietnam, with the Hoang Lien Son mountain range, Fansipan (3,143 m), border mountain ranges, plateaus, and small plains, significantly influencing rainfall and forecasting. Figure 1c Radar dataset from the Phadin station consisting of 2,425 images (June-July 2020), with a resolution of 150×150 pixels, collected every 10 min within a 300 km^2 scanning range, providing information on rainfall. **Data Division:** 60 images from July 10, 2020, divided in an 8:1:1 ratio: 48 training images (6:00 AM–2:00 PM), 6 testing images (2:10 PM–3:00 PM), and 6 validation images (3:00 PM–4:00 PM). The 8:1:1 ratio balances training and testing. Although the sample size is small, the diverse data with a 10-min frequency still ensures effective short-term forecasting. Expanding the sample size and collection time will improve accuracy. In this study, the data from July 10, 2020, was selected because it recorded a significant change in weather, making it suitable to illustrate the feasibility of the model in short-term rainfall extrapolation. However, we also recognize the need to expand the data to increase diversity and representativeness.

2.2 Related Models

The CNN model extracts spatial features from images, using Conv-L layers, ReLU activation layers, pooling layers for dimensionality reduction, and flattening layers to create a 1D vector for the regression network (Fig. 2).

– GRU (Gated Recurrent Unit): A simplified version of LSTM that addresses the vanishing gradient problem while using fewer parameters. It processes long data sequences with two gates: the update gate, which retains or adds new information, and the reset gate, which discards unnecessary past data. GRU updates the hidden state directly, enabling faster computations and lower resource usage than LSTM while maintaining long-term relationship learning (Fig. 3).

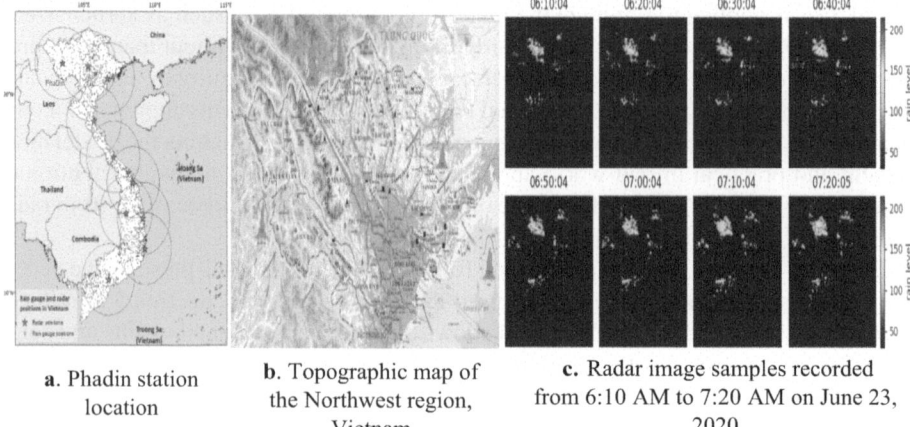

a. Phadin station location

b. Topographic map of the Northwest region, Vietnam

c. Radar image samples recorded from 6:10 AM to 7:20 AM on June 23, 2020

Fig. 1. Survey Area

– Fully Connected Layer (FC): The FC layer links every neuron to the previous layer, aggregating features to generate the final output. Each neuron in the FC layer is connected to all neurons in the preceding layer, enabling it to learn intricate relationships between features. This layer consolidates the learned features into outputs suitable for classification, regression, or prediction tasks. The output can be classification labels or predicted images, with the number of units corresponding to the image size, enabling reshaping to the actual dimensions.

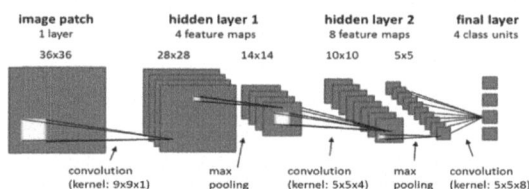

Fig. 2. Basic structure of a CNN model

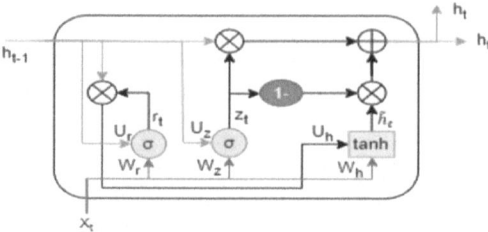

Fig. 3. Structure of the GRU model receiving input from the CNN

3 Proposed Model

3.1 Implementation Process

First, we will collect data from the radar image dataset at the Phadin station (as mentioned in the Data Collection section), then preprocess the data by converting the images to grayscale, resizing them appropriately, and denoising the images. Next, we will build the proposed model and train it alongside three other models (ConvLSTM, ConvGRU, and Bi-ConvLSTM), testing to identify the best-performing model. Following this, we will use the Genetic Algorithm (GA), as well as our improved version of GA (GA+), to find the best hyperparameters for the selected model and run these parameters to forecast results.

3.2 Data Preprocessing

Our specific data preprocessing steps are presented as in Fig. 4 below:

- Resize all images to standardize their dimensions. The original images with dimensions ($150 \times 150 \times 1$) will be resized to ($224 \times 224 \times 1$) to fit the proposed model and converted to grayscale matrices.
- Normalize the data using Min-Max Scaling, determining the minimum ($Xmin$) and maximum ($Xmax$) pixel values across all images. Each pixel value in the image ($Xpixel$) will then be normalized to the range [0–1] using the following formula:

$$(X_{pixel} - X_{min})/(X_{max} - X_{min}) \tag{1}$$

- Smooth and denoise the images with a Gaussian filter, using the kernel size (default 3×3) to calculate the sigma value. Then, create data batches with a time step of 4 and a stride of 1, where the input consists of 4 consecutive frames, and the output label corresponds to the 5th frame. Two data arrays are generated: one containing the input image sequences and another containing the labels. Each batch consists of 4 consecutive images; for instance, with a time step of 4, the images at time steps t-*3, t-2, t-1,* and t correspond to the label at *t + 1.*

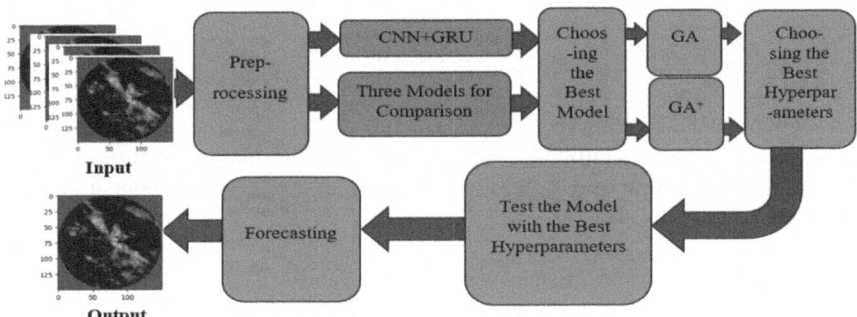

Fig. 4. Implementation Process

Once the batches and labels are created, divide the data into three sets: training, validation and testing, using a ratio of 8:1:1. The input data for the proposed model is structured as (T, H, W, C), where T represents the number of consecutive time steps, H and W denote the height of the images and the width of the images, and C indicates the number of color channels. The labels are formatted as (H, W, C).

3.3 Building and Training the Proposed Model

We propose the CNN + GRU model to forecast rainfall using radar images, with specific steps outlined (Fig. 5). The input sequence of radar images is passed through CNN layers, performing feature extraction on each image at each independent time step ttt (where $t \leq T$). The CNN layer produces an output tensor T with dimensions (H', W', C') for each time step t. After passing through the CNN layer, we obtain the feature size of each image at each time step t denoted as:

$$X_{\text{CNN}(t)} : X_{CNN(t)} \subset \mathbb{R}^{T \times H' \times W' \times C'} \tag{2}$$

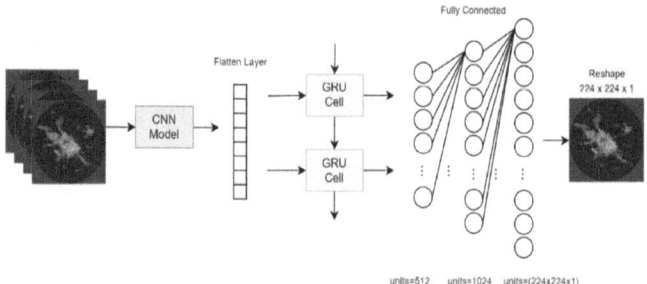

Fig. 5. The building of the Combined CNN + GRU

Flatten the spatial dimensions $H' \times W' \times C'$ of each time step t, transforming the output of each time step t into a 2D vector. The dimensions of the vector after flattening at time ttt are denoted as $X_{\text{flatten}(t)}$, representing the feature size of each image at each time step t after flattening:

$$X_{\text{fatten}(t)} \subset \mathbb{R}^{T \times (H'.W'.C')} \tag{3}$$

Subsequently, the feature vectors of each image at each time step ttt, after being flattened, will pass through GRU layers to predict the next sequence of 1D vectors. Each feature vector at each time step t after flattening is treated as one time step input t (from $t = 1$ to $t = T$), with an input size of (T,d), where d $= (H' \cdot W' \cdot C')$:

$$h_t = GRU(x_t, h_{t-1}) \tag{4}$$

where: $x_t \in \mathbb{R}^d$ represents the input vector at time t; $h_t \in \mathbb{R}^h$ is the hidden state at time t, h_{t-1} is the hidden state at the previous time step $t - 1$.

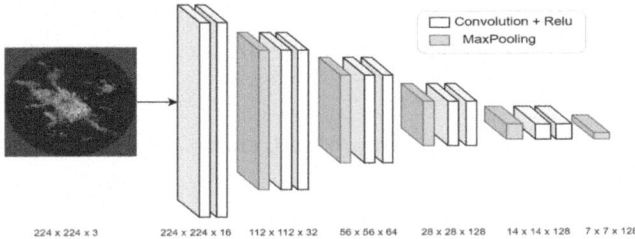

Fig. 6. Proposed CNN Architecture In which the white blocks represent Convolution layers with the ReLU activation function, and the pink blocks represent

The GRU layer processes each vector X_t sequentially from time steps $t = 1$ to $t = T$, using the hidden state h_{t-1} to retain information from previous time steps. The specific formulas for the GRU model receiving input from the CNN layer are as follows:

$$z_t = \sigma (b_z + U_z h_{t-1} + W_z.X_t) \tag{5}$$

$$r_t = \sigma (b_r + U_r h_{t-1} + W_r.X_t) \tag{6}$$

$$\tilde{h}_t = tanh(b_h + U_h(r_t \odot h_{t-1}) + W_h X_t) \tag{7}$$

$$h_t = (1 - z_t) \odot h_{t-1} + z_t \odot \tilde{h}_t \tag{8}$$

The reset gate r_t is computed from the input t and the previous hidden state h_{t-1}, while the update gate z_t controls the retention of information from h_{t-1}. The potential hidden state $\tilde{h}_t$ is influenced by r_t and derived from the current input X_t and h_{t-1}. The current hidden state h_t is then calculated using z_t, combining portions of h_{t-1} and $\tilde{h}_t$. The learned weights are W_z, W_z, W_h, U_z, U_r, U_h and the bias vectors are b_z, b_r, b_h. The symbols σ and tanh represent the sigmoid and hyperbolic tangent functions, respectively, while $\odot$ denotes the Hadamard product (element-wise multiplication). After passing through the GRU, the final hidden state of the GRU is taken as input for the FC layer. This final hidden state has a spatial dimension of $h_T \in \mathbb{R}^h$, at the last time step t $=$ T, where h represents the number of units in the final GRU layer. h_T is fed into the FC layer, which performs a linear transformation via the weight matrix W_{FC} and bias b_{FC}. Therefore, the output y is defined by the formula:

$$y = W_{FC} h_T + b_{FC} \tag{9}$$

In this equation, $W_{FC} \in \mathbb{R}^{o \times h}$ denotes the weight matrix of the FC layer, $b_{FC} \in \mathbb{R}^o$ represents the bias vector, and y $\in \mathbb{R}^o$ is the output of the FC layer. We used trial-and-error testing to select the CNN and FC architecture, consisting of 10 Conv-L and 5 MaxPooling layers in 5 blocks (2 Convolutional layers followed by 1 MaxPooling layer) for feature extraction and dimensionality reduction (see Fig. 6). GRU was chosen over LSTM for its simpler structure, effectively addressing the vanishing gradient problem while retaining long-term information with fewer parameters, using 2 consecutive GRU layers.

- *Fully Connected Layers:* There are three layers with 512, 1024 neurons, and the final layer has a number of units equal to the image size for aggregation. (Fig. 6. Proposed CNN Architecture).

3.4 Genetic Algorithm (GA) and Improved Genetic Algorithm (GA+) for Model Optimization

- *Genetic Algorithm (GA):* According to [5], the Genetic Algorithm (GA) simulates natural evolution through selection, using a population of solutions that undergo crossover, mutation, and selection based on fitness. The process involves three main steps: crossover, mutation, and selection. While random initialization is common, it can lead to low diversity, infeasible solutions, poor performance, slow convergence, and tuning difficulties for complex tasks.
- *Improved Genetic Algorithm (GA+):* To address the drawbacks of random initialization, we improve GA algorithm by individual initialization from value ranges. In this method, a continuous value range is divided into evenly sized segments. Each segment represents a distinct value range. Individuals are generated by randomly choosing values from specified ranges, ensuring that each individual falls within defined value limits. This approach promotes greater diversity and feasibility within the population.
- *Comparison with Random Initialization:* The range-based initialization method enhances feasibility by ensuring individuals stay within predetermined ranges, reducing invalid solutions and promoting diversity. This approach allows for faster convergence to feasible solutions compared to the slower convergence of random initialization. In summary, range-based initialization improves feasibility, diversity, and optimization performance, while the GA stages of crossover, mutation, and selection remain unchanged.

3.5 Implementation of Model Training Parameters

The CNN + GRU model comprises blocks with shared filters and kernel sizes: Block 1 {16, (3, 3), relu}, Block 2 {32, (3, 3), relu}, Block 3 {64, (3, 3), relu}, Block 4 {128, (3, 3), relu}, Block 5 {256, (3, 3), relu}. It includes two GRU layers with 512 units (tanh activation) and three Fully Connected layers: (512, relu), (1024, relu), and ((width * height * color channels), relu).

- For the parameters in the GA and GA+ algorithms, the default settings include a population size of 5, a number of individuals per population of 5, a crossover rate of 0.8 and a mutation rate of 0.2, and a number of evolutionary generations of 2. Both algorithms use the same parameters, differing only in the method of population and individual initialization.
- The CNN + GRU model parameters optimized with GA and GA+ include filters (filter1: 16–32, filter2: 32–64, and filter5 increasing accordingly), kernel sizes (randomly chosen from (3x3), (5x5), or (7x7)), and activation functions (selected from 'swish', 'relu', 'selu', and 'elu'). This results in 25 individuals, each represented as (filter1, …, filter5, kernel1, …, kernel4, activation1, …, activation4), forming 5 populations of 5 individuals each.

- The model is trained using the Adam algorithm with a learning rate of 10^{-4} and the Mean Squared Error (MSE) loss function. An early stopping method is implemented to halt training if the validation loss does not improve after 10 epochs. Training occurs on the training set and evaluation is performed on the validation set, with a total of 200 epochs and a batch size of 4. The best weights are saved after each epoch.
- To evaluate the proposed model, the following metrics have been used MAE, MSE and RMSE.

The CNN + GRU model consists of 5 CNN blocks (16–256 filters), 2 GRU layers (512 units), and 3 Fully Connected layers, optimized using GA/GA+ with 5 populations and 2 generations. Training is done using Adam (learning rate $10 - 4$), MSE loss, 200 epochs, batch size 4, and early stopping. The model combines CNN and GRU to extract image features and capture temporal dependencies, with parameter optimization improving forecast accuracy.

4   Experiments and Observations

4.1   Machine Configuration

The device used for training the models is the NVIDIA A100 GPU on Google Colab Pro, which is part of a powerful environment for training large AI models. Below are the key specifications of the A100: GPU Name: NVIDIA A100; VRAM (GPU Memory): 40GB HBM2; CUDA Cores: 6912 CUDA cores; Tensor Cores: 432; Memory Bandwidth: 1.6 TB/s; RAM: 25GB for Colab Pro.

4.2   The Forecast Results of CNN + GRU, Compared with ConvLSTM, ConvGRU, and Bi-ConvLSTM

The models have a default structure of 3 layers with parameters: Filters: 32, 16, 1; Kernels: (3, 3); Activation: Relu. The optimization algorithm is Adam with a learning rate of 10^{-4}, evaluated using the MSE metric. The objective function is the validation loss (val_loss), targeting the lowest value at each epoch. The training configuration consists of 200 epochs and a batch size of 4. Table 1 shows the results of the CNN + GRU model compared to other models.

Table 1. Results of CNN + GRU Compared to Other Models

Parameters and Standard Values	ConvLSTM	Bi-ConvLSTM	ConvGRU	CNN + GRU
Training Time	5min	8 min	4 min	**1 min**
Number of Epochs to Stop	56	95	200	**25**
MSE	0.01104	0.01108	0.01173	***0.01064***
MAE	0.06061	0.06143	0.06133	***0.05643***
R^2	0.62021	0.61903	0.59656	***0.55427***

The CNN + GRU model converged fastest at 25 epochs, outperforming ConvGRU (200), Bi-ConvLSTM (95), and ConvLSTM (56). It achieved the lowest MSE (0.01064) and MAE (0.05643), indicating high accuracy. ConvLSTM had the highest R^2 (0.62021), while CNN + GRU had the fastest training time.

Conclusion: CNN + GRU (default CNN + GRU) converges quickly and provides good predictions with the lowest MSE and MAE. ConvLSTM has the highest R^2 value. Bi-ConvLSTM and ConvGRU require more epochs and exhibit higher errors.

4.3 Results of the CNN + GRU Model Integrated with GA and GA+

Using Random GA: The Objective Function (Fitness Function) evaluates the CNN + GRU model by optimizing kernel size, filters, and activation function. It uses the Adam optimizer with MSE loss and implements early stopping after 10 epochs without improvement. Each individual's fitness value is based on the minimum validation loss achieved during training.

Using Improved GA (GA+): Dividing Value Ranges- A range is divided into segments; for example, 16 to 256 yields (16, 135) and (136, 256). Creating Individuals: Each individual has 5 random values from the ranges (f1 to f5), 4 random kernel sizes ((3, 3), (5, 5), (7, 7)), and 4 activation functions ('relu', 'elu', 'selu', 'swish'), forming a 13-element list. Initializing the Population: A population of 5 individuals is created with random values from the ranges (Table 2).

Table 2. Results of CNN + GRU, CNN + GRU Integrated with GA, and CNN + GRU GA$^+$

Metrics	Results of the Default CNN + GRU	CNN + GRU + GA	CNN + GRU + GA$^+$
MSE	0.01064	0.01050	**0.01048**
MAE	0.05643	0.05650	**0.05511**
R2	0.55427	0.56029	**0.56094**
Best Set	16, 32, 64, 128, 256	17, 39, 92, 164, 306	**26, 55, 103, 222, 433**
	(3, 3) (3, 3) (3, 3) (3, 3)	(3, 3) (3, 3) (7, 7) (3, 3)	**(7, 7) (3, 3) (7, 7) (3, 3)**
	relu relu relu relu	swish swish elu relu	**relu selu elu swish**
Train Time/epoch	2.6s/epoch	3s/epoch	2.72s/epoch

The results with optimal parameters are shown in Fig. 7a, 7b, and 7c. For CNN + GRU, CNN + GRU + GA, and CNN + GRU + GA+

The results of the analysis from the CNN + GRU model in forecasting rainfall using radar images indicate improved effectiveness when applying the Genetic Algorithm (GA) and the Enhanced Genetic Algorithm (GA+). A detailed analysis of the metrics is as follows:

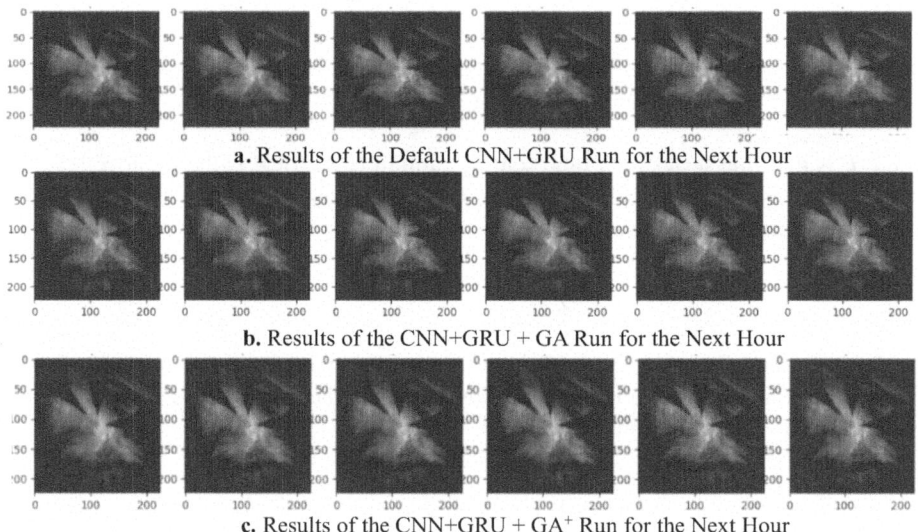

a. Results of the Default CNN+GRU Run for the Next Hour

b. Results of the CNN+GRU + GA Run for the Next Hour

c. Results of the CNN+GRU + GA+ Run for the Next Hour

Fig. 7. Forecasting results of the methods.

The default model had an MSE of 0.01064, which improved to 0.01050 with GA and 0.01048 with GA+, enhancing forecast accuracy. The MAE was 0.05643 for the default, 0.05650 for GA, and 0.05511 for GA+. RMSE decreased from 0.10316 to 0.10247 with GA and 0.10239 with GA+, showing consistent error reduction. The default model's RMAE increased to 0.23770 with GA but decreased to 0.23477 with GA+, indicating GA+'s optimization strength. The R^2 value improved from 0.55427 to 0.56029 with GA and 0.56094 with GA+, reflecting better predictive accuracy. The application of GA and GA+ algorithms to the CNN + GRU model has significantly improved key metrics such as MSE, MAE, RMSE, and R^2. While GA enhanced model accuracy compared to the default model, GA+ yielded the best results with lower error metrics and better fit. Although training time for the GA+ model increased to 2 min (compared to 1 min for GA), the accuracy improvement justifies this additional time. In summary, combining CNN and GRU with optimization algorithms like GA and GA+ has enhanced rainfall forecasting using radar images, with GA+ demonstrating superior error reduction and accuracy improvement. In terms of training time, GA+ has a faster training time (2.72s/epoch) compared to GA (3s/epoch).

4.4   Forecasting Rainfall Using the CNN + GRU + GA+ Model

After identifying the best-performing model, we use it to forecast the next sequence of images from the input. Using 4 consecutive images (10 min apart), the model predicts 6 images for the next hour, with each new predicted image replacing the first, creating a continuous flow. We also calculate 95% confidence intervals to assess reliability and uncertainty levels. After predicting the 6 images, we calculate rainfall based on the predicted radar images using a pixel-based, as detailed in reference [9], applying the

Marshall-Palmer formula:

$$R = (\frac{Z}{200})^{\frac{5}{8}} \tag{10}$$

where R is the time series data representing rainfall (mm/h); Z is the radar reflectivity (mm^6/mm^3). The radar reflectivity will be calculated based on the magnitude of each pixel in the grayscale image as follows:

$$Z = 10^{\frac{\frac{Pixel-0.5}{255}x70-10}{10}} \tag{11}$$

After applying the rainfall calculation formula, we obtain results for each image. The total rainfall forecast for 1 h is calculated by summing the rainfall from the 6 predicted images, as shown in the Table 3:

Table 3. Rainfall Forecast Results

Images	$t+1$	$t+2$	$t+3$	$t+4$	$t+5$	$t+6$	*Sum*
The forecasted rainfall (mm^6/mm^3)	0.096390	0.096419	0.096405	0.096385	0.096371	0.096371	**0.578339**

5   Conclusion

This paper presents a rainfall forecasting model (Nowcasting) that combines CNN and GRU to enhance performance. We developed a novel model with CNN and GRU, optimized using an improved Genetic Algorithm (GA). Compared to ConvLSTM, ConvGRU, and Bi-ConvLSTM, our model demonstrates superior performance and faster processing. We also enhanced the GA during initialization, resulting in an advanced version (GA+) integrated into the model.

The model, tested with radar data from the Phadin station on July 10, 2020, showed that the improved GA algorithm (GA+) outperformed control models in accuracy and forecasting time, highlighting its superiority for short-term rainfall forecasting.

The CNN + GRU model improved forecasting performance but still falls short compared to ConvLSTM, ConvGRU, and Bi-ConvLSTM. While the GA+ algorithm shows some enhancements, it lacks significant improvement over the original GA, and we haven't compared it with other global optimization algorithms like PSO or MPA. To address these limitations, we plan to:

- Develop a new model by experimenting with the combination of U-Net and GRU.
- Use additional variants of the GA such as Elitism GA, Steady-State GA, Parallel GA, or continue to improve the GA towards Hybrid GA, such as HGAPSO (combining GA and PSO) or HGAMPA (combining GA and MPA).

Real-time forecasting of rainfall intensity poses several challenges because of the impact of external factors such as temperature, wind speed, geographical location, and more. Utilizing CNN layers to extract spatial features and create a 2D matrix, which is then transformed into a 1D vector sequence and passed through LSTM or GRU layers to predict the next vector sequence, provides a significant advantage in forecasting spatiotemporal data from radar images. This method has the potential to capture complex features often overlooked by traditional models. Ultimately, the GA algorithm will be employed to optimize the model's parameters, significantly enhancing forecasting performance.

References

1. Camps-Valls, G., Tuia, D., Zhu, X.X., Reichstein, M.: Deep Learning for the Earth Sciences: A Comprehensive Approach to Remote Sensing, Climate Science, and Geosciences (2021). ISBN: 978-1-119-64614-3
2. Ayzel, G., Heistermann, M., Sorokin, A., Nikitin, O., Lukyanova, O.: All convolutional neural networks for radar-based precipitation nowcasting. Procedia Comput. Sci. **150**, 186–192 (2019)
3. Rojas-Campos, A., et al.: Deep learning models for generation of precipitation maps based on numerical weather prediction. Geoscientific Model Dev. **16**(5), 1467–1480 (2023)
4. Han, L., Liang, H., Chen, H., Zhang, W., Ge, Y.: Convective precipitation nowcasting using U-Net model. IEEE Trans. Geosci. Remote Sens. **60**, 1–8 (2022)
5. Ngan, T.T., et al.: A hybrid of RainNet and Genetic algorithm in nowcasting prediction. Earth Sci. Inf., vol. 16(4) (2023)
6. Pavlík, P., Rozinajová, V., Ezzeddine, A.B.: Radar-based volumetric precipitation nowcasting: a 3D convolutional neural network with U-Net architecture. CEUR-WS.Org/Vol-3207/Page-10.PDF
7. Shi, X., Chen, Z., Wang, H., Yeung, D.-Y., Wong, W.-K., Woo, W.-C.: Convolutional LSTM network: a machine learning 685 approach for precipitation nowcasting. In: Advances in Neural Information Processing Systems, vol. 28 (2015) https://doi.org/10.48550/arXiv.1506.04214
8. Han, D., Shin, Y., Im, J., Lee, J.: Key factors for quantitative precipitation nowcasting using ground weather radar data based on deep learning (2023).https://doi.org/10.5194/gmd-2022-276
9. Son, H.G., Tuan, T.H., Tan, N.H.: Rainfall forecast through radar images by combining ARIMA, LSTM and GRU. https://doi.org/10.15625/vap.2023.0044

Approach to Scalable Machine Learning Operations (MLOps) Architectures for Research Labs with Limited Hardware Resources

Pham Ba Tuan Chung[1,2], Tran Tuan Toan[3], Le Minh Tuan[4(✉)],
Phung Hong Quan[2], Ngo Duc Tam[2], Le Trong Minh[2], and Le Hoang Son[2]

[1] Information Technology Center, Hanoi University of Industry,
Hanoi 010000, Vietnam
chung.pham@haui.edu.vn

[2] Artificial Intelligence Research Center, VNU Information Technology Institute,
Vietnam National University, Hanoi 010000, Vietnam
{phunghongquan.business,minh140903}@gmail.com, sonlh@vnu.edu.vn

[3] Faculty of Information Technology, Electric Power University, Hanoi, Vietnam
toantt@epu.edu.vn

[4] Faculty of Technology and Engineering, Trade Union University, Hanoi, Vietnam
letuan@dhcd.gmail.com

Abstract. Machine Learning Operations (MLOps) has become increasingly essential for research labs aiming to streamline machine learning workflows and ensure the reproducibility, efficiency, and scalability of their models. However, many research labs face significant challenges due to limited hardware resources, which hinder their ability to implement robust and scalable MLOps systems. This paper aims to address these challenges by proposing scalable MLOps architectures specifically designed for research environments with constrained hardware capabilities. We have proposed a scalable MLOps architecture specifically designed for research labs with limited hardware resources. Our results show that the proposed architecture improves resource utilization, offering a more resource-efficient solution for research labs with limited hardware. Furthermore, we provide illustrative cases of real-world deployments and the benefits of this solution in practical research environments. The main contribution of this work lies in its ability to provide a practical and scalable solution for research labs operating under hardware constraints, ensuring they can continue conducting advanced research without being limited by computational capabilities. The solutions presented in this paper not only highlight the efficiency of the proposed MLOps architecture but also lay the foundation for future studies to further optimize workflows in resource-constrained environments.

Keywords: MLOps architecture · Hardware limitation · Research labs · Containerization

Artificial Intelligence Research Center, VNU Information Technology Institute, Vietnam National University.

ⓒ ICST Institute for Computer Sciences, Social Informatics and Telecommunications Engineering 2025
Published by Springer Nature Switzerland AG 2025. All Rights Reserved
H. X. Huynh et al. (Eds.): GOODTECHS 2024, LNICST 648, pp. 94–105, 2025.
https://doi.org/10.1007/978-3-032-01472-6_8

1   Introduction

Machine Learning Operations (MLOps) has emerged as a critical discipline that integrates the principles of software engineering with machine learning (ML) to automate the deployment, monitoring, and management of ML models in production environments. MLOps aims to streamline the entire ML life cycle, from data preparation and model training to deployment and monitoring, ensuring that models remain accurate, efficient, and reliable over time [14].

However, despite the growing recognition of MLOps as essential to successful ML projects, many research labs, especially those with limited hardware and financial resources, struggle to implement these practices effectively. The primary challenge lies in the resource-intensive nature of traditional MLOps frameworks, which often require substantial computational power and robust infrastructure to support large-scale, automated ML pipelines [1]. For smaller labs, these requirements can be prohibitive, leading to bottlenecks in model deployment and a lack of scalability.

In this paper, we proposed an architecture that introduces several key innovations designed to address the challenges faced by labs with limited resources. First, we leverage containerization and lightweight orchestration tools to enable efficient deployment and scaling of machine learning models, reducing overhead and resource consumption. Second, our approach includes fine-grained resource management strategies that dynamically allocate computing power based on real-time model demands, ensuring efficient hardware usage without waste. Third, we incorporate distributed system [4] techniques that allow labs to pool their limited hardware resources, creating a virtualized, more powerful infrastructure to support larger-scale ML workloads.

This paper presents a scalable, lightweight, and adaptable MLOps solution designed for research labs with limited hardware resources. For the experimental environment, we conducted our study at the Artificial Intelligence Research Center, VNU Information Technology Institute, Vietnam National University, Vietnam, using a setup that reflects the typical resource constraints encountered by small research labs. In our case study on Visual Relationship Detection (VRD), we processed input images through a data pipeline using JupyterHub for coding and Kubeflow for model training.

2   Overview of MLOps

MLOps represents a new concept and emphasizes how to optimally coordinate data scientists and operations staff for the efficient development, deployment, and monitoring of models since machine learning productization is difficult. In this regard, machine learning, data engineering, and software engineering are involved in MLOps paradigm discipline [6].

A standard MLOps infrastructure typically consists of various components and layers that ensure smooth and efficient collaboration between data scientists, machine learning (ML) engineers, and DevOps teams. These components work

Table 1. Standard MLOps Component

Component	Purpose	Key Features
Data Ingestion Layer	Collect and aggregate data from different sources for ML model training.	- Handles batch or real-time data ingestion. - Supports multiple data formats (CSV, JSON, Parquet, etc.). - Scalable for large datasets.
Data Processing and Transformation	Clean, normalize, and transform raw data for feature engineering and ML training.	- Parallel and distributed processing for large datasets. - Automates data cleaning and preprocessing steps.
Model Development Environment	Provide an environment for data scientists and ML engineers to experiment, develop, and train ML models.	- Easy access to compute resources (CPU, GPU, TPU). - Collaboration and shared development environments. - Versioning for both code and data.
Model Training and Hyperparameter Tuning	Train ML models on large datasets and optimize their performance using hyperparameter tuning.	- Scalable training infrastructure to handle large datasets. - Automated hyperparameter tuning to optimize model performance. - Support for both single-node and distributed training.
Model Registry and Versioning	Store, manage, and version ML models for easy retrieval and deployment.	- Tracks model versions, metadata, and performance metrics. - Provides roll-back and comparison options for models. - Ensures traceability and reproducibility.
Model Deployment and Serving	Deploy trained models into production environments for inference.	- Real-time and batch inference. - Scalable and highly available deployment infrastructure. - A/B testing and canary deployments for model rollouts.
Continuous Integration/Continuous Deployment (CI/CD)	Automate the process of integrating new models and deploying them into production.	- Continuous integration of new code and models. - Automated testing and validation of ML models. - Seamless deployment into production environments.
Monitoring and Observability	Monitor model performance, detect issues, and ensure the ML model is functioning correctly in production.	- Real-time monitoring of models for accuracy and latency. - Alerts for issues like performance degradation or data drift. - Automated retraining of models when performance drops.
Data and Model Governance	Ensure compliance with regulatory standards and maintain the quality of data and models.	- Compliance with data privacy regulations (GDPR, HIPAA). - Ensures that models are auditable and explainable. - Versioning and lineage tracking of both data and models.
Security and Compliance	Secure the entire MLOps life cycle from data collection to model deployment and inference.	- Secure model training and inference environments. - Data privacy and encryption throughout the pipeline. - Role-based access for sensitive data and models.

together to streamline the entire ML life cycle, from data preparation to model deployment and monitoring Below is a structured presentation of the standard infrastructure components for MLOps (Table 1):

This component supports scalability, automation, and collaboration while maintaining high-quality standards for model development and deployment. However, the majority of the software mentioned in this documentation consists of paid solutions, which may not be suitable for the needs of research labs with limited hardware and financial resources. Paid solutions like Amazon Sage-Maker, Azure Machine Learning, MLflow, and H2O.ai offer robust functionality but come with high costs that can pose significant barriers (Fig. 1).

3 Purpose-Driven MLOps for Research Labs with Limited Hardware Resources

3.1 Background

DevOps-based software development supports to speed up the delivery time and frequency of delivering while supporting quality, reliability, and security [13]. The

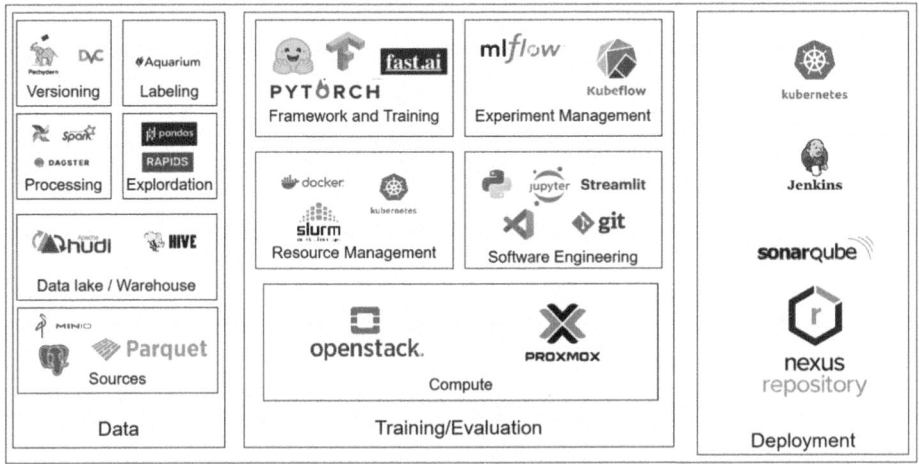

Fig. 1. List of Open Source software for the MLOps

MLOps practice brings ML models into the software solution production process. It bridges the ML applications with DevOps principles, where deployments and maintenance of ML models can be automated in the production environment as show in Fig. 2 [5]. The integration of Machine Learning (ML) into software development is closely tied to Continuous Integration and Continuous Deployment (CI/CD) practices. The ML development life cycle involves a range of roles, skill sets, and tools, and consists of multiple stages such as model requirements gathering, data collection and pre-processing, design and development, evaluation, deployment, and ongoing monitoring.

3.2 MLOps Roadmap

In building scalable MLOps architectures for research labs with limited hardware resources, it is crucial to understand the core components and their interconnections. The MLOps landscape intersects with traditional DevOps principles while incorporating specialized tools and processes for managing machine learning workflows. The roadmap presented in Fig. 3 visualizes these key elements, highlighting the essential technologies and practices that underpin a robust MLOps infrastructure.

At the center of this roadmap Programming, which serves as the foundation for MLOps implementation. Common languages and formats like Python, YAML,... enable development of machine learning pipelines. Version Control is fundamental for tracking changes, ensuring reproducibility, and fostering collaboration, with Git being the most widely adopted tool.

Virtualization and Containerization technology introduce the scalability needed for handling resource constraints in research environments. Tools such

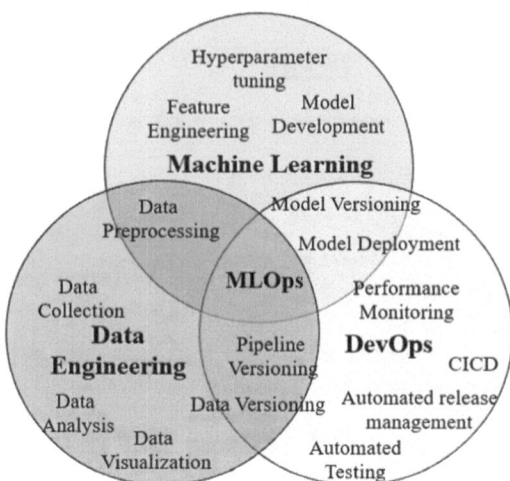

Fig. 2. MLOps combination [5]

as OpenStack or Proxmox enable virtualization, while Docker and Kubernetes provide container management solutions.

Machine Learning is the core component, supported by frameworks for creating Data Pipelines, managing Data Lakes and Data Warehouses, and transforming raw Data into models. Lastly, the successful integration of these components culminates in MLOps Components, which encompass training, evaluation, deployment, and monitoring processes. Monitoring ensures the continuous tracking of model performance, helping detect data drift or model degradation in production environments.

This roadmap serves as a guide for research labs, providing a strategic overview of how to construct an MLOps architecture tailored to the constraints of limited hardware, while still embracing scalability and flexibility through cloud-native and container-based solutions.

3.3 Proposed System Architecture

The proposed architecture (Fig. 4) integrates a variety of open-source tools and platforms to create a scalable, efficient MLOps pipeline tailored for research labs. At its core, the system using Kubernetes to manage containerized workloads, offering flexibility in deploying and scaling machine learning models across multiple nodes. Each node in the cluster is responsible for running specific services (data processing, training, etc.), while the NFS (Network File System) handles storage management. This setup ensures efficient use of hardware, with the ability to scale as more resources become available [11]. All components are authenticated using Keycloak to ensure secure access and integration.

The architecture begins with data ingestion from multiple sources such as images, PDFs, IoT devices, web data,... The data is funneled through Airflow,

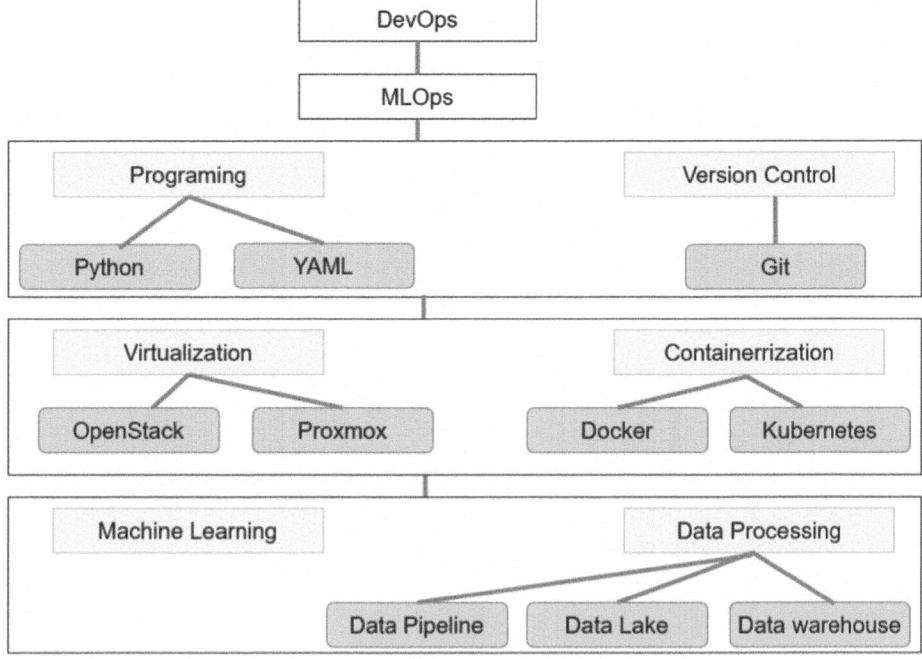

Fig. 3. MLOps Roadmap for research labs

which performs data filtering and processing. Apache Airflow orchestrates tasks in the data pipeline, allowing for a modular and scalable approach to handling data. This step is crucial as it prepares the data for downstream machine learning tasks while efficiently managing computational resources. [8]. Processed data is stored in MinIO and database. MinIO can handle large datasets and seamlessly integrate with the rest of the pipeline, ensuring that the architecture is both scalable and reliable [16].

For model training and evaluation, the system integrates Kubeflow, a powerful platform designed for orchestrating machine learning workflows on Kubernetes. Kubeflow interacts with JupyterHub, where users can experiment and develop machine learning models in an interactive notebook environment. This allows researchers to perform experiments in a controlled manner and easily transition from development to production. The architecture supports continuous model training and evaluation, essential for ongoing research projects. This aligns with recent research highlighting the importance of containerized workflows for optimizing resource usage and accelerating model iteration in constrained environments [15].

Once models are trained, they are deployed using a CI/CD pipeline facilitated by GitLab, Jenkins, and Nexus Repository. This combination allows for automated version control, testing, and deployment, ensuring models are consistently integrated into production environments with minimal manual intervention. The

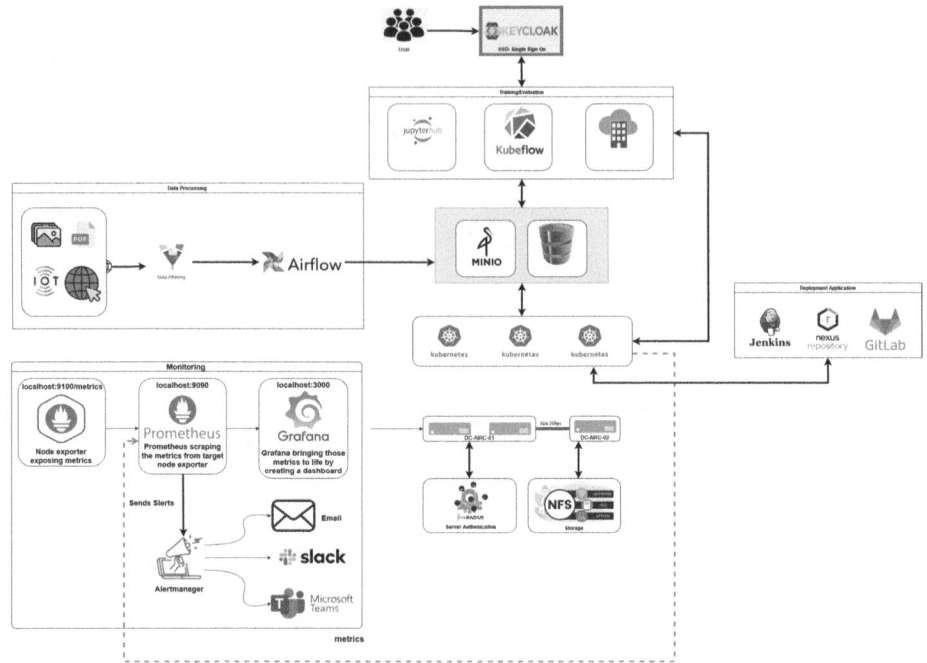

Fig. 4. Proposed MLOps Architecture for research labs

use of containerization through Kubernetes ensures that the deployment process remains efficient even under limited hardware resources.

After training, models are deployed via GitLab, Jenkins, and Nexus Repository, facilitating CI/CD workflows. The deployment process is monitored through a stack combining Prometheus and Grafana, which visualizes system metrics and triggers alerts via Slack, Microsoft Teams, or Email through Alert manager [8].

This system architecture efficiently manages machine learning life cycles while maintaining operational performance through robust monitoring, cloud services, and container orchestration. Recent research has shown that hybrid cloud architectures using containerization, as adopted in this system, significantly improve performance scalability, especially when hardware resources are limited [8].

4   Case Study

4.1   Problem

4.1.1   Problem Statement

We chose the **Scene Graph Generation (SGG)** task to experiment with our system architecture. This problem has garnered significant attention from the research community. The goal of scene graph generation is to analyze an image and generate a structured representation, bridging the gap between visual perception and semantic understanding, ultimately leading to a comprehensive understanding of visual scenes. Typically, generating a scene graph involves grouping elements into triplets and connecting them to construct the complete scene graph. The core challenge lies in identifying the relationships (also called the **Visual Relationship Detection (VRD)** [12] task) between objects within the image, specifically in the form of *(subject, relation, object)* triplets, abbreviated as *(s, r, o)* as shown in Fig. 5.

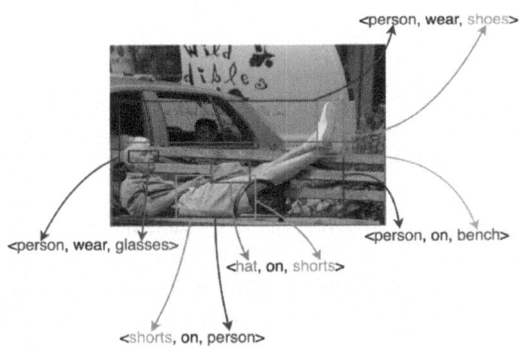

Fig. 5. Illustration of detecting triplets in Visual Relationship Detection task [3]

The problem statement of the task can be formulated as follows: given an input image, the objective is to generate triplets that represent the relationships between objects in the picture, which can then be used to construct a complete scene graph.

The input image undergoes a series of processing steps orchestrated by Apache Airflow. Processed image with included meta data are stored MinIO. Kubeflow facilitates the orchestration of machine learning workflows, using the preprocessed data to train Image Relationship model.

To address the Scene Graph Generation (SGG) challenge, we adopted a newly released one-stage model called **EGTR (Extracting Graph from Transformer)** [7]. By leveraging the multi-head self-attention mechanism of the DETR (DEtection TRansformer) [2] decoder, EGTR extracts rich relational information between objects without requiring additional modules for triplet detection. This lightweight approach enhances both efficiency and accuracy, offering effective multi-task learning by incorporating a relation-smoothing technique. The model demonstrates competitive results on well-established benchmark datasets for SGG, such as **Visual Genome** [9] and **Open Images V6** [10]. The detailed architecture of the EGTR model is illustrated in Fig. 6.

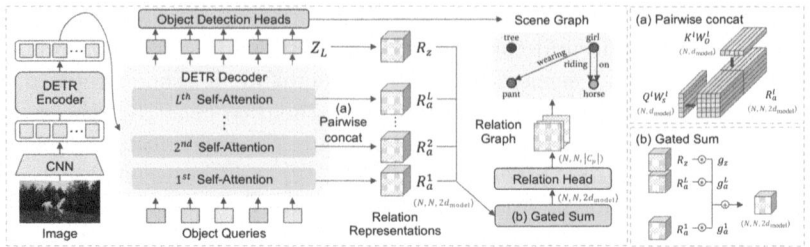

Fig. 6. The overall architecture of EGTR

4.2   Experiments and Results

4.2.1   Hardware Resources

In our case study, we use hardware resources at the Artificial Intelligence Research Center, VNU Information Technology Institute, Vietnam National University. The hardware setup consisted of two machines with same specifications. Both machines were equipped with the following specifications: CPU Intel Core i7 - 14700KF, 32GB Memory, SSD 500GB, GPU Nvidia RTX 4080 Supper 16GB.

The manual setup machine was configured to operate locally, utilizing all libraries and tools directly on the system. This machine was responsible for performing tasks without any MLOps pipeline support, relying on manual processes for data preparation, model training, and deployment.

The MLOps machine was dedicated to running the full MLOps pipeline using MLOps Architecture in Fig. 4. It utilized containerization technologies like Docker, orchestration tools like Kubernetes, and a range of MLOps frameworks such as Kubeflow for model training and deployment.

4.2.2   Evaluation Metrics and Results

We conducted the evaluation using two key metrics: model accuracy and execution time. The accuracy of the SGG model is assessed using two widely recognized metrics: Recall@K and mean Recall@K. Recall@K (R@k) measures the ability of the model to correctly predict the ground-truth relationships among all the top-k most confident predictions made by the model while mean Recall@k (mR@k) addresses the limitations of R@k by averaging recall values across different relationship categories. The specific formulas for these two metrics are presented in Eqs. 1 and 2.

$$R@k = \frac{|Top_k \cap GT|}{|GT|} \tag{1}$$

$$meanR@k = \frac{1}{C} \sum_{c=1}^{C} R@k_c \tag{2}$$

where:

- Top_k: top-K triplets extracted from an image based on ranked model predictions.
- GT: a set of ground truth triplets.
- $R@k_c$: R@k for category c.
- C: total number of relationship categories.

The specific evaluation results are shown in the Table 2. Both machines produced equivalent results in terms of model accuracy and performance, but there were significant differences in terms of processing time and workflow automation. The manual setup without MLOps required manual intervention for each step, from data preparation to model deployment, leading to slower overall performance. In contrast, the MLOps system (Second machine) automated these processes, reducing the time required for model training and deployment significantly.

Table 2. Evaluation Metrics Between First machine and Second machine

Test Metric	Manual setup	MLops System
Images	57,723	57,723
Processing time	2h36m	2h18m
R@100	0.384759	0.384760
R@20	0.259948	0.259949
R@50	0.334665	0.334667
mR@100	0.097777	0.097778
mR@20	0.055871	0.055875
mR@50	0.080139	0.080141

5   Conclusion

In this study, we presented an MLOps-based architecture designed to address the challenges faced by research labs with limited hardware resources. Our experiments demonstrated that the use of MLOps pipelines, which incorporate containerization, orchestration, and automation, significantly improves efficiency without compromising the accuracy of machine learning models.

By comparing two systems—one relying on manual processes and local tools, and the other leveraging a fully automated MLOps framework—we observed substantial reductions in execution time across all stages of the machine learning life cycle, including data preparation, model training, and deployment. Both systems achieved the same level of model accuracy, but the MLOps system was able to streamline workflows, drastically reducing the time required for model development and deployment.

The results underscore the importance of adopting scalable MLOps frameworks, especially for research institutions operating with constrained resources. With automation reducing manual intervention and optimizing resource usage, MLOps provides a practical and effective solution for achieving high performance in machine learning projects, even in hardware-limited environments.

Future work will focus on further optimizing resource management within the MLOps pipeline and exploring how distributed and cloud-based infrastructures can enhance scalability and real-time processing capabilities, particularly for more complex machine learning tasks.

References

1. Breck, E., Cai, S., Nielsen, E., Salib, M., Sculley, D.: The ml test score: a rubric for ml production readiness and technical debt reduction. In: 2017 IEEE International Conference on Big Data (Big Data), pp. 1123–1132 (2017). https://doi.org/10.1109/BigData.2017.8258038
2. Carion, N., Massa, F., Synnaeve, G., Usunier, N., Kirillov, A., Zagoruyko, S.: End-to-end object detection with transformers (2020). https://arxiv.org/abs/2005.12872
3. Deeplab: Semantic visual objects relationship detection (2024). https://deeplab.ai/project/visual-relationship-detection/. Accessed 24 Sep 2024
4. Donta, P.K., Murturi, I., Casamayor Pujol, V., Sedlak, B., Dustdar, S.: Exploring the potential of distributed computing continuum systems. Computers **12**(10) (2023). https://doi.org/10.3390/computers12100198, https://www.mdpi.com/2073-431X/12/10/198
5. Hewage, N., Meedeniya, D.: Machine learning operations: a survey on MLOps tool support (2022). https://doi.org/10.48550/ARXIV.2202.10169
6. Heydari, M., Rezvani, Z.: Challenges and experiences of Iranian developers with MLOps at enterprise (2023). https://doi.org/10.1109/ICAEA60387.2023.10414442
7. Im, J., Nam, J., Park, N., Lee, H., Park, S.: EGTR: extracting graph from transformer for scene graph generation (2024). https://arxiv.org/abs/2404.02072
8. Kreuzberger, D., Kühl, N., Hirschl, S.: Machine learning operations (MLOps): overview, definition, and architecture (2022). https://arxiv.org/abs/2205.02302
9. Krishna, R., Zhu, Y., Groth, O.: Visual genome: connecting language and vision using crowdsourced dense image annotations (2017). https://doi.org/10.1007/s11263-016-0981-7
10. Kuznetsova, A., et al.: The open images dataset v4: unified image classification, object detection, and visual relationship detection at scale. Int. J. Comput. Vis. **128**(7), 1956–1981 (2020). https://doi.org/10.1007/s11263-020-01316-z
11. Li, H.: Alluxio: A Virtual Distributed File System. Ph.D. thesis, EECS Department, University of California, Berkeley (2018)
12. Lu, C., Krishna, R., Bernstein, M., Fei-Fei, L.: Visual relationship detection with language priors (2016). https://arxiv.org/abs/1608.00187
13. Meedeniya, D.A., Rubasinghe, I.D., Perera, I.: Software artefacts consistency management towards continuous integration: a roadmap. Int. J. Adv. Comput. Sci. Appl. **10**(4) (2019). https://doi.org/10.14569/IJACSA.2019.0100411

14. Sculley, D., et al.: Hidden technical debt in machine learning systems. In: NIPS, pp. 2494–2502 (2015)
15. Tabassam, A.I.U.: MLOps: a step forward to enterprise machine learning (2023). htttps://arxiv.org/abs/2305.19298
16. Čop, A., Bertalanič, B., Fortuna, C.: An overview and solution for democratizing AI workflows at the network edge (2024). htttps://arxiv.org/abs/2407.11905

A New Architecture for Controlling IoT Devices of Smart Room Using ESP32 Microcontroller

Nguyen Thi Van Anh[1,3] , Nguyen Xuan Duc Anh[2], Le Hoang Son[2] ,
and Duong Quang Khanh[2(✉)]

[1] University of Transport Technology, Trieu Khuc 54, Hanoi 120000, Vietnam
[2] Artificial Intelligence Research Center, VNU Information Technology Institute, Vietnam
National University, Xuan Thuy 144, Hanoi 122000, Vietnam
khanhdq@vnu.edu.vn
[3] VNU Information Technology Institute, Vietnam National University, Xuan Thuy 144, Cau
Giay, Hanoi 122000, Vietnam

Abstract. This paper introduces a framework that adopts ESP32 microcontroller-based devices aimed at smart controlling of Internet of Things (IoT) devices via the Message Queuing Telemetry Transport (MQTT) protocol for communication. Based on that framework, two scenarios were demonstrated to switch on/off automatically lights and fans using fuzzy control. The ESP32 microcontroller and the proposed framework are highlighted for their ability to enhance the control and automation of electrical devices within IoT ecosystems, as well as for their capability to scale to various use cases.

Keywords: IoT device · ESP32 microcontroller · smart control

1 Introduction

Internet of Things (IoT) represents a significant change in the ways we interact with devices, with applications ranging from smart home, school, and classroom automation to industrial control systems. The advent of low-cost, highly capable microcontrollers like the ESP32 [1] has further accelerated this trend, enabling the development of various IoT solutions accessible to a wider range of users. The built-in connection features and supported protocols, such as Wi-Fi and Message Queuing Telemetry Transport (MQTT) allow IoT devices to communicate with each other within the ecosystem and with the computer via a cloud platform.

Several use cases utilizing the features of the central microcontroller have been introduced. In the field of home automation, the ESP32 microcontroller with MQTT protocol were also used in a smart nursing home solution proposed by Li [2], in which data were collected from various sensing devices and transmitted to users in real-time. IoT device control can be combined with other technologies such as computer vision. This approach was applied in the smart pest monitoring method proposed by Cardoso

© ICST Institute for Computer Sciences, Social Informatics and Telecommunications Engineering 2025
Published by Springer Nature Switzerland AG 2025. All Rights Reserved
H. X. Huynh et al. (Eds.): GOODTECHS 2024, LNICST 648, pp. 106–117, 2025.
https://doi.org/10.1007/978-3-032-01472-6_9

et al. [3], which employed cameras and deep neural models. However, these approaches did not propose any database to collect data for further processing or analysis.

Babiuch et al. [4] proposed the home monitoring system using ESP32-CAM and MariaDB in which collected data is stored. The presentation of the camera in the proposed system is only for recording and no computer vision functionality was implemented. The smart home control system proposed by Taiwo and Ezug-wu [5] was based on ESP8266 and ESP32-CAM boards, including smartphone monitoring, and a simple SVM-based intruder detection. Data storage in this method was a cloud database of the Blynk app [5]. This cloud platform was also used in the classroom monitoring system introduced by Ritheesh et al. [6] for receiving and displaying sensors' data. The above-mentioned approaches either employed built-in database design or did not incorporate sophisticated computer vision functionalities. Another application of IoT in smart classroom proposed by Paudel et al. [7] is a context-aware architecture for reducing power consumption employing sensors and video action recognition. Although they used Raspberry Pi and MySQL for collecting and managing data [7], along with an activity detection function, the proposed method mainly aimed at power saving purpose.

Addressing the potential functionalities that were not completely employed in the related field, this paper introduces a framework adopting the ESP32 microcontroller for smart control of electrical devices such as lights and fans. Communication between devices in the system is ensured by using the MQTT protocol. Data collected from the environment is stored in a MongoDB database. They are then processed by fuzzy control to switch on/off electrical devices for power consumption saving.

2 Proposed Framework and Device

2.1 IoT-Based Controlling System Architecture

The room is equipped with IoT devices such as lights, fans, air conditioners, as well as sensors including light sensors, temperature sensors, humidity sensors and Passive Infrared (PIR) sensors. The overall model of the IoT system controlling electrical devices using ESP32 microcontroller via the MQTT protocol of each room is illustrated in Fig. 1.

The MQTT broker functions as an intermediary, receiving data from sensors, IoT devices, and control systems via "publish" and "subscribe" methods. Data such as temperature, humidity, light intensity, and the number of people is collected and transmitted to the MQTT broker through the "publish" method. Applications use the "subscribe" method to receive this data, process it, and send control commands back to the MQTT broker via the "publish" method. Similarly, devices transmit their status and receive control commands through the MQTT "subscribe" and "publish" methods (Fig. 2).

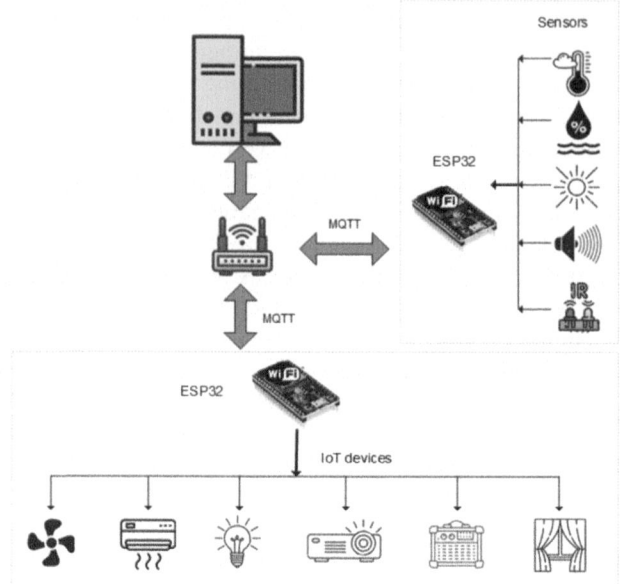

Fig. 1. Smart room control diagram using ESP32 microcontroller.

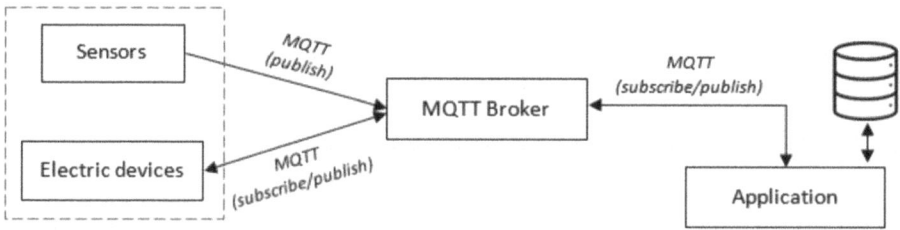

Fig. 2. Illustration of "publish" and "subscribe" operations.

2.2 Hardware Design

ESP32 controller is a series of low-cost, low-power system-on-chip microcontrollers with integrated WiFi and dual-mode Bluetooth. The ESP32 series includes microcontrollers in both dual-core and single-core variations, up to 240 MHz, built-in antenna switches, RF balun, power amplifier, low-noise receive amplifier, filters, and power management modules.

The design board has a function of collecting environmental data such as temperature, light, humidity. They are then sent to the server through WiFi modem for analysis, adjusting the consumption power of electrical devices in the room. The power circuit amplifies control signals and provides feedback monitoring actual status of the device.

The Message Queueing Telemetry Transport (MQTT) protocol is used in communication ensuring high stability in the transmission process, avoiding data loss and delay. The MQTT protocol is designed for connections with remote locations that have devices with resource constraints or limited network bandwidth. So, it is suitable for IoT applications. The FreeRTOS operating system is used for real-time embedded systems.

Figure 3 illustrates the algorithm flowchart of the ESP32 microcontroller based PCB in two phases: transmit sensor data and directly control devices by pushing buttons via the MQTT protocol.

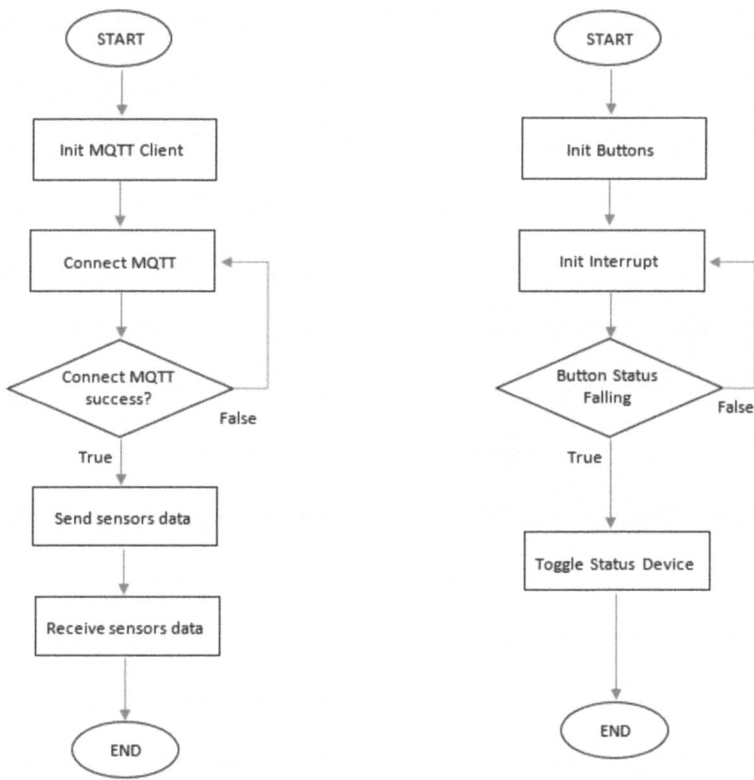

Fig. 3. The algorithm flowchart of the ESP32 controller-based PCB.

There are two set modes of the control box: manual mode and automatic mode. In manual mode, electrical devices are controlled by pushing buttons in all cases even if WiFi connection is not available. The LCD screen mounted on the box displays actual status of electrical devices (ON/OFF), environmental parameters and error notifications (Figs. 4 and 5).

In automatic mode, the demonstration was carried out at the computer laboratory at the University of Transport Technology. To reduce power consumption of electrical devices installed in the room, low-cost sensors such as the AHT30 sensor measuring humidity and temperature, the BH1750 sensor for light intensity, and the PIR sensor for counting individuals were added to the laboratory.

Fig. 4. Designed control box for IoT devices.

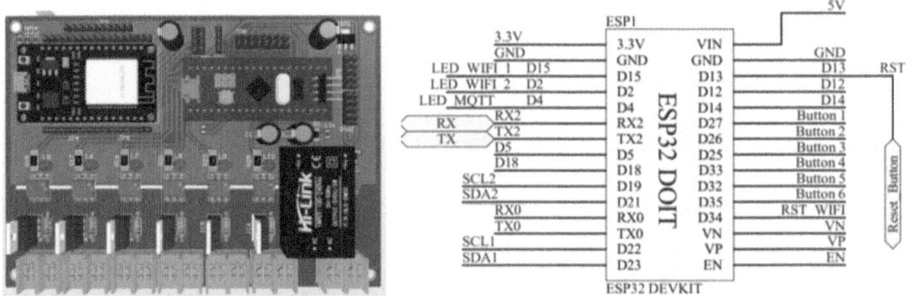

Fig. 5. ESP32 module based dedicated PCB for IoT applications.

2.3 Software Design

The operational model of the fan control system is illustrated in Fig. 6. Information on temperature, humidity, and number of individuals from environmental sensors are read through the MQTT broker. The collected data is stored in a MongoDB database and then processed by fuzzy control to switch on/off electrical devices and to reduce energy consumption.

The fuzzy based fan controller has three inputs: temperature, humidity, and number of individuals present in the room, and one output representing the fan level (level 0, level 1, level 2 and level 3). The temperature range in the room is defined from 0 to 50 degrees Celsius, with five triangular fuzzy value sets: Cold ($0^0 - 15^0$C), Cool ($12^0 - 20^0$C), Normal ($18^0 - 27^0$C), Warm ($25^0 - 38^0$C), and Hot ($35^0 - 50^0$C). The humidity range in the room is defined from 0 to 100 RH%, with three triangular fuzzy value sets: Low (0 – 45), Normal (40 – 75), and High (70 – 100). The membership functions for the input and output variables are illustrated in Fig. 7.

Table 1 explains the rules based on the value ranges of temperature and humidity to control the speed of fan when the number of people present in the room is between 1 and 15 (few people). Similarly, Table 2 explains the case when the number of people is between 16 and 30 (many people).

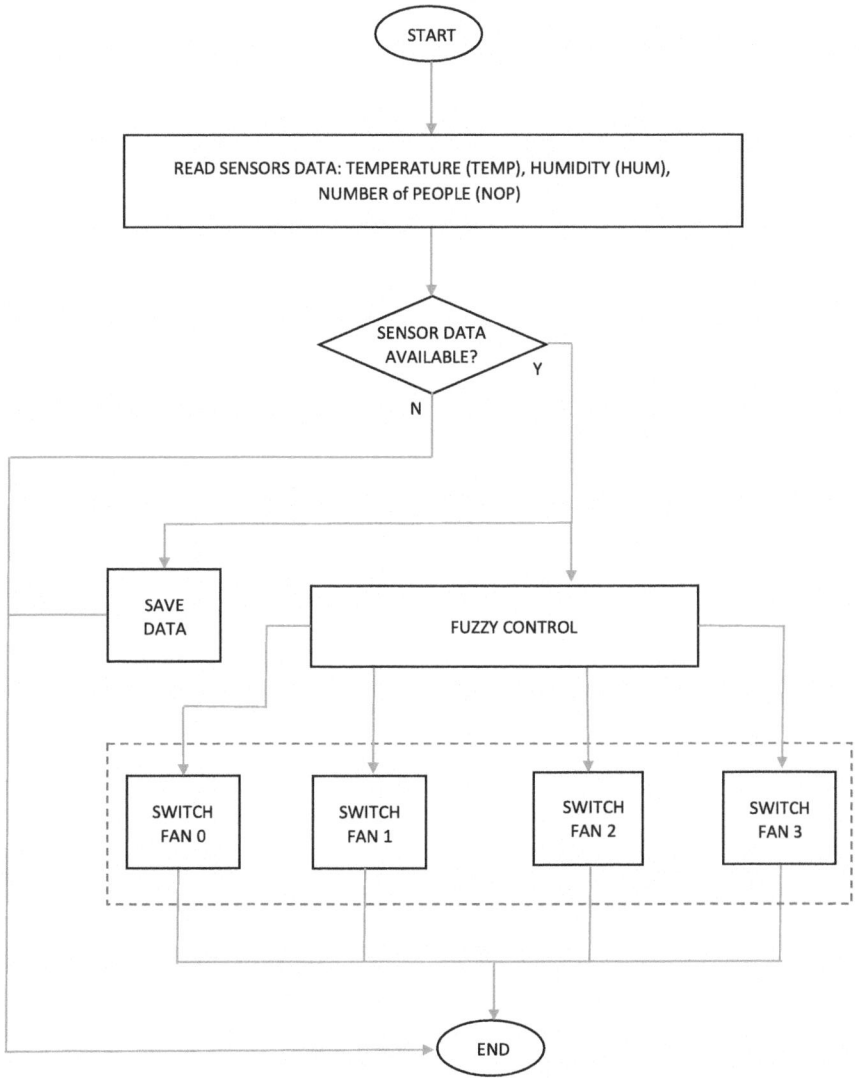

Fig. 6. Fan control system.

The second scenario conducted in this study is to switch on/off the lights automatically when a person is detected in the room and the light intensity exceeds the permissible threshold. The operational diagram of the light control system is shown in Fig. 8.

The rules used to switch on/off lights with the appropriate luminance threshold (L) are as follows:

IF *NUMBER OF PEOPLE* < 1 THEN *Turn OFF light*
IF *NUMBER OF PEOPLE* > 1 AND *LUMINANCE* > L THEN *Turn OFF light*
IF *NUMBER OF PEOPLE* > 1 AND *LUMINANCE* <= L THEN *Turn ON light*

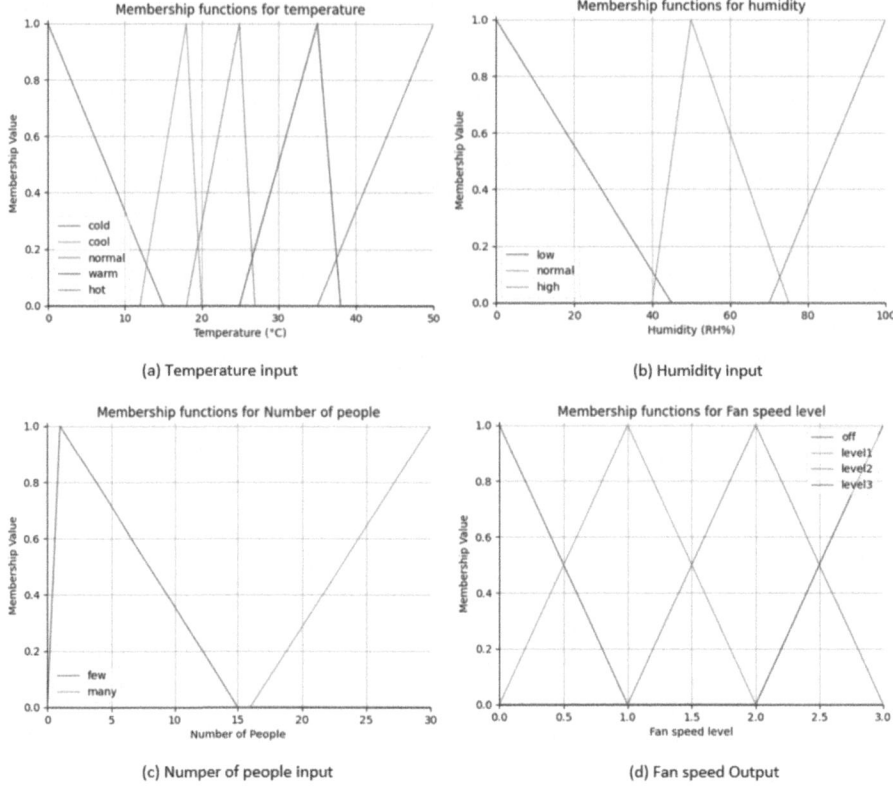

(a) Temperature input

(b) Humidity input

(c) Numper of people input

(d) Fan speed Output

Fig. 7. The membership functions for the input and output variables.

3 Demonstration Result

The designed control box was tested in a room with dimensions of 10 m in length, and 5 m in width. In Vietnam, the deployment of widespread WiFi coverage has been effectively implemented. The WiFi speed, measured using an application from the Vietnam Internet Center under the Ministry of Information and Communications, recorded 21.09 Mbps for download and 21.87 Mbps for upload, with an overall connection quality rating of 3/5. At this speed, the system's processing time ranged from 0.2 s to nearly 0.7 s, as illustrated in Tables 3 and 4, (Figs. 9 and 10).

Realtime status of electrical devices is displayed on the user interface created on the computer. This interface built in C# environment also allows users to control devices through buttons (Fig. 11).

Table 1. Fuzzy rules to control fans in the presence of few people.

Temperature (°C)	Humidity (RH%)	Fan level
Cold	Low	0
Cold	Normal	0
Cold	High	1
Cool	Low	0
Cool	Normal	1
Cool	High	1
Normal	Low	1
Normal	Normal	2
Normal	High	2
Warm	Low	2
Warm	Normal	2
Warm	High	3
Hot	Low	2
Hot	Normal	3
Hot	High	3

Table 2. Fuzzy rules to control fans in the presence of many people.

Temperature (°C)	Humidity (RH%)	Fan level
Cold	Low	0
Cold	Normal	0
Cold	High	1
Cool	Low	1
Cool	Normal	1
Cool	High	2
Normal	Low	2
Normal	Normal	2
Normal	High	3
Warm	Low	2
Warm	Normal	3
Warm	High	3
Hot	Low	3
Hot	Normal	3
Hot	High	3

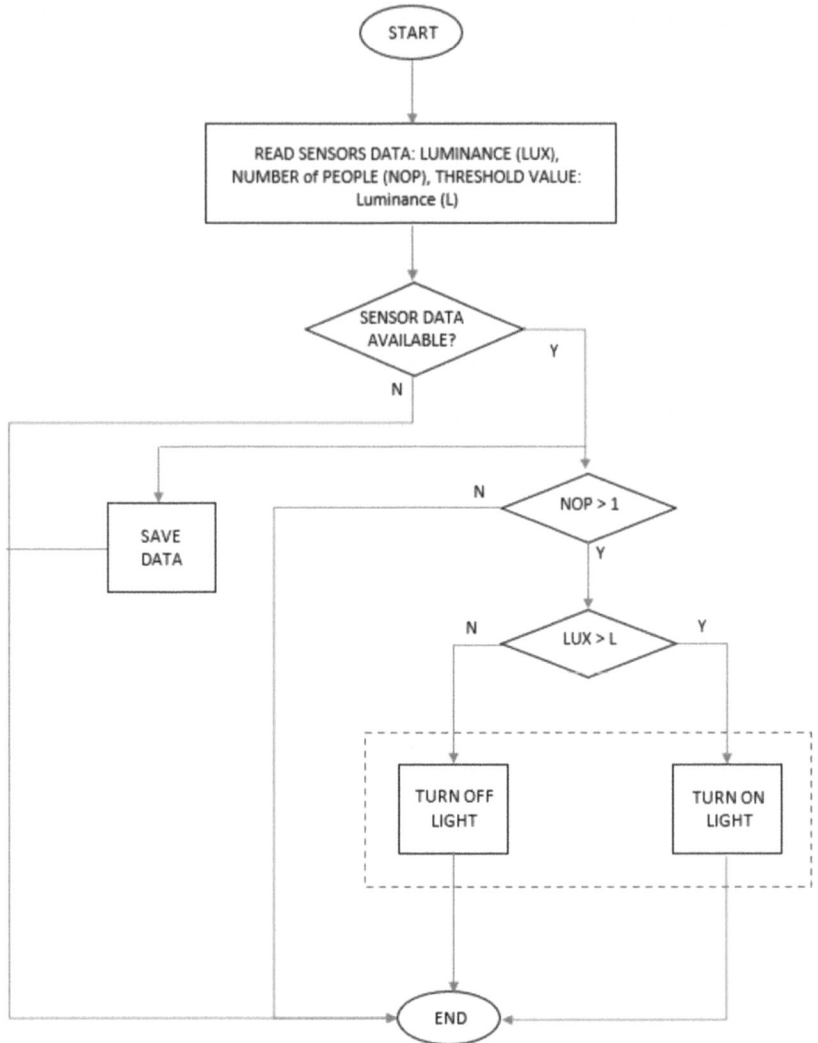

Fig. 8. Operational model of light control system.

Fig. 9. The computer laboratory at the University of Transport Technology.

Table 3. Some results of fan control system.

Temperature input (°C)	Humidity input (RH%)	Number of people	Fan level (Output)
10	55	10	1
15	50	10	2
17	45	10	2
27	42	20	3
29	39	10	3
30	54	10	3

Table 4. Execution time for fan control.

No.	Execution time (second)
1	0.2970
2	0.5377
3	0.2995
4	0.3035
5	0.6221
6	0.3164
7	0.5012
8	0.2997
9	0.3045
10	0.3022

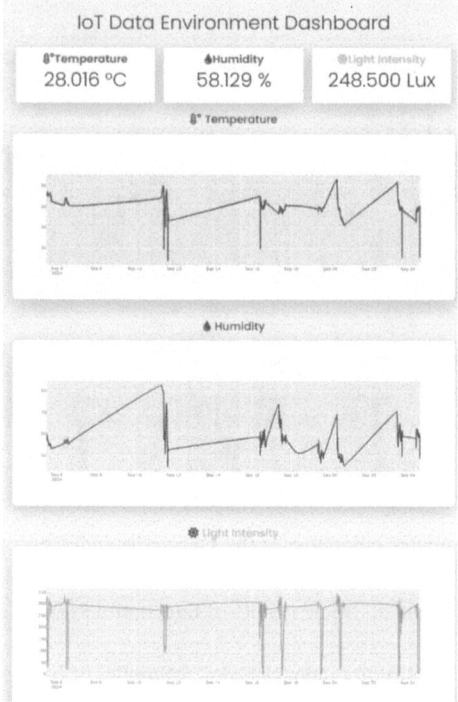

Fig. 10. User interface for monitoring sensor values.

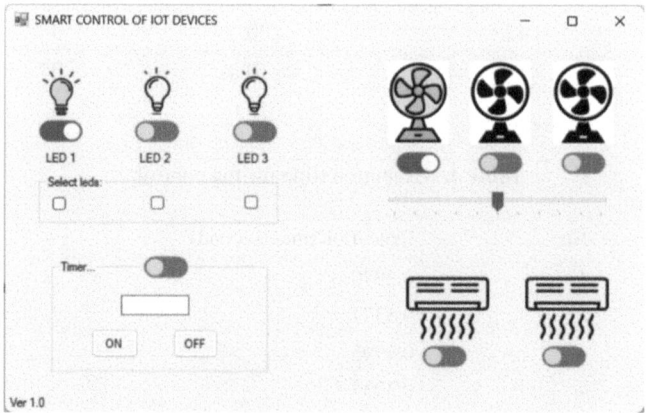

Fig. 11. User control interface for smart IoT devices.

4   Conclusion

In this paper, the framework based on the ESP32 microcontroller and MQTT protocol were presented with the aim of controlling IoT electrical devices. Based on the proposed framework, collected data from the ambient environment were processed by fuzzy control to switch on/off electrical devices and energy consumption saving. Two scenarios of fan and light control systems were conducted at the computer laboratory at the University of Transport Technology to demonstrate applicability. For future work, the scalability of the proposed framework for applying in various scenarios including the integration of a camera for control, multiple devices, multi-users, or use-cases of smart classroom or smart office will be implemented.

References

1. ESPRESSIF Homepage. https://www.espressif.com/en/products/socs/esp32. Accessed 23 Sep 2024
2. Li, S.: IoT healthcare system based on ESP32 for smart home. In: IEEE International Conference on Mechatronics and Automation (ICMA), pp. 1768–1772 (2023)
3. Cardoso, B., Silva, C., Costa, J., Ribeiro, B.: Internet of things meets computer vision to make an intelligent pest monitoring network. Appl. Sci. **12**(18), 18 (2022)
4. Babiuch, M., Postulka, J., Babiuch, M., Postulka, J.: Smart home monitoring system using ESP32 microcontrollers. Internet of Things, IntechOpen (2020)
5. Taiwo, O., Ezugwu, E.: Internet of things-based intelligent smart home control system. Secur. Commun. Netw. **2021**, e9928254 (2021)
6. Ritheesh, P., Kumar, K., Singh, K.: Smart classroom: real time monitoring of classroom through IoT. In: 2023 Third International Conference on Secure Cyber Computing and Communication (ICSCCC), pp. 202–206 (2023)
7. Paudel, P., Kim, S., Park, S., Choi, K.-H.: A context-aware IoT and deep-learning-based smart classroom for controlling demand and supply of power load. Electronics **9**(6), 6 (2020)

Energy Correlation-Based EBM for Skin Lesion Classification: A Novel Approach

Quyen Van Vo[1,2]([⊠]) [ID] and Ba Van Huynh[2] [ID]

[1] Can Tho University, Can Tho, Vietnam
vovanquyen@ctump.edu.vn
[2] Can Tho University of Medicine and Pharmacy, Can Tho, Vietnam
hvba@ctump.edu.vn

Abstract. Skin lesion classification presents significant challenges in medicine, especially due to the increasing complexity of data. Traditional methods often face difficulties when dealing with heterogeneous datasets, particularly those in the medical domain, which frequently exhibit class imbalance and uneven distribution of disease types. In this paper, we propose a novel approach that integrates Energy-Based Models (EBMs) with Energy Correlation to classify skin lesion images. Our method optimizes the relationship between features and labels by minimizing intra-class energy while maximizing inter-class differences. Experiments conducted on the ISIC 2019 dataset demonstrated promising results, achieving 72.94% accuracy, 53.45% sensitivity, and 95.30% specificity. This approach significantly enhances classification performance and introduces a new paradigm for addressing complex medical classification problems.

Keywords: Energy-Based Models · Energy Correlation; Skin lesion Classification

1 Introduction

The classification of skin lesions is an urgent and significant task in medicine, aimed at supporting the early diagnosis of dermatological diseases such as skin cancer or other dangerous skin lesions. Many previous studies have focused on the application of Deep Learning and Machine Learning methods to improve the classification of skin lesion images [6–8, 10–14]. Convolutional Neural Networks (CNNs) have been widely employed in medical image classification and have achieved encouraging results [16–18]. A notable study utilizing CNNs on the ISIC dataset reached an accuracy of up to 86.6% in skin lesion classification [15]. However, traditional CNN-based methods require large amounts of data and often struggle when dealing with heterogeneous datasets, such as the imbalance between different types of lesions in medical data [4]. This leads to difficulties in achieving high accuracy on datasets with a high degree of variability. Moreover, these methods usually focus on optimizing the neural network architecture without thoroughly considering the correlation between features and classification labels, which limits the effectiveness of the classification process.

© ICST Institute for Computer Sciences, Social Informatics and Telecommunications Engineering 2025
Published by Springer Nature Switzerland AG 2025. All Rights Reserved
H. X. Huynh et al. (Eds.): GOODTECHS 2024, LNICST 648, pp. 118–130, 2025.
https://doi.org/10.1007/978-3-032-01472-6_10

The application of Energy-Based Models (EBMs) [1] in the medical field has been receiving significant attention recently. Particularly in medical imaging diagnostics, these models help improve performance in segmentation, image reconstruction, and multimodal data processing, contributing to enhanced accuracy and efficiency in diagnosis and treatment planning [24–26]. EBMs are particularly effective in handling complex medical image segmentation tasks. They have the ability to model the energy distribution of the data, improving segmentation accuracy, especially when applied to multimodal data such as CT and MRI [26]. Additionally, EBMs can reduce computational load by focusing on specific features rather than reconstructing the entire image. This makes EBM-based models lightweight and more suitable for real-time applications or resource-constrained environments [27]. Besides, a few papers provide a comprehensive view of energy correlation and the application of Artificial Intelligence (AI) in optimizing energy within the field of machine learning Energy Correlation in Machine Learning [19, 20]. Energy Correlation has the ability to detect both linear and nonlinear relationships between variables, which is very useful in complex datasets with interactions that are not easily detectable [21]. Additionally, Energy Correlation does not require assumptions about data distribution. This makes it more flexible, especially in applications with diverse data that do not follow a normal distribution [22]. Energy Correlation is particularly effective when applied to high-dimensional data, helping to process complex datasets with many features. This makes it very suitable for applications in deep learning and large-scale data analysis [23].

In this paper, we propose a novel approach to integrate the Energy Correlation method into the Energy-Based Model to optimize the classification of skin lesions. Energy Correlation improves the correlation between features and class labels, allowing the model to more accurately differentiate between various classes, even when the data is imbalanced. The experiment was conducted on the ISIC 2019 dataset, aiming to enhance the model's accuracy in classifying complex skin lesions. Despite these advantages, the proposed model also faces limitations related to computation time due to the precise tuning of the loss function and model structure required to achieve optimal performance.

The rest of this paper is organized as follows: Sect. 2 presents the skin lesion image representation and Energy Correlation Loss function. Section 3 describes the proposed EBM model and algorithm. Section 4 details our experimental setup and results. Finally, Sect. 5 concludes the paper and suggests future research directions.

2   Skin Lesion Image Representation and Energy Correlation Loss

2.1   Skin Lesion Image

Skin lesion images, from a mathematical and machine learning perspective, can be represented in a way that allows computer models to process and analyze them. Skin lesion images can be expressed as a matrix of weights or as feature vectors, with each element in the matrix or vector representing a specific attribute of the image.

Representation of Skin Lesion Images as a Pixel Matrix. Skin lesion images are represented as a matrix of weights, where each value represents the brightness intensity of a pixel at the corresponding position. Suppose there is a skin lesion image with dimensions M x N, where M is the number of rows (horizontal) and N is the number of columns (vertical): $A \in R^{M \times N}$ (Fig. 1).

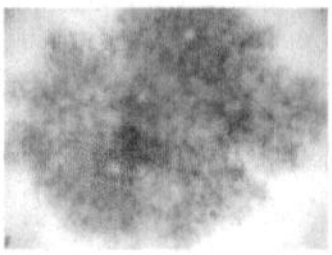

$$\rightarrow A = \begin{pmatrix} a_{11} & a_{12} & ... & a_{1N} \\ a_{21} & a_{22} & ... & a_{2N} \\ \vdots & \vdots & \ddots & \vdots \\ a_{M1} & a_{M2} & \cdots & a_{MN} \end{pmatrix}$$

Fig. 1. Skin lesion image [3] → Weight matrix A with a_{ij} being the pixel value at coordinates (i, j)

Representation of Skin Lesion Images Using Feature Vectors

To represent a skin lesion image as a general feature vector, it is necessary to extract important features from the image and represent them by a mathematical vector. Suppose there is a skin lesion image A, the features of the image can be represented by a vector F, where each element of the vector represents a specific feature of the image.

$$F = \begin{bmatrix} f_1 \\ f_2 \\ \vdots \\ f_k \end{bmatrix}$$

F is a feature vector with k elements, each element fi represents a feature extracted from the skin lesion image.

2.2 Loss Function According to Energy Correlation (L_{EC})

Energy Correlation (EC) is a concept used in statistical analysis and machine learning, particularly in classification or regression tasks. It is based on measuring the correlation between variables using the energy distance between them, rather than relying on linear correlation measures like Pearson correlation.

Suppose we have two data distributions from skin lesion images, P and Q, with feature vectors sampled from two different probability distributions. We can calculate the Energy Correlation between these two distributions using the formula:

$$EC(P, Q) = \frac{EneryDistance(P, Q)}{\sqrt{EnergyDistance(P, P).EnergyDistance(Q, Q)}} \tag{1}$$

where:

– Energy Distance is a distance measure based on the energy function between probability distributions [2, 9]:

$$ED(P, Q) = 2 \cdot Ex_p \sim P, x_q \sim Q[d(x_p, x_q)] - Ex_p, x_p' \sim P\left[d\left(x_p, x_p'\right)\right]$$
$$- Ex_q, x_q' \sim Q\left[d\left(x_q, x_q'\right)\right] \tag{2}$$

$$d(x_p, x_q) = \|x_p - x_q\|_2 = \sqrt{\sum_{i=1}^{d}(x_p^{(i)} - x_q^{(i)})^2} \tag{3}$$

ED(P,Q) is the energy distance between P and Q; E denotes the mathematical expectation; and $d(x_p, x_q)$ is a distance function between two data points x_p and x_q.

- When EC(P,Q) is equal to 1, the two variables are perfectly correlated; when it is close to 0, the two variables are independent of each other.

Loss function in EBM [1] can be customized to include Energy Correlation to optimize the correlation between features and classes.

Energy Correlation Loss (L_{EC}). EBM learns to minimize the energy level for the correct class while maintaining a distinction between unrelated classes, which helps improve classification accuracy:

$$L_{EC} = \sum_{i=1}^{N}(E(x_i, y_i) - \beta.EC(x_i, y_i)) \tag{4}$$

where:

- $E(x_i, y_i)$ is the predicted energy of layer y_i with feature x_i
- $EC(x_i, y_i)$ is the energy correlation function between x_i and y_i
- β is the weight adjustment factor of Energy Correlation during the optimization process

2.3 EBM Model for Skin Lesion Classification

The EBM model uses the energy function $E(X;\theta)$ to assess the suitability of the skin image features X with a classification label, represented as a feature vector.

The energy function: $E(X,y;\theta)$ is constructed based on the conditional probability of the classification label y given the input features X, as follows:

$$E(X, y; \theta) = -\log P(y|X; \theta) \tag{5}$$

where θ represents the model parameters, with the task of optimizing the energy function to identify the most likely classification label y for each skin lesion image.

The EC calculation function is expressed as a weighted sum of the features:

$$E(X; \theta) = \sum_{i=1}^{n} w_i f_i(X) \tag{6}$$

where:

- $f_i(X)$ is the specific features extracted.
- w_i are the weights learned during training, reflecting the importance of each feature.

Model parameter update: The parameters θ of the model are updated using the Gradient Descent method [12] to minimize the loss function L_{EC}:

$$\theta \leftarrow \theta - \eta \nabla_\theta L_{EC}(\theta) \tag{7}$$

where: η is learning rate, $\nabla_\theta L_{EC}(\theta)$ is the gradient of the loss function with respect to the parameters θ.

This process continues until the model converges to the optimal value of the parameters, meaning when the energy difference between samples of the same class and different classes is clearly distinguished.

Classification calculation: After the model is trained, classification for a new skin lesion image X^* is performed by selecting the class y such that the energy function $E(X^*,y;\theta^*)$ is minimized:

$$y^* = \arg\min E\left(X^*, y; \theta^*\right) \tag{8}$$

The expected outcome is an efficient classification system that utilizes the Loss Function L_{EC} with Energy Correlation to achieve high accuracy in classifying different types of skin lesions.

3   Proposed EBM Model for Skin Lesion Classification

3.1   Overview Diagram

The overview diagram of the system is designed to illustrate the entire process from data input to result evaluation. This diagram is divided into four main functional blocks: Image Acquisition, Image Preprocessing and Feature Extraction, Energy Modeling, and Skin Lesion Classification. The steps in the diagram are sequentially connected, ensuring that the input data is processed, modeled, and ultimately classified accurately and efficiently (Fig. 2).

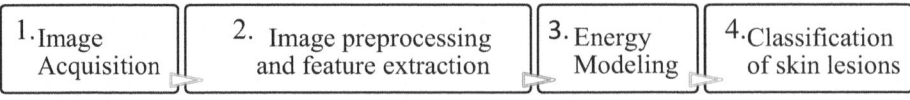

Fig. 2. System overview diagram

3.2 Main Functions and Algorithms

Feature Extraction: Extract features from the ISIC 2019 dataset and save as features.csv file

---

Begin
    dataset_path = "path/to/ISIC_2019_images"
    labels_csv = "path/to/ISIC_2019_Training_GroundTruth.csv"
    image_size = 128
    batch_size = 32
    labels = pandas.read_csv(labels_csv) // *Load label file*
    function preprocess(image):
      Resize image(image_size, image_size)
      Normalize pixel value: image = image / 255.0
      Convert image to tensor
      return image
    model = Load pretrained ResNet50 from torchvision.models
    Initialize DataLoader với batch_size // *Extract Features*
      Create empty list to store features and labels
      for batch_images, batch_labels in DataLoader:
      Convert batch_images to tensor
      features = model(batch_images)
      Save features and batch_labels to list
    Save features and labels to "features.csv"
End

Definition of the Energy Correlation Loss function (L_ED): Using Energy Correlation Loss to optimize the EBM model in classifying skin lesion images. Energy Correlation enhances the distinction between classes and optimizes the correlation between features and classification labels.

Begin
CLASS EnergyCorrelationLoss:
    def initialize class_weights
    def forward:
      energy_loss = (Energy compatibility value between predicted label and actual label)
    return energy_loss
End

Skin lesion classification with EBM using Energy Correlarion Loss (L_{ED}):

Input: Preprocessed image (128x128x3) from the ISIC 2019 dataset, The feature vector is extracted and Label of each image (1 of 8 types of lesions - 8 classes)

Output: - Energy Score: EBM calculates the energy for each input image).

      - Label Output: The result is a predicted label (one of 8 lesion types).

Begin
```
# Train_EBM
FUNCTION Train EBM with epochs = 500:
    Create empty list to save loss history
    FOR epoch FROM 1 TO epochs DO:
        FOR each batch (images, labels) IN dataloader DO:
            loss = Cal EnergyCorrelationLoss with output and correct label
            Execute optimizer(), backward() to calculate gradient of loss
            total_loss += value of loss
            predicted = Get predicted label with highest energy value from
        output
            correct += Total number of correct predicted labels compared to
        actual labels
            total += Number of labels in current batch
        average_loss = total_loss / Number of batches in dataloader
        accuracy = correct / total * 100
        add average_loss to loss_history
        Print "Epoch [epoch/epochs], Loss: average_loss, Accuracy: accuracy%"
```
End

Starting with a dataset consisting of feature vectors extracted from skin lesion images of the ISIC 2019 dataset and the corresponding labels for various types of skin lesions. The model calculates the Energy Correlation Loss between the feature vectors, which is the ratio of inter-class energy to intra-class energy. During training, the model adjusts the parameters to minimize the Energy Correlation Loss. In the final result, the model computes the energy values for each classification label, and the label with the lowest energy value is selected as the predicted label, as it has the highest probability (Fig. 3).

4 Experimental Results and Discussion

4.1 Dataset Used

The ISIC_2019 skin image dataset is used in the model experiments (Table 1).

Characteristics and challenges in the dataset: Imbalanced class distribution, uneven lighting in images, varying angles, noisy images, and multi-class classification.

To prepare the data for training and testing, the dataset is split into two parts: 80% for training and 20% for testing.

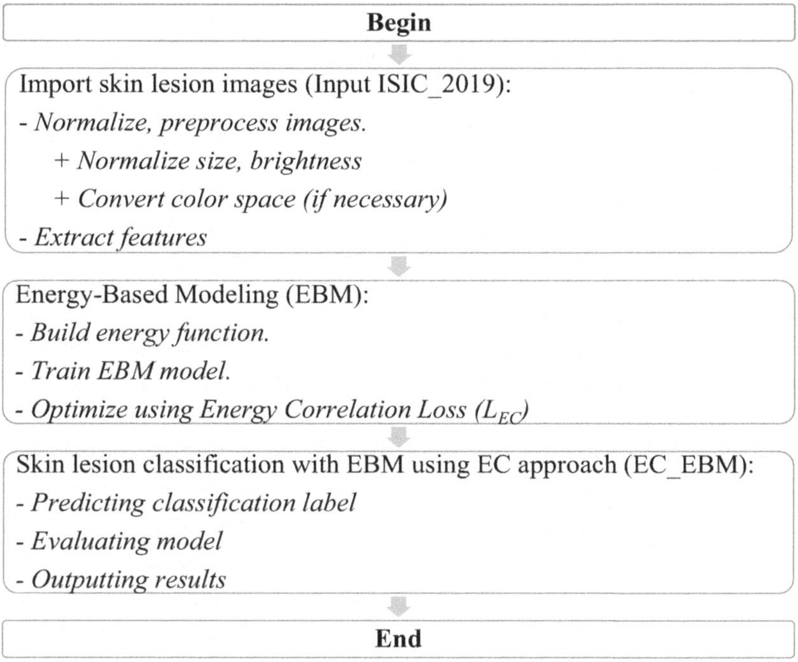

Begin

⬇

Import skin lesion images (Input ISIC_2019):
- *Normalize, preprocess images.*
    + *Normalize size, brightness*
    + *Convert color space (if necessary)*
- *Extract features*

⬇

Energy-Based Modeling (EBM):
- *Build energy function.*
- *Train EBM model.*
- *Optimize using Energy Correlation Loss (L_{EC})*

⬇

Skin lesion classification with EBM using EC approach (EC_EBM):
- *Predicting classification label*
- *Evaluating model*
- *Outputting results*

⬇

End

Fig. 3. Main system function diagram

Table 1. Summary of the ISIC_2019 dataset [3]

Diagnostic Label	Abbreviation	Number of Skin Image
Melanoma	MEL	4,522
Melanocytic Nevus	NV	12,722
Basal Cell Carcinoma	BCC	3,452
Actinic Keratosis / Bowen's Disease	AKIEC	867
Benign Keratosis	BKL	2,694
Dermatofibroma	DF	239
Vascular Lesion	VASC	253
Squamous Cell Carcinoma	SCC	628
Unknown	UNK	954

4.2 Tools Used

EBMEC (Energy-Based Model Energy Correlation) is a tool built on the Python platform, utilizing the PyTorch, TensorFlow/Keras, and Energy libraries. This tool enables efficient model training, experimentation, and deployment of the EBM model, covering processes such as data preprocessing, feature extraction, energy correlation calculation, model building, skin lesion classification, and result evaluation.

4.3   Experimental Scenario for Skin Lesion Classification with EBM and Energy Correlation

The results of skin lesion classification using the EBM approach with Energy Correlation were experimented with the EBM model on the ISIC 2019 dataset.

Training Results and L_{EC} Chart Across Epochs
From the chart Fig. 4, it can be observed that the Train Loss decreases steadily throughout the training process. Specifically, after about 100 epochs, the Train Loss reaches a very low stable level and remains there in the subsequent epochs. This indicates that the model has learned quite well from the training data and is not overfitting.

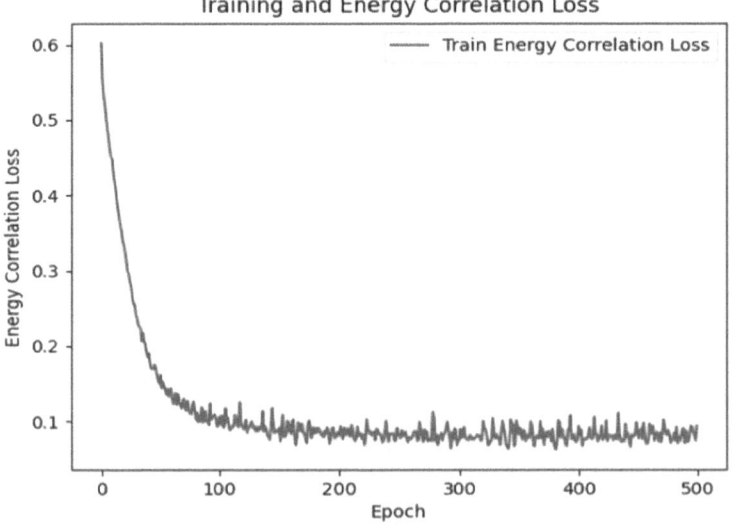

Fig. 4. Training EBM with Energy Correlation Loss (L_{EC}), Epoch = 500

Classification Results
The result from Fig. 5 indicate that the model was able to classify all diagnostic labels with fairly high accuracy. Some labels were classified with particularly good results, achieving high accuracy rates, such as Nevus (88.50%) and Basal Cell Carcinoma (68.27%). This suggests that the model accurately learned the distinguishing features for these types of lesions. However, for certain lesions like Dermatofibroma and Benign Keratosis, the model encountered more difficulty in accurate classification, showing a high misclassification rate.

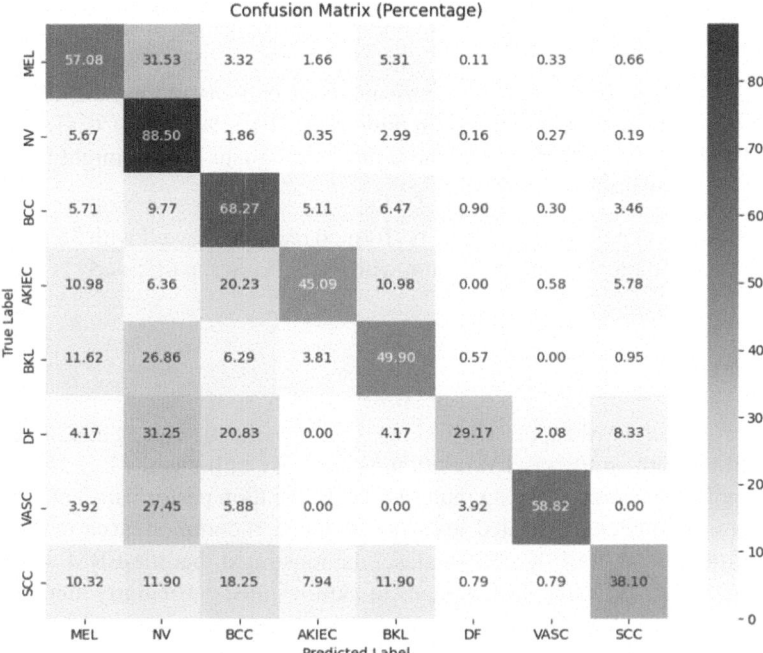

Fig. 5. Confusion Matrix

Melanoma (MEL). The model correctly classified 57.08% of melanoma cases. However, a significant 31.53% of melanoma cases were misclassified as NV (nevus), which indicates confusion between these two classes. This confusion might be due to similar visual features between melanoma and nevus lesions, which can sometimes appear alike in dermoscopic images.

Melanocytic Nevus (NV). The model performed well with 88.50% accuracy in classifying nevi, which is a good result, showing that the model distinguishes this class relatively well. There are minor misclassifications, such as 5.67% of nevus cases being incorrectly classified as MEL.

Basal Cell Carcinoma (BCC). The accuracy for basal cell carcinoma was 68.27%, which shows a moderate performance. Notable confusion is seen with NV (9.77%) and MEL (5.71%), suggesting that some features overlap between these classes.

Actinic Keratoses and Intraepithelial Carcinoma (AKIEC). This class had a relatively low correct classification rate of 45.09%, with significant misclassifications into BKL (benign keratosis) at 20.23%, showing that the model struggles with distinguishing these two classes. Misclassifications into other classes, such as NV and BCC, also occurred.

Benign Keratosis (BKL). The model correctly classified 49.90% of BKL cases, but a large percentage (26.86%) were misclassified as NV. This confusion suggests that the features of benign keratosis might overlap with those of nevus, leading to these misclassifications.

Squamous Cell Carcinoma (SCC). For squamous cell carcinoma, the accuracy was low (38.10%), with significant confusion with MEL (10.32%) and BCC (18.25%). The overlap in features between SCC and these other malignant classes might be the cause of these misclassifications.

Vascular Lesions (VASC). The model performed reasonably well with 58.82% correct classification, but there was still confusion with other classes, particularly NV and BCC.

5   Conclusion

The study proposed a novel approach to skin lesion classification using the Energy-Based Model (EBMs) with an Energy Correlation method. By utilizing the L_{EC} loss function, the model not only achieved strong multiclass classification performance but also effectively addressed challenges related to data imbalance, a common issue in the medical field. Experiments on the ISIC 2019 dataset demonstrated that the EBM model effectively distinguishes between various types of skin lesions, particularly dangerous ones such as skin cancer. Additionally, the research opens numerous avenues for developing medical diagnostic support systems, ranging from expanding datasets to improving modeling techniques, preprocessing, and feature extraction. Deploying the model in real-world clinical applications to ensure transparency and decision accuracy represents a critical next step in translating this research into practice.

In conclusion, the proposed method not only contributes to the classification of skin lesions but also broadens the potential applications of Energy-Based Models (EBMs) in both the medical and machine learning fields.

References

1. Lecun, Y., Chopra, S., Hadsell, R., et al.: A tutorial on energy-based learning. Predicting Struct. Data 191–246 (2006)
2. Energy Distance. https://en.wikipedia.org/wiki/Energy_distance
3. International Skin Imaging Collaboration (ISIC): ISIC 2019: skin lesion analysis towards melanoma detection (2019). https://www.isic-archive.com/
4. He, H., Garcia, E.A.: Learning from imbalanced data. IEEE Trans. Knowl. Data Eng. **21**(9), 1263–1284 (2009). https://doi.org/10.1109/TKDE.2008.239
5. Gradient descent. https://en.wikipedia.org/wiki/Gradient_descent
6. Jha, A., Ananthanarayana, V.S.: An interpretable deep learning model for skin lesion classification. In: Advances in Computing and Data Sciences. ICACDS 2023, vol. 1848. Springer, Cham (2023). https://doi.org/10.1007/978-3-031-37940-6_44
7. Subramanian, M.: Deep learning techniques in skin cancer detection: a survey. In: 1st International Conference on Computational Science and Technology (ICCST), Chennai, India, pp. 378–381 (2022). https://doi.org/10.1109/ICCST55948.2022.10040424
8. Naqvi, M., et al.: Skin cancer detection using deep learning-a review. Diagnostics (Basel, Switzerland) **13**(11), 1911 (2023). https://doi.org/10.3390/diagnostics13111911

9. Rizzo, M.L., Székely, G.J.: Energy distance. WIREs Comput. Stat. **8**, 27–38 (2016). https://doi.org/10.1002/wics.1375

10. Debelee, T.G.: Skin lesion classification and detection using machine learning techniques: a systematic review. Diagnostics **13**(19), 3147 (2023). https://doi.org/10.3390/diagnostics13193147

11. Grignaffini, F., et al.: Machine learning approaches for skin cancer classification from dermoscopic images: a systematic review. Algorithms **15**(11), 438 (2022). https://doi.org/10.3390/a15110438

12. Kassem, M.A., Hosny, K.M., Damaševičius, R., Eltoukhy, M.M.: Machine learning and deep learning methods for skin lesion classification and diagnosis: a systematic review. Diagnostics **11**(8), 1390 (2021). https://doi.org/10.3390/diagnostics11081390

13. Zia Ur Rehman, M., Ahmed, F., Alsuhibany, S.A., Jamal, S.S., Zulfiqar Ali, M., Ahmad, J.: Classification of skin cancer lesions using explainable deep learning. Sensors **22**(18), 6915 (2022). https://doi.org/10.3390/s22186915

14. Hosny, K.M., Kassem, M.A., Foaud, M.M.: Classification of skin lesions using transfer learning and augmentation with Alex-net. PLoS ONE **14**(5), e0217293 (2019). https://doi.org/10.1371/journal.pone.0217293

15. Viknesh, C.K., Kumar, P.N., Seetharaman, R., Anitha, D.: Detection and classification of melanoma skin cancer using image processing technique. Diagnostics **13**(21), 3313 (2023). https://doi.org/10.3390/diagnostics13213313

16. Nie, Y., Sommella, P., Carratù, M., O'Nils, M., Lundgren, J.: A deep CNN transformer hybrid model for skin lesion classification of dermoscopic images using focal loss. Diagnostics **13**(1), 72 (2023). https://doi.org/10.3390/diagnostics13010072

17. Musthafa, M.M., et al.: Enhanced skin cancer diagnosis using optimized CNN architecture and checkpoints for automated dermatological lesion classification. BMC Med. Imaging **24**, 201 (2024). https://doi.org/10.1186/s12880-024-01356-8

18. Höhn, J., Hekler, A., Krieghoff-Henning, E., et al.:. Integrating patient data into skin cancer classification using convolutional neural networks: systematic review. J. Med. Internet Res. **23**(7), e20708 (2021). https://doi.org/10.2196/20708

19. McDonagh, J.L., Silva, A.F., Vincent, M.A., Popelier, P.L.A.: Machine learning of dynamic electron correlation energies from topological atoms. J. Chem. Theory Comput. **14**(1), 216–224 (2018). https://doi.org/10.1021/acs.jctc.7b01157

20. Margraf, J.T., Reuter, K.: Making the coupled cluster correlation energy machine-learnable. J. Phys. Chem. A 2018 **122**(30), 6343–6348 (2018). https://doi.org/10.1021/acs.jpca.8b04455

21. Foorotan, M.M., Larki, I., Zahedi, R., Ahmadi, A.: Machine learning and deep learning in energy systems: a review. Sustainability. **14**(8), 4832 (2022). https://doi.org/10.3390/su14084832

22. Shahcheraghian, A., Ilinca, A.: Advanced machine learning techniques for energy consumption analysis and optimization at UBC campus: correlations with meteorological variables. Energies **17**(18), 4714 (2024). https://doi.org/10.3390/en17184714

23. Mira, K., Bugiotti, F., Morosuk, T.: Artificial intelligence and machine learning in energy conversion and management. Energies **16**(23), 7773 (2023). https://doi.org/10.3390/en16237773

24. Guan, Y., Tu, Z., Wang, S., Wang, Y., Liu, Q., Liang, D.: Magnetic resonance imaging reconstruction using a deep energy-based model. NMR Biomed. **36**(3), e4848 (2023). https://doi.org/10.1002/nbm.4848

25. Tiwary, P., Bhattacharyya, K.: Cycle consistent twin energy-based models for image-to-image translation. Med. Image Anal. **91**, 103031 (2024). https://doi.org/10.1016/j.media.2023.103031

26. Tu, Z., Jiang, C., Guan, Y., Liu, J., Liu, Q.: K-space and image domain collaborative energy-based model for parallel MRI reconstruction. Magn. Reson. Imaging **99**, 110–122 (2023). https://doi.org/10.1016/j.mri.2023.02.004

27. Cai, S., Shen, C., Wang, X.: Energy-based MRI semantic augmented segmentation for unpaired CT images. Electronics **12**(10), 2174 (2023). https://doi.org/10.3390/electronics12102174

Caught in the Lens: Zero-Shot BioCLIP Struggles with Camera Trap Wildlife Images

Ali Reza Sajun[1]([📧]) [ID], Maryam Gharaibeh[1], Nesreen Rahmeh[1], Imran Zualkernan[1] [ID], Altaf Habib[2], and Andrew Gardner[2]

[1] American University of Sharjah, Sharjah, UAE
{b00068908,g00093023,g00092745,izualkernan}@aus.edu
[2] Emirates Nature-WWF, Dubai, UAE
{ahabib,agardner}@enwwf.ae

Abstract. The decline of wildlife populations and rising species extinctions is an increasing threat do global biodiversity. Camera traps are vital for monitoring animals in their natural habitats. However, manually labeling the resulting images is time-consuming and expensive. This study evaluates the performance of BioCLIP, a specialized Vision Language Model (VLM) for biological images, in classifying camera trap images using zero-shot predictions. We utilized a private dataset from Emirates Nature-WWF, comprising of 65,919 images from the Hajar Mountains in the United Arab Emirates, categorized into 15 classes with significant class imbalance and a dominant "Ghost" class representing non-animal triggers. Using accuracy and F1-score metrics, the zero-shot analysis revealed limited effectiveness, with genus-level prediction accuracy at only 18%, and family and order accuracies at 36% and 42%, respectively. Restricting outputs to the 14 animal genera improved genus accuracy to 38%, but this remains insufficient for practical use. These results indicate that BioCLIP struggles with camera trap images when used directly, highlighting limitations of large vision models trained on idealistic datasets when applied to real-world problems. We recommend fine-tuning or few-shot training to optimize the model for ecological monitoring, suggesting that incorporating object detection could enhance performance and support biodiversity conservation efforts.

Keywords: BioCLIP · LVM · Wildlife Conservation · Generalizability · Image Classification

1 Introduction

In recent times, wildlife is experiencing a continual decline in diversity. Ecosystems that once thrived are now on the brink of collapse due to the growing pressures of habitat destruction, climate change, poaching, and pollution, and much of it is driven by human interventions [1]. Species extinctions, once rare, are becoming a disturbingly common and in order to keep track of what is happening in wildlife habitats and maintain biodiversity, continuous monitoring through devices like camera traps are used as a non-invasive

H. X. Huynh et al. (Eds.): GOODTECHS 2024, LNICST 648, pp. 131–145, 2025.
https://doi.org/10.1007/978-3-032-01472-6_11

analytical tool to capture pictures and record wildlife species. The significance of camera traps extends far beyond their mechanical simplicity. For ecologists, each captured image represents a critical data point, emphasizing the complex behaviors of wildlife. These snapshots offer insight into animal migration patterns, predator-prey dynamics, and the delicate balance of ecosystems. In some cases, camera traps have even documented the presence of species previously thought to be extinct or undiscovered, providing critical evidence that informs conservation strategies [2]. However, a significant challenge associated with this approach is the large volume of image data that ecologists must process manually. Cameras have captured up to tens of thousands of images that take significant amount of time to go through manually [3]. To solve the problem, ecologists seek the help of automation to process and analyze the camera trap data.

Over the past decade, generative computer vision models became more advanced, with the introduction of multimodal models that combine both visual and linguistic elements [4]. Large vision models, like CLIP, merge transformer architecture with vision and language, enabling them to process and encode both text and images. Trained on large-scale datasets, CLIP functions as an image encoder within multimodal frameworks, transforming how AI interprets human instructions across vision and language tasks [4–6]. One such model is that of BioCLIP [7] which is a specialized version of the CLIP model and was trained and tested on biological text and imagery. This model is designed to identify, classify, and provide hierarchical labeling of animals in any setting [5]. This work aims to investigate the performance of BioCLIP model on data of camera traps collected in mountainous terrains. In doing so, we hope to leverage advancements in the field of large vision models towards solving a critical problem faced by ecologists and therefore aid them in the battle against animal extinction while also aligning with the UN goal of life on land.

2   Literature Review

2.1   Previous Work

In an initial study, deep learning models were trained and evaluated using WWF data with the goal of developing a system for classifying camera trap images on an edge device in real-time [2]. This approach aimed to provide ecologists with timely information about animal sightings, which could be delayed for months with traditional camera trap monitoring methods. The results were that Xception was the best-performing model, achieving a 0.98 average accuracy and a 0.94 macro F1-score. In addition, transfer learning, which is the technique of leveraging a pre-trained model on a new but related task, was employed to utilize pre-trained weights from these models, significantly enhancing performance and reducing training time. However, the study acknowledges a significant performance drop in classifying images from minority classes after optimizing the model for edge deployment.

Subsequent work aiming to address this issue have experimented with a variety of approaches towards achieving efficient camera trap inferencing such as semi-supervised learning and model generalization approaches. This research is summarized in Table 1.

Table 1. Summary of models used for camera trap image

Model	References	Domain	Data	Architecture	Result (Score)	Year
Xception	[5]	Camera trap image classification (edge device)	WWF camera trap images	Depthwise separable convolution layers	Accuracy: 0.98, Macro F1-Score: 0.94	2015
Inception- V3	[6]	Camera trap image classification (IoT system)	WWF camera trap images	CNN	Accuracy: 94%, Macro F1-Score: 0.93	2017
Inception-V3 (TensorFlow Lite)	[6]	Camera trap image classification (IoT system)	Camera trap images of wildlife from ecological monitoring	CNN	Accuracy: 92%, Macro F1-Score: 0.90	2017
WilDect-YOLO	[8]	Wildlife detection and conservation	Images of endangered wildlife species for monitoring and conservation efforts	YOLOv4	Precision: 97.18% F1-score: 97.87%	2015

2.2   What are Large Vision Models

Large Vision Models (LVMs) are advanced artificial intelligence (AI) models that process and interpret visual data like images and videos, similar to the way Large Language Models process textual data. They are called "Large" models, because they have a large number of parameters, often millions or even billions, which can be used to learn complex patterns from visual data [9]. LVMs are built primarily using deep learning principles and convolutional neural networks (CNNs) with a significant number of parameters, which helps the models understand visual content. However, more recently some have used transformer models for different vision tasks, providing more accurate results in some cases [10]. Large vision models are highly used in our day to day lives, some LVM use cases include health care, where they are used to analyze X-rays, MRIs and CT scans. Other uses include autonomous vehicles to interpret and respond to visual cues and surroundings [9]. Large vision models face many challenges which include computational resources since using these models requires huge computational power and memory, another challenge these models face is the difficulty of providing enough data that is collected, labeled and processed which can be expensive and hard to do which leads us to another challenges such as generalization since these models struggle to work on data that is different to what they were trained on [11]. Some of the most well-known LVMs include OpenAI's GPT-4o which is a large multimodal model that is able to interact using sound, image or video. Another well-known model is Landing AI's LandingLens is an industry-leading AI Computer Vision software platform from landing AI. It was designed for quickly developing and deploying visual classification systems using domain experts and artificial intelligence experts [12].

Large Vision Models (LVMs) are being increasingly used in wildlife conservation efforts since they rely on vast amounts of visual data. Models such as WilDect-YOLO which build upon YOLOv4 is a high-precision, single-stage object detection model, YOLO models are known for their speed and accuracy in simultaneously classifying and locating objects within an image by predicting bounding boxes and class probabilities [8]. The model was used in a study where the authors aimed to use it for automated detection and localization of endangered wildlife species in images [8]. The main problem that was addressed in the study is the need for an accurate, efficient, and robust system to assist in wildlife monitoring and conservation efforts. Some of the key architectural improvements done on WilDect-YOLO are the improvement of discriminative feature extraction, preserving critical feature information, receptive field enhancement and preserving fine-grain localized information [8]. This made the model robust to challenges and achieve high accuracy and fast detection speed [8]. However, the model also came with some challenges like limited generalizability and high computational resources for training and deployment.

2.3   OpenAI's CLIP

OpenAI's CLIP or Contrastive Language-Image Pre-training which was first introduced in 2021 is one of the most successful large vision models [13]. The model is an image and text embedding model, essentially mapping text and images to the same embedding space. It was trained using a diverse set of 400 million images and text pairs in a self-supervised way. An example of this is how CLIP can map an image of a cat with the sentence "an image of a cat", this pair would be close to each other in the vector space and have very similar embeddings [14].

Using these capabilities CLIP is able to interpret images using natural language to perform a multitude of vision-related tasks, including zero-shot classification. This type of classification allows the model to predict a class that it didn't see during training. This is particularly useful when there is a limited amount of labeled data to work with [15]. CLIP can also be used to generate captions for images, describe visual concepts, and generalize to other tasks in the same domain. Additionally, CLIP can be used to transfer knowledge across different tasks and domains [16].

2.4   BioCLIP

BioCLIP is a large-scale multimodal model designed to answer biology questions about images [17]. This model uses a large number of images available for plants, animals and fungi sourced from a dataset called TreeOfLife-10M, consisting of 10 million images containing over 450,000 classes. This dataset combines images from three major sources;

iNaturalist, BIOSCAN-1M, and the Encyclopedia of Life (EOL) [17]. The images represent a wide variety of living organisms including plants, animals, and fungi, and cover different taxonomic ranks from species to kingdoms. The model was designed for broad biological applications, including species identification, biodiversity monitoring, and ecological research. BioCLIP is trained using the CLIP objective, which means that it learns to match images to textual descriptions. The text encoder used in BioCLIP is autoregressive, meaning it processes text in a specific order, with each word influencing the interpretation of the next. BioClip's output depends highly on the task at hand. The model's primary outputs are text-image similarity scores which represent how closely an image aligns with a given textual description. The higher the score, the more relevant the image is to the text. It also outputs predicted classes or labels for classification tasks, based on its interpretation of the image and corresponding textual prompts typically in the form of kingdom, phylum, class, order, family, genus, species epithet, species, common name, and score. Finally, the model also produces ranked image-text pairs, rank multiple images or text descriptions according to how well they match, based on their similarity scores. BioCLIP has high accuracy where it consistently outperforms existing baselines in biology-related classification tasks, exceeding them by 17% to 20%. BioCLIP also has claims to have strong generalizability since it can accurately classify even unseen species based on their visual features and their position within the biological hierarchy.

3 Methodology

3.1 Dataset

The dataset used in this work was a private dataset of camera trap images provided by Emirates Nature-WWF. The data originates from surveys conducted within the Hajar Mountains of the United Arab Emirates. The primary goal is to identify biodiversity hotspots and aid in establishing protected areas. Due to the practical nature of this dataset, it serves as a useful test case to examine the efficacy of the BioCLIP model in handling real life data. The dataset comprised of 65,919 images which included both night and day images, categorized into 15 classes. Fourteen classes represent specific animal species, while one class, labeled "Ghost", accounts for images triggered by non-animal factors like wind, vegetation movement, heat etc. Sample images from the dataset can be seen in Fig. 1.

A significant challenge posed by the dataset is the considerable class imbalance between the species. The "Ghost" class dominates, accounting for 52.55% of the total images. Meanwhile, classes like "Camel" and "Rat" have very few instances. Table 2 summarizes the class distribution.

While the BioCLIP model is able to perform inference to the species level, the WWF dataset used for this work had labeled data at the genus level and therefore the genus was used as the lowest level of prediction. The corresponding family and order of each genus were also extrapolated e.g. the genus Vulpes (fox) was assigned the family Canidae and the order Carnivora.

a. Camelus   b. Capra   c. Ghost

Fig. 1. Sample images of EN-WWF Dataset

Table 2. Distribution of Images in EN-WWF Dataset

Class	Number of images	Percentage
Ghost	34,642	52.55%
Capra	15,617	23.69%
Vulpes	9,275	14.07%
Equus	3,284	4.98%
Ammoperdix	821	1.25%
Ovis	779	1.18%
Canis	475	0.72%
Spilopelia	327	0.50%
Oenanthe	287	0.44%
Felis	216	0.33%
Acomys	196	0.30%
Total	**65,919**	**100%**

3.2 Validation Methodology

A series of tests were conducted on the data in order to fully analyze the efficacy of the BioCLIP model when dealing with real-life camera trap data. In the first stage, the animal images in the dataset were extracted leaving the ghost images out. The BioCLIP model was then used to generate genus, family and order predictions for all the animal images. This was done in order to be able to evaluate the BioCLIP model in three different levels of abstraction, the assumption being the results of the order being greater than that of family which would be greater than that of genus. The top-1 predictions were then compared with the true label and a variety of metrics such as accuracy, precision, recall, macro average f1-score and weighted f1-score were computed in order to properly analyze the efficacy of the BioCLIP model.

Next, an analysis was conducted on the mistakes made by the model for each class by mapping the class to how many unique genera predictions existed and what the top 5 most common genera predictions were for each class. A confusion factor was computed in order to analyze the confusion of the model when handling different genus classes. This would allow an insight into which of the genera were easily identifiable. The equation for the confusion factor can be found below.

$$Confusion\ Factor = \frac{Number\ of\ Images}{Unique\ Genera\ of\ Predictions} \tag{1}$$

In order to investigate how far the model was from the true predictions, a subsequent analysis was conducted where in addition to the top-1 genus predictions, the performance of the model was also computed with the number of top genus predictions considered being varied from 1 to 5. For example, in the top-3 analysis, if any of the BioCLIP model's top 3 genus predictions corresponded with the correct genus of the image, the prediction was considered correct. Consequently, in order to minimize the effect of non-relevant classes on the prediction process, a CustomLabelsClassifier was used to fix the possible genus outputs to the 14 genera present in the animals subset. The performance of the BioCLIP model's predictions was then evaluated and compared with the results obtained from the initial test. Finally, an analysis was conducted on the previously discarded ghost images by generating genus predictions for all of the images using the BioCLIP model and analyzing the top-10 orders, families and genera predictions across the ghost images.

4   Results and Analysis

4.1   Zero-Shot Analysis

In the first test, the animals data from the WWF Camera trap image dataset was fed into the BioCLIP model in a zero-shot prediction analysis. The metrics computed by comparing the resulting predictions with the actual class labels revealed a number of interesting trends. Firstly, despite the input images being across 14 genus classes, the BioCLIP model's genus predictions for the data was spread across a vast collection of 665 genera. This clearly meant the model had a difficult time differentiating between the intricacies in different genera it was trained on when it came to assigning a genus label on the camera trap images. This could be due to a variety of factors such as the presence of a large number of infrared night images in the camera trap data or the specific mountainous terrain which is the backdrop for all images. Consequently, this resulted in the predictions showing a low accuracy of 18% and a macro average f1-score of 0.3%. This significantly low f1-score is a direct result of the number of classes in the model predictions and therefore the weighted average f1-score was also computed to be an unimpressive 27.9%.

Building upon the assessment that these low results were due to the intricacies between the various genera, consequent analysis focused on abstracting the problem further by predicting first the family and then the order of the animals in the images, with the idea of simplifying the problem for the BioCLIP model These results are summarized in Table 3 below.

As expected, with the generalization of the problem, the performance metrics of the predictions rose with the family level predictions having a total of 314 unique predictions, showing an accuracy of 36.2% and a weighted average f1-score of 47.9% while the order level predictions had a total of 119 unique predictions with an accuracy of 42.0% and a weighted average f1-score of 49.7%. These results are in contrast to the state-of-the-art on this dataset achieved by Ramesh et al. [18] who achieved an accuracy of 72.7% and a weighted f1-score of 95.7% using ImageNet transfer learning applied to CNN models such as DenseNet and ImageNet.

Table 3. BioCLIP Zero-Shot results for EN-WWF dataset

Category	Accuracy (%)	M. Avg F1-score (%)	W. Avg F1-score (%)	Unique Predictions
Genus	18.0	0.30	27.9	665
Family	36.2	0.70	47.9	314
Order	42.0	1.70	49.7	119

Due to the large number of predicted genera classes, an analysis was then conducted into the class-wise genus predictions for each of the animal classes within the camera trap dataset. For each class, the number of instances of that class was mapped alongside the number of unique genera predicted and the model's confusion factor was computed in order to prevent bias resulting from a class with a large number of images having a corresponding large number of unique Genera from skewing the analysis. Table 4 shows the results of the analysis conducted.

As the table demonstrates, the classes with a high number of images had a higher confusion factor, meaning that the model displayed a lack of consistency between inferencing images within the same genus. This assessment is further supported by the fact that the two classes with the highest confusion factors i.e. Capra and Vulpes had the correct genus as the prediction of most frequency and yet had a very large number of classes that the non-correct predictions were associated with. On the other hand, the classes with the two least confusion factors i.e. Ammomanes and Emberiza didn't have the correct genus among the top 5 most frequent predictions at all. This suggests that in these cases, the model was more consistent but with the *wrong* predictions.

Generally, it was noted that Camelus, Canis, Capra, Equus, Ovis and Vulpes had the correct genus as the outcome with most predictions whereas Acomys, Ammomanes, Ammoperdix, Emberiza, Spilopelia, all of which are birds and Rattus did not have the correct predictions in any of the top 5 predicted genera. Finally, in the case of Felis and Oenanthe the correct genus was the second most predicted genus with the most predicted genus in both cases being Neotoma (pack rat).

The case of the Neotoma is most interesting, with 5 classes having it as their most predicted class and 5 others having it within their top 5 genus predictions. Indeed, out of the 31,881 total animal images, 4050 (12%) are predicted as Neotoma, making it the most predicted class overall. This is interesting the class is not in the input images at all. A closer analysis needs to be conducted into the properties of Neotoma images that make

Table 4. Zero-shot Predictions of Genus from BioCLIP

Actual Genus	Images of the Genus in dataset	Total unique Genera predicted	Confusion Factor	5 most predicted Genera in descending order
Acomys	195	13	15	*Neotoma*, Dasyurus, Pseudantechinus, Allactaga, Gehyra
Ammomanes	150	41	3.66	Eberlanzia, Amphispiza, *Neotoma*, Ovis, Chinchilla
Ammoperdix	834	107	7.79	*Neotoma*, Eberlanzia, Alectoris, Crotalus, Scelorchilus
Camelus	100	19	5.26	**Camelus**, Alcelaphus, Taurotragus, Panthera, Ovis
Canis	476	48	9.92	**Canis**, Caracal, Equus, Ovis, Vulpes
Capra	15626	436	35.85	**Capra**, *Neotoma*, Ursus, Ovis, Canis
Emberiza	186	50	3.72	Sauromalus, Phymaturus, Uta, Phainopepla, Metriopelia
Equus	3286	183	17.95	**Equus**, Asian, Tragelaphus, *Neotoma*, Ovis
Felis	216	33	6.55	*Neotoma*, **Felis**, Canis, Puma, Bettongia
Oenanthe	288	68	4.24	*Neotoma*, **Oenanthe**, Amphispiza, Toxostoma, Ovis
Ovis	779	72	10.82	**Ovis**, Capra, Bos, Canis, Ursus
Rattus	138	8	17.25	*Neotoma*, Mus, Otus, Agapornis, Streptopelia
Spilopelia	327	71	4.61	Amphispiza, *Neotoma*, Crotalus, Metriopelia, Oena
Vulpes	9280	287	32.33	**Vulpes**, *Neotoma*, Canis, Lycalopex, Macropus

the BioCLIP model attribute camera trap images across all classes to this specific pack rat genus. A further analysis of this phenomenon of Neotoma predictions is conducted below alongside the Ghost image analysis.

In order to investigate how far the model was from the true predictions, the performance of the model was also computed with the number of top genus predictions considered being varied from 1 to 5. Figure 2 below shows the results seen from the analysis.

As the figure shows, the overall accuracy does improve, reaching as high as 45% for the Top-5 predictions, indicating that in 45% of cases, the model was able to predict the

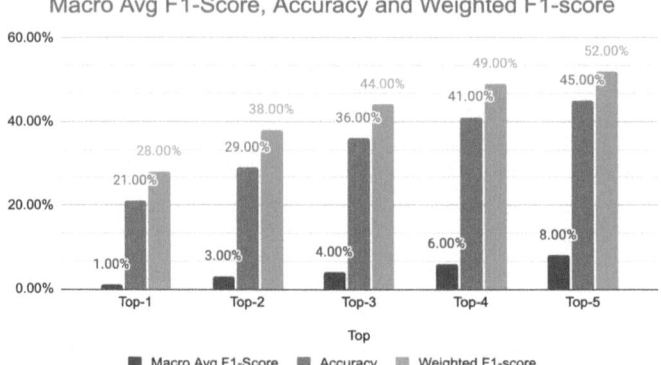

Fig. 2. Macro Average F1-Score, Weighted F1-Score and Accuracy

correct genus within the top-5 predictions. This is still far from favorable performance, especially when compared to the approach followed by the state-of-the-art results by tuning a pre-trained CNN model.

4.2 Fixing the BioCLIP Output Classes

In an effort to progress beyond the zero-shot approach followed by the majority of experiments, a further experiment was conducted where the possible genus predictions of the BioCLIP model were fixed to the genus classes present within the camera trap image dataset. While this would not be considered zero-shot since the model is being given background information about the data, analyzing the model behavior with such a constraint would shed further light on the intricacies of the BioCLIP predictions. The results of this analysis can be seen in the Table 5 below.

Table 5. Predictions of Genus from BioCLIP after fixing outputs

Metric	Value (%)
Accuracy	38
Macro-average F1-score	18
Weighted F1-score	48

As expected, this shows a considerable jump in genus prediction performance, with the accuracy jumping to 38% up from the 21% seen with zero-shot genus prediction and macro-average f1-score jumping to 18% up from 1%. However, this still demonstrates the BioCLIP model's inadequacy in working for camera trap images, with the fixed output analysis still falling considerably short of the required performance. In order to see the class-wise performance of the model with this added constraint, the confusion matrix is seen in Fig. 3 below.

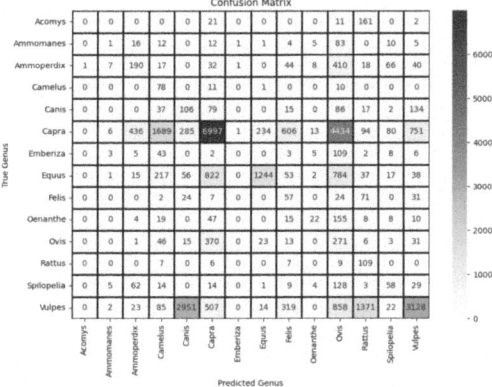

Fig. 3. Confusion Matrix of predictions after fixing the BioCLIP output

A number of interesting observations can be made from this confusion matrix. Firstly, a look along the diagonal reveals that in the case of two classes, Acomys and Emberiza, none of the images of those classes were correctly predicted. Sample images from those two classes can be seen in Fig. 4 below.

a. Acomys   b. Emberiza

Fig. 4. Images of Acomys and Emberiza from the EN-WWF Dataset

While Acomys had over 80% of its images classified as Rattus, an understandable confusion between the two rodent genera, the interesting misclassification is the case of Emberiza, a bird which had 58% of its images classified as Ovis and 23% of its images classified as Camelus. A look at the Emberiza images indicates that the bird is generally of colors that blend into the background, which could prevent the model from identifying its features and therefore getting confused in the predictions.

Other notable features in the confusion matrix are the misclassification of a large number of Capra as Ovis which is understandable given the similarity between the animals which both belong to the Bovidae family. Similarly, a large amount of confusion was seen in the case of Vulpes images being classified as Canis. This is again understandable due to both these genera belonging to the same Canidae family. However, this trend was not seen in many cases, such as a considerable number of Vulpes being confused as Rattus, Capra being confused as Camelus and Equus being confused with both

Capra and Ovis. In these cases, despite there being no obvious similarities between the genera, the model wasn't able to distinguish between them. This exposes a considerable limitation in using BioCLIP for camera trap image classification, even with the output classes being constrained.

4.3 Analysis of Ghost Images

As a final step of analysis, the previously discarded ghost images were fed into the BioCLIP model and the top-10 orders, families and genera predictions across the images were analyzed. Table 6 shows a summary of the results obtained.

Table 6. Frequent Ghost Image Predictions

Metric	Values
Top 10 Orders	Passeriformes, Rodentia, Squamata, Galliformes, Artiodactyla, Caryophyllales, Columbiformes, Lagomorpha, Perissodactyla, Macroscelidea
Top 10 Families	Cricetidae, Phasianidae, Bovidae, Mimidae, Liolaemidae, Muscicapidae, Columbidae, Aizoaceae, Passerellidae, Chinchillidae
Top 10 Genera	Neotoma, Centrocercus, Ovis, Oreoscoptes, Phymaturus, Myrmecocichla, Eberlanzia, Amphispiza, Toxostoma, Crotalus

In order to gain a better understanding of what classes the Ghost images were attributed to, Table 7 shows the top 3 most frequent genus predictions alongside a sample image of that genus class from the iNaturalist dataset used for training BioCLIP and a sample Ghost image that was classified as that genus.

For many of the genera, it appears their native terrain is somewhat similar to the terrain seen in this specific set of camera trap images (rocky mountainous backdrops). However, the most interesting case is that of the Neotoma as mentioned earlier.

4.4 The Neotoma Conundrum

Neotoma was also the most frequent prediction for the ghost images. As mentioned earlier, the Neotoma also appeared in the top-1 prediction of 5 animals and in the top-5 of 5 other animals. Therefore, an analysis needs to be made on the possible reasons for this persistent classification.

Figure 5 displays a sample image of a Vulpes in the dataset which was classified as Neotoma alongside a sample image of Neotoma from the iNaturalist dataset - the data used to train the BioCLIP model.

Firstly, it is evident that the Neotoma image has a dark background, similar to the setting of the Vulpes camera trap image. This is justifiable because the Neotoma is considered a nocturnal species and therefore it is reasonable to assume that a large number of Neotoma images used to train the BioCLIP model would have dark backgrounds,

Table 7. Images of Genus from iNaturalist and WWF Dataset

Genus	Ghost Images	iNaturalist Images
Neotoma		
Centrocercus		
Ovis		

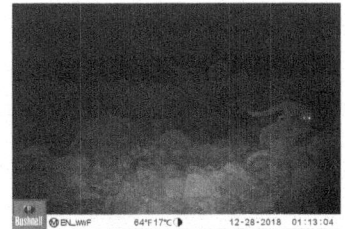

(a) Vulpus in WWF dataset classified as Neotoma

(b) Neotoma in iNaturalist dataset

Fig. 5. Vulpes image classified as Neotoma alongside a Neotoma from training dataset

closely resembling the background in the infrared night images in the camera trap dataset. Secondly, one of the common habitats in which Neotoma are observed is that of hillsides and valleys, consistent with backdrop of the camera trap images from the EN-WWF dataset which are sourced from mountain and valley terrains. Therefore, it is possible that these factors make the camera trap images more prone to being associated with this specific genus by the BioCLIP model thereby resulting in the large bias seen by the model in predicting the WWF dataset images to be from the Neotoma genus.

5   Conclusion

This paper aims to evaluate the performance of the newly proposed BioCLIP model on camera trap animal images by utilizing zero-shot predictions made by the model on the EN-WWF dataset. Consequently, BioCLIP's accuracy, performance and prediction behaviors were analyzed through a variety of experiments. Initial approaches focused on generating top-1 predictions for the genus, family and order of the images and comparing them with true labels using metrics like accuracy, precision, recall, and F1-scores to assess performance. Through this methodology, the model was able to achieve 42% accuracy when predicting the order but a mere 18% accuracy at predicting the genus correctly. Error analysis was conducted consequently by examining incorrect genus predictions and analyzing the top-5 most common errors per class. Furthermore, the number of considered correct predictions were varied from top-1 to top-5, improving performance by recognizing partial accuracy, pushing genus prediction accuracies to 45%. In a departure from the zero-shot approach, an analysis was done on restricting genus outputs to the 14 animal genera in the dataset, thereby achieving an enhanced performance of 38% accuracy. Finally, the final analysis applied the model to "Ghost" images, examining frequent taxonomic predictions. Across the experiments, the case of frequent Neotoma predictions was highlighted and attempts were made to justify the bias of the BioCLIP model towards predicting that particular genera.

It can therefore be seen that BioCLIP model, despite its promise, struggles with dealing with camera trap images, especially when handling them in a zero-shot mythology. This exposes limitations of a large vision model trained on idealistic datasets, such as iNaturalist, when dealing with real world problems. However, the vast amount of information learnt by such large vision models can easily be utilized by performing certain initial steps. One possible approach to leveraging the BioCLIP's learned information would be to perform an initial step of object detection upon the real-world images, thereby identifying the animal within the image and preventing the model from being misled by unnecessary terrain data. Another natural approach would be to retrain specific parts of the BioCLIP model through various strategies such as few shot learning or simply fine tuning the classification layers. Recently, techniques such as LoRa (Low-Rank Adaptation) have been used to fine-tune large models efficiently [19]. Through these approaches, the promise of BioCLIP in aiding real life camera trap data persists, however for now, despite its promise, BioCLIP finds that the wild remains a tough terrain for zero-shot models to capture.

References

1. Friese, C.: Cloning Wild Life: Zoos, Captivity, and the Future of Endangered Animals. NYU Press (2013)
2. Wearn, O.R., Glover-Kapfer, P.: Camera-trapping for conservation: a guide to best-practices (2017)
3. Sajun, A.R., Zualkernan, I.: Exploring semi-supervised learning for camera trap images from the wild. In: Proceedings of the 2022 5th Artificial Intelligence and Cloud Computing Conference, pp. 143–149. Association for Computing Machinery, New York, NY, USA (2023). https://doi.org/10.1145/3582099.3582122

4. Liu, Y., et al.: SORA: a review on background, technology, limitations, and opportunities of large vision Models, http://arxiv.org/abs/2402.17177 (2024)
5. Zualkernan, I., Dhou, S., Judas, J., Sajun, A.R., Gomez, B.R., Hussain, L.A.: An IoT system using deep learning to classify camera trap images on the edge. Computers. **11**, 13 (2022). https://doi.org/10.3390/computers11010013
6. Zualkernan, I., et al.: Towards an IoT-based deep learning architecture for camera trap image classification. Presented at the December 12 (2020). https://doi.org/10.1109/GCAIoT51063.2020.9345858
7. Stevens, S., et al.: BioCLIP: a vision foundation model for the tree of life. http://arxiv.org/abs/2311.18803 (2024)
8. Roy, A.M., Bhaduri, J., Kumar, T., Raj, K.: WilDect-YOLO: an efficient and robust computer vision-based accurate object localization model for automated endangered wildlife detection. Eco. Inform. **75**, 101919 (2023). https://doi.org/10.1016/j.ecoinf.2022.101919
9. Bai, Y., et al.: Sequential modeling enables scalable learning for large vision models. http://arxiv.org/abs/2312.00785 (2023). https://doi.org/10.48550/arXiv.2312.00785
10. Han, K., et al.: A survey on vision transformer. IEEE Trans. Pattern Anal. Mach. Intell. **45**, 87–110 (2023). https://doi.org/10.1109/TPAMI.2022.3152247
11. Lin, F., et al.: Universal object detection with large vision model. Int. J. Comput. Vis. **132**, 1258–1276 (2024). https://doi.org/10.1007/s11263-023-01929-0
12. Strickland, E.: Andrew Ng, AI minimalist: the machine-learning pioneer says small is the new big. IEEE Spectr. **59**, 22–50 (2022). https://doi.org/10.1109/MSPEC.2022.9754503
13. CLIP: Connecting text and images. https://openai.com/index/clip/. Accessed 27 Sep 2024
14. Understanding OpenAI's CLIP model | by Szymon Palucha | Medium. https://medium.com/@paluchasz/understanding-openais-clip-model-6b52bade3fa3. Accessed 27 Sep 2024
15. Wang, W., Zheng, V.W., Yu, H., Miao, C.: A survey of zero-shot learning: settings, methods, and applications. ACM Trans. Intell. Syst. Technol. **10**, 13:1–13:37 (2019). https://doi.org/10.1145/3293318
16. Laba, N.: Engine for the imagination? Visual generative media and the issue of representation. Media, Cult. Soc. (2024). https://doi.org/10.1177/01634437241259950
17. Imageomics/Bioclip hugging face. https://huggingface.co/imageomics/bioclip. Accessed 29 Sep 2024
18. Ramesh, K., et al.: Exploring the generalizability of transfer learning for camera trap animal image classification., presented at the European Conference on Machine Learning and Principles and Practice of Knowledge Discovery in Databases 2023, Turin, Italy (2023). https://2023.ecmlpkdd.org/
19. Hu, E.J., et al.: LoRA: Low-Rank Adaptation of large language models. arXiv arXiv:2106.09685 (2021). https://doi.org/10.48550/arXiv.2106.09685

Blending Federated Learning and Value-Sensitive Design for Ethics and Privacy-Preserving in Education

Nguyen Ha Cong Ly[1], Nguyen Thanh Thau[2], and Nguyen Thanh Quan[3(✉)]

[1] Department of Mathematics, FPT University, Can Tho, Vietnam
lynhc@fe.edu.vn
[2] Thoi Thuan Secondary School and High School, Thuan An City, Vietnam
nt_thau.c23thoithuan@cantho.edu.vn
[3] Faculty of Computer Science and Engineering, Ho Chi Minh City University
of Technology (HCMUT), Vietnam National University Ho Chi Minh City
(VNU-HCM), Ho Chi Minh City, Vietnam
ntquan.sdh20@hcmut.edu.vn

Abstract. As applied artificial intelligence (AI) continues to advance in education, addressing the ethical and privacy concerns related to machine learning (ML) systems becomes increasingly important. These concerns often necessitate compromises among project collaborators involved in designing and deploying these systems, which can affect teachers, students, and other stakeholders. Our work emphasizes the integration of value-sensitive design (VSD) principles into the technical design and performance of ML systems within educational environments. To achieve this, we propose utilizing distributed and federated learning (FL) frameworks as decentralized approaches to training ML models, effectively tackling key issues such as data privacy and security. These frameworks enable us to maintain privacy and ethical standards while leveraging the collective expertise of educational and ML partners. We conclude by identifying potential directions for future research aimed at enhancing the capabilities of privacy-preserving ML in education. By combining VSD principles with technical innovation, we promote responsible and ethical ML practices in education while ensuring practical application.

Keywords: Federated Learning · Educational Project ·
Privacy-Preserving · Value-Sensitive Design · Ethics

1 Introduction

Educational data mining has emerged as a pivotal application of artificial intelligence and data mining over the past decades. Its primary goal is to uncover patterns and trends within educational data that can be leveraged to enhance both teaching and learning processes [2,4,26,27]. Beyond these direct improvements, educational data mining also offers the potential to optimize the effectiveness of educational materials and resources. Furthermore, it holds promise

H. X. Huynh et al. (Eds.): GOODTECHS 2024, LNICST 648, pp. 146–159, 2025.
https://doi.org/10.1007/978-3-032-01472-6_12

in streamlining the broader educational system, enhancing efficiency at various levels.

However, despite these numerous advantages, the implementation of educational data mining is not without its challenges. A critical issue is the variability in the quality and accessibility of educational data, often rendering it difficult to use [31]. Additionally, concerns surrounding data privacy, security, and ethical guidelines arise frequently when dealing with sensitive educational information [15]. It is also essential to approach data mining outcomes with caution, as they may be influenced by a multitude of factors beyond just the learning process or the underlying algorithms.

In this context, Nguyen *et al.* conducted a thematic analysis of existing ethical frameworks and reports, proposing a set of ethical principles intended to guide stakeholders in developing and deploying trustworthy AI in education [22]. They highlight that, while no universal ethical consensus has been reached, embedding AI ethics within educational contexts—focusing on principles such as responsibility, inclusion, fairness, security, and explainability—can have profound implications for AI governance and policy-making.

The European Commission's Directorate-General for Education, Youth, Sport and Culture has also addressed these concerns by issuing ethical guidelines on AI and data use in teaching and learning [1]. Their guidelines emphasize key considerations, including human agency, fairness, humanity, and justified decision-making in AI applications. Among the essential requirements for trustworthy AI are privacy and data governance—encompassing respect for privacy, data quality and integrity, and controlled access to data—as well as technical robustness and safety, which ensure accuracy, reliability, and resilience to potential threats.

These concerns have motivated the exploration of federated learning (FL) as a promising solution for advancing machine learning (ML) in educational contexts while adhering to strict privacy standards. FL enables ML applications to utilize data in a distributed manner without the need to exchange raw data directly, thereby preventing the inference of private information from other parties involved [36]. This approach addresses three fundamental challenges in educational projects: protecting personally identifiable information, enabling the interoperable exchange and sharing of machine-learning-driven learning management systems, and fostering ethical AI practices [1,8,23]. By constructing learner models that aggregate data from multiple systems, FL enhances pedagogical strategies by improving the robustness of insights drawn from educational data.

Moreover, value-sensitive design (VSD) serves as a comprehensive design strategy aimed at embedding human values throughout the technology development process. VSD operates through an iterative methodology comprising conceptual, empirical, and technical investigations, all focused on the integration of human values into technological design [13]. Conceptual investigations involve philosophical analyses to identify the stakeholders impacted by the design and the core values that should guide the design process. Empirical investigations gather insights from direct and indirect stakeholders, shedding light on the values they prioritize in their interactions with technology. Finally, technical investigations focus on the technology's design and performance to ensure it aligns with identified values [10]. VSD emphasizes that every design decision has repercussions for usability, stakeholder engagement, and equitable access to technology.

Incorporating VSD principles into federated learning aligns the technology with the ethical and privacy-preserving needs of educators, students, and other stakeholders involved in educational projects [9,30]. FL inherently respects privacy by ensuring that data remains on local devices and only model updates are shared. VSD extends this by incorporating advanced privacy-preserving techniques such as differential privacy or secure multi-party computation to safeguard sensitive information throughout the collaborative model training process.

Furthermore, VSD promotes ethical data use by ensuring compliance with legal and ethical guidelines throughout the FL lifecycle. This ensures that data collection, model training, and deployment adhere to principles of fairness, informed consent, and data protection. Educators can confidently deploy FL, knowing that it respects the rights and privacy of students and other participants.

By integrating VSD principles, FL can also address fairness and bias concerns. Aggregating data from diverse sources allows for the creation of more inclusive and representative models. Educators can use FL to minimize biases by ensuring demographic representation and preventing disproportionate impacts on any specific group. Additionally, FL facilitates collaborative knowledge sharing among educators and institutions while safeguarding data privacy. VSD ensures that this collaboration respects individual autonomy and confidentiality, promoting both technical and ethical robustness in educational models [14].

In the following sections, we first provide a brief review of related work. Subsequently, we present our vision of federated learning systems in education, followed by an in-depth exploration of FL deployment, including our experimental results. Finally, we conclude by discussing the potential synergy between FL and VSD, underscoring the promising future of this combined approach.

2 Related Work

This section briefly summarizes related works focusing on the intersection between FL and privacy protection and ethics protocols in education. The literature witnesses no standalone surveys or reviews on FL in education. Instead, FL in education research appears in the application section of several other domains' surveys [32,38]. This lack of interest and research will be a premise for interdisciplinary studies in the future. Fortunately, many individual works have gradually gained attention to combining computer science, educational data mining, and policymakers under the guidance of teaching-learning science to develop FL systems in education.

Schleiss *et al.* raised the awareness of any distributed computing and design responsible for organizational and technical measures to ensure privacy [28].

Labba *et al.* practically exploited FL on edge computing-based system for distributed analytics to support real-time K-12 learners' assessment. Still, they did not provide the experimental data and codes to confirm the results [18]. In addition, their FL deployment seems unstable when scaling.

Several educational data analysis frameworks based on FL have been introduced, such as Federated Deep Knowledge Tracing for personalized and adaptive learning [34] and FEEDAN [16] for the exchange of analytical capabilities of educational data. Another Hierarchical Personalized Federated Learning model addressed the inconsistent clients for the task of user modeling [35]. Fochola *et al.* presents the application of federated learning techniques to a well-known learning analytics problem: student dropout prediction [11].

Although understandably, FL is a very new trend in ML, researchers and educators have seen it as a potential methodology to effectively disentangle privacy resolution and ethical guidelines on using artificial intelligence in education. New privacy-preserving ML refers to modifying traditional ML pipelines and properties to protect sensitive information; see Fig. 1. To our knowledge, we are the first to formalize the application of FL in a particular educational project.

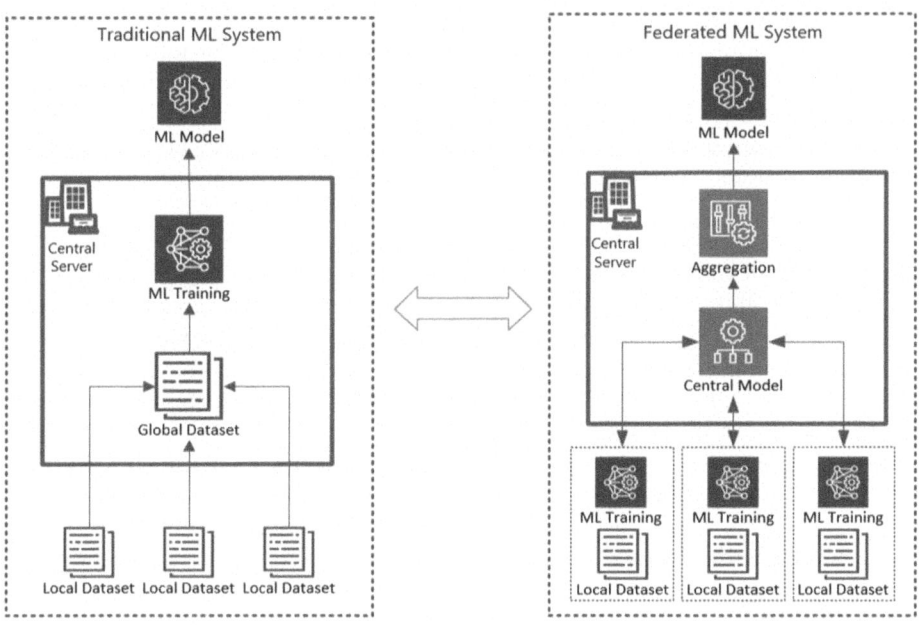

Fig. 1. Comparison between traditional machine learning and federated learning.

3   Federated Learning System in Education

In traditional ML, a model is trained using a large dataset stored and processed in a central location. This data is typically collected from various sources, e.g., data islands, and then moved to a central repository for training a model [19]. However, there are many situations where this approach could be more feasible and desirable. For example, in cases where the data is sensitive, private, or distributed across multiple devices or organizations, moving the data to a central location can pose security, privacy, and ethics risks. The strict regulations and sharing protocols make training a good machine learning model on the appropriate large quantity of data impractical. Additionally, collecting, moving, and maintaining large amounts of data can be time-consuming and costly. When the data partners send data around, they might lose control over how it will be manipulated.

FL was first introduced by Google [20] to address the problem of data islands while protecting data privacy and ethics protocols by training models directly on the decentralized computing nodes without the need to move the data to a central location [3, 24, 25, 33, 37]. In this scenario, the data partners maintain complete control over how they will share, the anonymity level, and how long they want to share the data, making it especially suitable for highly sensitive information environments. In an FL system, a central server coordinates the training process by sending a model to multiple participating devices or organizations, each of which trains the model on its local data and hardware configuration, e.g., laptops, workstations, mobiles, and IoT devices. The devices or organizations then return their updated model parameters to the central server, accumulating them to create a new global model by averaging contributions. Hence, only the model weights are communicated among partners, not the dataset. The comparison between traditional machine learning systems and FL systems is presented in Fig. 1.

FL presents significant benefits when applied to educational projects within the framework of value-sensitive design. This approach allows multiple computers or devices to collaborate in constructing a shared global ML model by utilizing locally stored data on each device. The process involves iterative interactions, where each device trains a local model using its data and then shares only the model updates (without sharing the actual data) to enhance the global model. The improved global model is then distributed back to the devices for further local training, continuing this cycle until a specified level of accuracy is achieved. Within the applied AI in education, we refer to two levels of ethical guidelines and privacy protection. The first level lies in general policies and regulations [17, 22] reflected in Ethics & Privacy Policies and Data Processing Pipeline components. The other components are part of the FL methodology. We present Fig. 2 as a proof of concept.

When considering value-sensitive design in educational projects, FL offers several advantages. Firstly, it allows for including locally-protected data from a diverse and representative range of users, devices, and other sources. This inclusivity ensures that the global ML models in educational projects are trained on data that reflects the unique characteristics, needs, and perspectives of the shareholders involved. This consideration promotes fairness and accuracy in the educational system. Furthermore, FL accommodates data-sharing restrictions

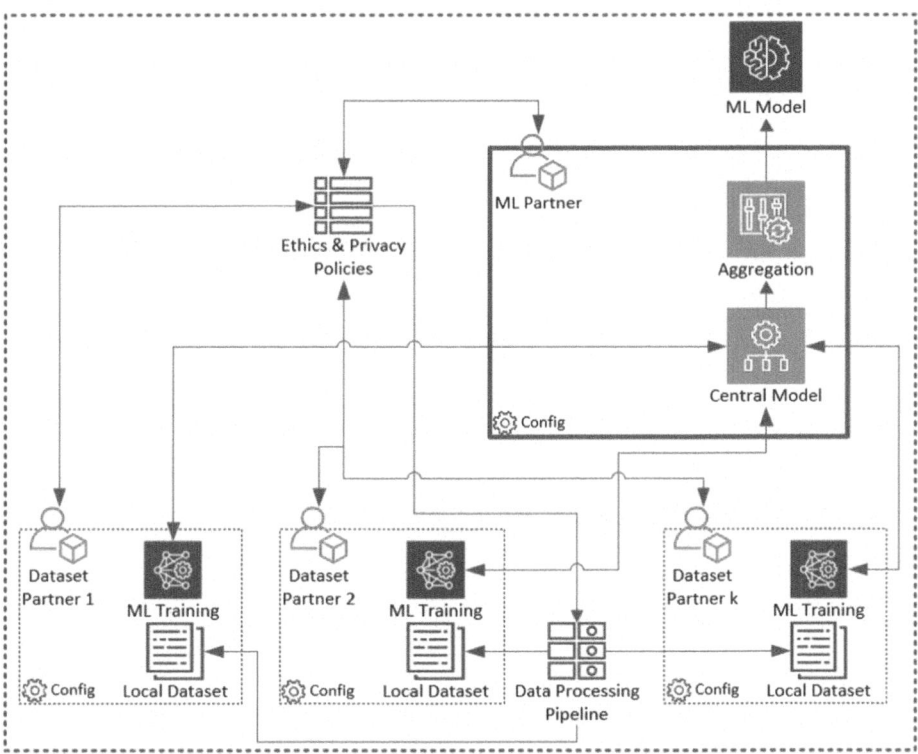

Fig. 2. An abstraction of a federated learning system in education.

that may arise due to competitive, regulatory, or privacy concerns. This is particularly relevant in education, where student privacy and data protection are paramount. By keeping the actual data locally and sharing only model updates, FL respects, and safeguards privacy while still allowing for collaborative model improvement. Another key benefit of FL in educational projects is its capacity to process confidential information securely. Handling sensitive student data, such as grades, personal information, or learning patterns, is critical for delivering personalized and effective educational experiences. FL ensures that this confidential information remains on the respective devices, protecting students' privacy and complying with data protection regulations.

Next, we briefly formalize FL and the federated average algorithm. Hundreds or thousands of clients can cooperatively create a global model w for a prototypical FL. The learning process at the central server is to optimize the objective function as follows.

$$\min_{w} F(w), \text{ where } F(w) = \sum_{i=1}^{K} \frac{n_i}{n} F_i(w) \tag{1}$$

where K and n are the total numbers of participants/clients contributing to the training and the entire data of all participants, respectively. We denote $D = \cup_{i=1}^{K} D_K$ as the whole available dataset such that $n_i = |D_i|$ is that number of observations at the ith participant.

We denote x_j and y_j as the input value and the corresponding label in a particular supervised learning scenario. Let's denote $D = \cup_{j=1}^{n}\{x_j, y_j\}$ is the total sample-target pairs. Then, each client i contains a fraction $D_i \cup_{j=1}^{n_i}\{x_{ij}, y_{ij}\}$ Hence, the local objective function at i^{th} participant is defined as follows.

$$F_i(w) = \frac{1}{n_i} \sum_{j \in D_i} f_j(w) \tag{2}$$

where $f_j(w) = f(\{x_j, y_j\}, w)$ is the loss function generated by the trained model when learning on each pair $\{x_j, y_j\}$ in D_i to update parameters w.

4   Federated Learning Deployment

4.1   Dataset

In our implementation, we consider the Slideimages[1] for the task of classifying educational illustrations into seven different classes, as a benchmark dataset [21]. We executed a random regular 80%-20% train-test partition on each client. By the time of conducting experiments, some parts of the Slideimages data were unavailable, compared to the original release, due to the change of authorship and copyright information.

4.2   Client-Server Framework

Many FL systems require reliable, scaleable, open-source frameworks to deploy federated models in business scenarios. The framework should provide basic infrastructure to servers and clients to quickly build federated solutions. The platform would also support APIs and templates that allow machine learning developers to invoke existing and self-developed federated functions, which seamlessly fuse with the FL pipeline. Scholars and developers might find many existing frameworks such as Intel OpenFL [12], Google Tensorflow Federated[2], Flower [5], IBM Federated Learning[3], and OpenMined PySyft [39].

We presented the overview of the FL system in education in Fig. 2, which accords to a client-server architecture. The server is a trusted ML partner in charge of developing and providing ML models to clients. Every client acts as a data partner and is responsible for receiving and training the model using their local data sources. Clients can encompass various devices such as computers, laptops, workstations, or IoT devices that store the data. Hence, only the model's

---

[1] https://data.uni-hannover.de/dataset/slideimages.
[2] https://www.tensorflow.org/federated.
[3] https://www.ibm.com/docs/en/watsonx/saas?topic=models-federated-learning.

gradient and weights are communicated among partners in the aggregation process, which use as much local data as possible to guarantee privacy information protection. By our experiments on a variety of educational collaborations where there is one machine learning partner and many data providers, we mimic it in our implementation where a server $\in \{1\}$ and client $\in \{1, 2, 3, 4, 10, 20\}$. Technically, the experimented federated framework can quickly scale up the number of servers and clients. In this paper, the authors use Flower [6], which provides the facilities to execute large-scale FL experiments and seamlessly implement them on a wide range of richly heterogeneous devices. Flower can perform in a large-scale deployment of up to 15M clients.

4.3   Baseline Model

Convolutional neural networks (CNNs) have been widely applied to multimedia data due to their excellent performance and scale-up flexibility. Since the local model's weights get calculated on the client side, a partner might want to save the operational cost and compute on less computationally expensive hardware without compensation of prediction power [7]. Therefore, we build a tiny CNNs network as a baseline; see the model design in Table 1. In this case, a FL design turns out to be a cheaper approach for training machine learning models [29].

Table 1. The architecture of our baseline tiny CNNs model. Note that 800×600 is an example of image resolution.

Layer (type)	Output Shape	# Param
Conv2d-1	[-1, 100, 800, 600]	2800
ReLU-2	[-1, 100, 800, 600]	0
MaxPool2d-3	[-1, 100, 400, 300]	0
Dropout-4	[-1, 100, 400, 300]	0
Conv2d-5	[-1, 100, 400, 300]	90100
ReLU-6	[-1, 100, 400, 300]	0
MaxPool2d-7	[-1, 100, 200, 150]	0
Dropout-8	[-1, 100, 200, 150]	0
Flatten-9	[-1, 3000000]	0
Linear-10	[-1, 7]	179207

Total params: 272107
Trainable params: 272107
Input size (MB): 5.49
Forward/backward pass size (MB): 1167.30
Params size (MB): 1.04
Estimated Total Size (MB): 1173.83

Algorithm 1. General Federated Averaging

1: **Input:** Number of clients $i \in \{1, 2, \ldots, K\}$, number of rounds $t \in \{1, 2, \ldots, T\}$,
   number of epochs $e \in \{1, 2, \ldots, E\}$, global weight w, local dataset $D_i \in$
   $\{D_i^{train}, D_i^{test}\}$ for each client i
2: **Output:** Global weight w
3: Initialize global weight w_0
4: **for** each round $t = 1, 2, \ldots, T$ **do**
5:    **for** each client i in parallel **do**
6:       **Client i:**
7:       Download current global model w_t
8:       Train local model w_t^i in e epoch using local dataset D_i
9:       Upload updated local model w_t^i to server
10:    **end for**
11:    **Server:**
12:    Average all uploaded local models: $w_{t+1} \leftarrow \frac{1}{k} \sum_{i=1}^{k} w_t^i$
13: **end for**

The FL algorithm, see Algorithm 1, proceeds in rounds among server and clients w.r.t. updating the model weights. Each round consists of the following steps: the current global model is downloaded by each client; each client trains a local model using its local dataset; the updated local models are uploaded to the server. Finally, the server averages all uploaded local models to obtain a new global model. The process is repeated for several rounds, after which the final global model returns as the output. This global model is a weighted average of all local models, with each local model contributing equally to the final result.

We evaluate the performance using a vanilla accuracy score for the multiclass classification task to observe the accuracy prediction of four server-client scenarios. In particular, the authors do not apply any preprocessing data engineering, hyperparameters tuning, or design of machine learning models. The core idea of our paper is to show how to use FL straightforwardly and practically in any educational project to protect the privacy and sensitive information. We set the number of rounds and epoch as $100, 150$ and 1, respectively. The optimizer is stochastic gradient descent with momentum: learning rate and momentum are 0.01 and 0.95, respectively.

4.4   Experimental Results

We conducted a series of experiments to evaluate the performance of the proposed approach, and the results provide valuable insights for leveraging VSD. Each experiment was repeated three times using different random seeds, and the average accuracy scores and standard deviation are presented in Table 2. To address the issue of device heterogeneity, we trained the model asynchronously on both CPU and GPU, ensuring the effectiveness of FL.

The experimental results revealed some important observations. Firstly, the test performance remained stable regardless of the number of clients participating in the process. It suggests that even without data exchange between clients, the FL algorithm converged in the correct direction. This stability is crucial for maintaining accurate and reliable learning outcomes. Secondly, as the number of clients increased, FL demonstrated expected behavior. More training rounds were required for parameter updates, leading to increased stability in the learning process. This observation is supported by the findings illustrated in Fig. 3, which clearly depict the trend. The authors also conducted experiments with a higher number of data clients, which produced similar results.

Another significant finding is that the baseline CNN and the experimental dataset can be replaced while preserving the integrity of the ML pipeline. This flexibility enables researchers and practitioners to explore different models and datasets, allowing for adaptation to specific educational contexts and requirements. By leveraging these experimental results, VSD can be informed and guided to address critical challenges in the educational domain. The stability of test performance across different client participation scenarios and the ability to scale up effectively in FL demonstrate the reliability and scalability of the approach. Moreover, the flexibility to replace the CNN and dataset opens avenues for customization and tailoring to meet diverse educational needs. These insights can guide the design and implementation of value-sensitive educational systems, ensuring personalized and compelling learning experiences while upholding ethical considerations and promoting fairness, inclusivity, and privacy.

Table 2. Report of accuracy scores of experimental usecases.

No. Data Clients	Accuracy Scores	
	train	test
1	0.9541 ± 0.0131	0.7926 ± 0.0078
2	0.9918 ± 0.0044	0.7391 ± 0.0077
3	0.9950 ± 0.0038	0.7927 ± 0.0073
4	0.9882 ± 0.0117	0.8095 ± 0.0234
10	0.8713 ± 0.0171	0.7884 ± 0.0239
20	0.8452 ± 0.0049	0.7818 ± 0.0078

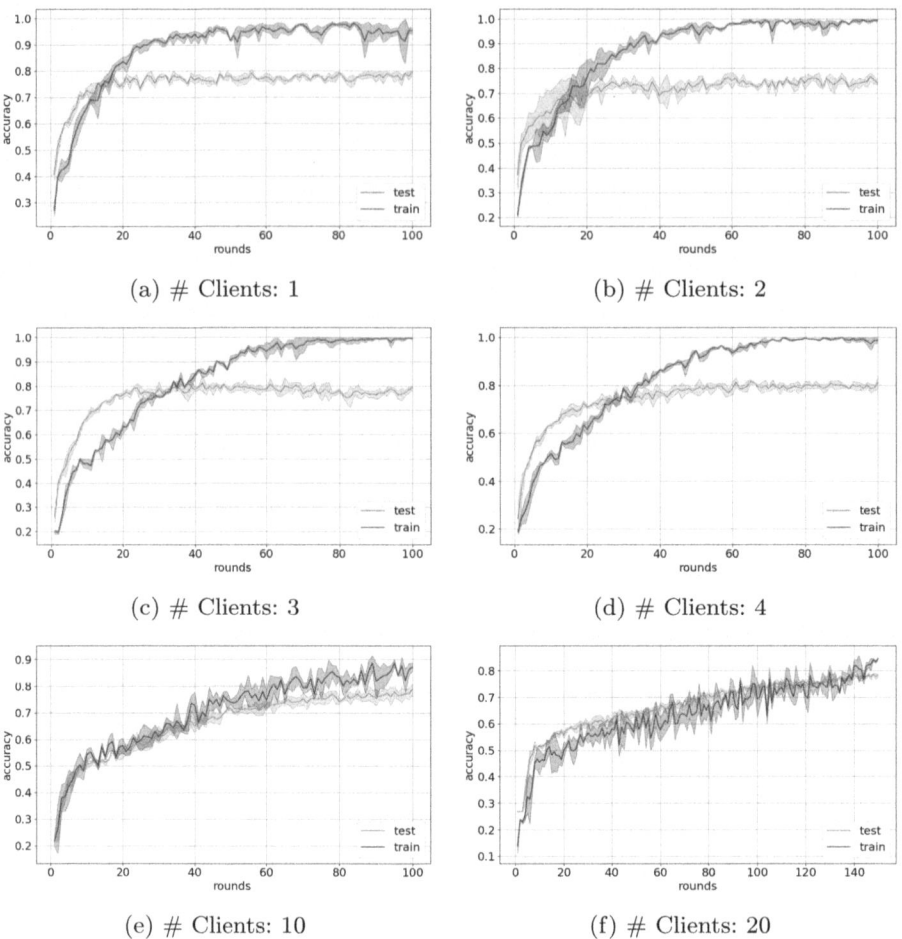

Fig. 3. Accuracy score and standard deviation w.r.t scaling up the number of data clients.

5   Conclusion

The integration of Federated Learning (FL) and Value-Sensitive Design (VSD) presents a promising approach to addressing the multifaceted challenges of data privacy, ethics, and security in educational settings. Through the decentralization of data, FL allows educational institutions to harness the power of machine learning without the need to transfer sensitive data, preserving the privacy of students and other stakeholders. By embedding VSD principles, we ensure that this technical innovation aligns with core human values, such as fairness, inclusivity, and autonomy.

FL facilitates secure collaboration between multiple educational institutions or devices by only sharing model updates, thereby eliminating the need for raw data exchange. This not only preserves privacy but also allows for the development of models that are more representative of diverse educational environments. The combination of these techniques fosters a more responsible use of AI in education, which can significantly enhance pedagogical strategies while adhering to strict ethical standards.

The research presented in this paper highlights the practical deployment of FL in educational projects, demonstrating the feasibility and effectiveness of this approach in real-world scenarios. The experimental results validate the capability of FL to maintain high levels of accuracy, even as the number of participating clients increases, showcasing its scalability and robustness. Moreover, the flexibility of the FL framework, combined with the ethical safeguards provided by VSD, offers an adaptable solution that can be applied across various educational contexts.

Looking ahead, there is immense potential for further exploration of the synergy between FL and VSD, particularly in developing more advanced privacy-preserving techniques, such as differential privacy and secure multi-party computation. These innovations can further strengthen the ethical use of AI in education by ensuring that models are not only accurate and efficient but also transparent, fair, and respectful of the privacy and rights of all individuals involved.

In conclusion, the blending of FL and VSD represents a pivotal step towards creating more ethical, secure, and inclusive educational technologies. As these fields continue to evolve, they hold the potential to reshape the landscape of AI in education, offering robust solutions to the challenges of data protection and ethical responsibility. Future research should aim to enhance the capabilities of these frameworks, ensuring that they can adapt to the rapidly changing needs of educational environments while maintaining a strong focus on ethical integrity and privacy.

References

1. Ethical guidelines on the use of artificial intelligence (AI) and data in teaching and learning for educators (2022). https://op.europa.eu/en/publication-detail/-/publication/d81a0d54-5348-11ed-92ed-01aa75ed71a1/language-en
2. Ahmad, K., et al.: Data-driven artificial intelligence in education: a comprehensive review. IEEE Trans. Learn. Technol. (2023)
3. Banabilah, S., Aloqaily, M., Alsayed, E., Malik, N., Jararweh, Y.: Federated learning review: fundamentals, enabling technologies, and future applications. Inf. Process. Manage. **59**(6), 103061 (2022)
4. Batool, S., Rashid, J., Nisar, M.W., Kim, J., Kwon, H.Y., Hussain, A.: Educational data mining to predict students' academic performance: a survey study. Educ. Inf. Technol. **28**(1), 905–971 (2023)
5. Beutel, D.J., et al.: Flower: a friendly federated learning framework (2022)
6. Beutel, D.J., et al.: Flower: a friendly federated learning research framework. arXiv preprint arXiv:2007.14390 (2020)
7. Bonawitz, K., et al.: Towards federated learning at scale: system design. Proc. Mach. Learn. Syst. **1**, 374–388 (2019)

8. Boyd, K.: Designing up with value-sensitive design: building a field guide for ethical ml development. In: 2022 ACM Conference on Fairness, Accountability, and Transparency, pp. 2069–2082 (2022)
9. Chen, B., Zhu, H.: Towards value-sensitive learning analytics design. In: Proceedings of the 9th International Conference on Learning Analytics & Knowledge, pp. 343–352 (2019)
10. Dexe, J., Franke, U., Nöu, A.A., Rad, A.: Towards increased transparency with value sensitive design. In: Artificial Intelligence in HCI: First International Conference, AI-HCI 2020, Held as Part of the 22nd HCI International Conference, HCII 2020, Copenhagen, Denmark, July 19–24, 2020, Proceedings 22, pp. 3–15. Springer (2020)
11. Fachola, C., Tornaría, A., Bermolen, P., Capdehourat, G., Etcheverry, L., Fariello, M.I.: Federated learning for data analytics in education. Data **8**(2), 43 (2023)
12. Foley, P., et al.: Openfl: the open federated learning library. Phys. Med. Biol. **67**(21), 214001 (2022)
13. Friedman, B., Hendry, D.G.: Value Sensitive Design: Shaping Technology with Moral Imagination. MIT Press (2019)
14. Gerdes, A.: A participatory data-centric approach to AI ethics by design. Appl. Artif. Intell. **36**(1), 2009222 (2022)
15. Guan, X., Feng, X., Islam, A.: The dilemma and countermeasures of educational data ethics in the age of intelligence. Humanit. Soc. Sci. Commun. **10**(1), 1–14 (2023)
16. Guo, S., Zeng, D.: Pedagogical data federation toward education 4.0. In: Proceedings of the 2020 The 6th International Conference on Frontiers of Educational Technologies, pp. 51–55 (2020)
17. Holmes, W., et al.: Ethics of AI in education: towards a community-wide framework. Int. J. Artif. Intell. Educ. **32**(3), 504–526 (2022)
18. Labba, C., Ben Atitallah, R., Boyer, A.: combining artificial intelligence and edge computing to reshape distance education (case study: K-12 learners). In: International Conference on Artificial Intelligence in Education, pp. 218–230. Springer (2022)
19. Li, L., Fan, Y., Lin, K.Y.: A survey on federated learning. In: 2020 IEEE 16th International Conference on Control & Automation (ICCA), pp. 791–796. IEEE (2020)
20. McMahan, B., Moore, E., Ramage, D., Hampson, S., y Arcas, B.A.: Communication-efficient learning of deep networks from decentralized data. In: Artificial Intelligence and Statistics, pp. 1273–1282. PMLR (2017)
21. Morris, D., Müller-Budack, E., Ewerth, R.: Slideimages: a dataset for educational image classification. In: European Conference on Information Retrieval, pp. 289–296. Springer (2020)
22. Nguyen, A., Ngo, H.N., Hong, Y., Dang, B., Nguyen, B.P.T.: Ethical principles for artificial intelligence in education. Educ. Inf. Technol. 1–21 (2022)
23. Prabhakar, A., Koizumi, K.: National AI research and development strategic plan 2023 - the white house (2023). https://www.whitehouse.gov/wp-content/uploads/2023/05/National-Artificial-Intelligence-Research-and-Development-Strategic-Plan-2023-Update.pdf
24. Qi, P., Chiaro, D., Guzzo, A., Ianni, M., Fortino, G., Piccialli, F.: Model aggregation techniques in federated learning: a comprehensive survey. Futur. Gener. Comput. Syst. **150**, 272–293 (2024)
25. ur Rehman, M.H., Gaber, M.M.: Federated Learning Systems: Towards Next-Generation AI, vol. 965. Springer Nature (2021)

26. Romero, C., Ventura, S.: Educational data mining and learning analytics: an updated survey. Wiley Interdisc. Rev. Data Mining Knowl. Discov. **10**(3), e1355 (2020)
27. Salloum, S.A., Alshurideh, M., Elnagar, A., Shaalan, K.: Mining in educational data: review and future directions. In: The International Conference on Artificial Intelligence and Computer Vision, pp. 92–102. Springer (2020)
28. Schleiss, J., Günther, K., Stober, S.: Protecting student data in ml pipelines: an overview of privacy-preserving ml. In: International Conference on Artificial Intelligence in Education, pp. 532–536. Springer (2022)
29. Verma, D.C.: Federated AI for Real-World Business Scenarios. CRC Press (2021)
30. Viberg, O., Jivet, I., Scheffel, M.: Designing culturally aware learning analytics: a value sensitive perspective. In: Practicable Learning Analytics, pp. 177–192. Springer (2023)
31. Wang, J., Liu, Y., Li, P., Lin, Z., Sindakis, S., Aggarwal, S.: Overview of data quality: examining the dimensions, antecedents, and impacts of data quality. J. Knowl. Econ. **15**(1), 1159–1178 (2024)
32. Wen, J., Zhang, Z., Lan, Y., Cui, Z., Cai, J., Zhang, W.: A survey on federated learning: challenges and applications. Int. J. Mach. Learn. Cybern. 1–23 (2022)
33. Wen, J., Zhang, Z., Lan, Y., Cui, Z., Cai, J., Zhang, W.: A survey on federated learning: challenges and applications. Int. J. Mach. Learn. Cybern. **14**(2), 513–535 (2023)
34. Wu, J., et al.: Federated deep knowledge tracing. In: Proceedings of the 14th ACM International Conference on Web Search and Data Mining, pp. 662–670 (2021)
35. Wu, J., et al.: Hierarchical personalized federated learning for user modeling. In: Proceedings of the Web Conference 2021, pp. 957–968 (2021)
36. Yang, Q., Fan, L., Tong, R., Lv, A.: IEEE federated machine learning. IEEE Federated Mach. Learn. White Paper 1–18 (2021)
37. Ye, M., Fang, X., Du, B., Yuen, P.C., Tao, D.: Heterogeneous federated learning: state-of-the-art and research challenges. ACM Comput. Surv. **56**(3), 1–44 (2023)
38. Yu, B., Mao, W., Lv, Y., Zhang, C., Xie, Y.: A survey on federated learning in data mining. Wiley Interdisc. Rev. Data Mining Knowl. Discov. **12**(1), e1443 (2022)
39. Ziller, A., et al.: Pysyft: a library for easy federated learning. In: Federated Learning Systems, pp. 111–139. Springer (2021)

Missing Data Imputation for Sensor Observation Streams Leveraging Data Correlation and Message Propagation

Nguyen Thanh Quan[1][(✉)] and Nguyen Ha Cong Ly[2]

[1] Faculty of Computer Science and Engineering, Ho Chi Minh City University
of Technology (HCMUT), Vietnam National University Ho Chi Minh City
(VNU-HCM), Ho Chi Minh City, Vietnam
ntquan.sdh20@hcmut.edu.vn
[2] Department of Mathematics, FPT University, Can Tho, Vietnam

Abstract. Sensor data streams are commonly used in many real-time
Internet of Things (IoT) applications. However, some values are missing
in the streams because of issues such as sensor malfunctions, intermittent
communication errors, or drained batteries. These gaps in data can affect
the accuracy of real-time analytics and other dependent processes. Current imputation methods either rely on predefined assumptions about
observed streams or do not take advantage of the nature of data correlation, so these methods sometimes impute values inaccurately. It is
for this reason that we aim to develop a more accurate and efficient
imputation solution addressing missing values in data streams in order
to ensure the operations of real-time applications. Firstly, we rely on a
true assumption about the correlation between data points measured by
sensors when they collect the same kinds of information. Secondly, we
calculate the degree of correlation based on historical data of problem-
atic sensors and others so as to eliminate data bias. After that, once the
optimal correlative dataset is ready, we adapt and feed the continuous
imputation framework MPIN with that dataset. Extensive experiments
on a real environmental dataset show that our method achieves better
results when taking data correlation into account compared to purely
using the original one.

Keywords: Missing data imputation · Data stream imputation · Data
correlation · Continuous imputation

1 Introduction

The Internet of Things (IoT) is one of the most important and promising technological topics today. Some market researchers estimate that there will be more
than 82 billion worldwide installed base of IoT devices in 2030 [13]. By itself,
a sensor is useless, but when it is used in systems including medical services

© ICST Institute for Computer Sciences, Social Informatics and Telecommunications Engineering 2025
Published by Springer Nature Switzerland AG 2025. All Rights Reserved
H. X. Huynh et al. (Eds.): GOODTECHS 2024, LNICST 648, pp. 160–172, 2025.
https://doi.org/10.1007/978-3-032-01472-6_13

[4, 28], meteorology [5, 25], transportation [1, 20], and energy [24], a sensor makes it possible to become an irreplaceable factor in providing data streams for various applications to operate. For example, the solar power data [7] reflects 21 different solar power plants, which establish the sensor networks deployed by the City Municipality of Aarhus in different solar power plants distributed over the city. These sensors continuously measure the power output of the plants. Therefore, such a system produces continuous and infinite sequences of streaming observation instances.

In reality, however, some values are missing in data streams because sensors have their own hardware restrictions and sometimes perform data collection in hostile environments or face sensor failures, communication errors, etc., making data more imprecise and uncertain. Thus, deficiencies on sensor data streams cannot be ignored but tackled in order to reduce information misunderstanding, assist experts in the decision-making process, and more importantly, assure the accurate operation of applications using that data. To illustrate this point, there would be a critical impact for all other activities, including industrial plant production, and the daily routine of citizens in Aarhus city when the measurements of the sensors are inaccurate because of the high missing data rate in the solar power dataset that we use to experiment in this paper. Consequently, real-time, reliable recovery of missing values from data streams is essential.

Missing data can be divided into three types according to the relationship between the missing and the observed values: Missing Completely at Random (MCAR) if there is no dependency on any of the variables, Missing at Random (MAR) if the missingness depends only on the observed variables, Missing Not at Random (MNAR) if the missing value depends on both observed variables and the unobserved variables [14, 19]. Moreover, when dealing with sensor data streams, aperiodicity, concurrency, heterogeneity, and sparsity are the challenging characteristics [15] that must be addressed properly. Figure 1 illustrates the status of possible missing data happening with each sensor s_i in a stream $stream_i$ at a time window t_i, $i \in [1..n]$.

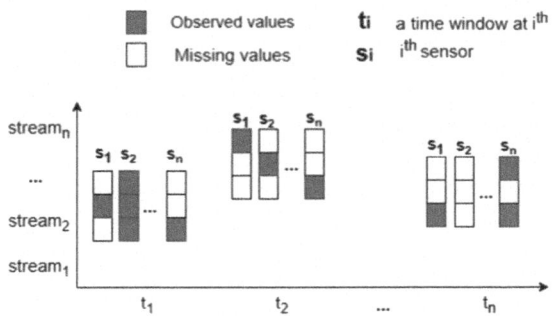

Fig. 1. Sensor data stream instances at a time window.

The work in [15] proposed MPIN framework for continuous missing data imputation that can tackle efficiently the aforementioned challenges and outperform former approaches. The authors created a similarity graph to connect data instances that come from several streams or timestamps within a time range. Besides, they did not have any assumptions about the origin and periodicity of data streams. Subsequently, they developed an imputation network that can take advantage of the correlations between instances and attributes and suggest a message propagation method on the similarity graph that they believe is accurate for imputing missing values. Nevertheless, their problem is viewed as the whole instances with missing values from all sensors to be recovered in a time window, so the similarity graph sometimes can not have enough data points to express the correlation between instances, especially when many missing values are in the observation instances. Furthermore, the distribution and variability of historical data instances among can not be also taken into account. Nevertheless, we believe that such information is very useful to be exploited before creating the similarity graph so that weak correlation data points and data bias can be eliminated in advance. Therefore, our work which is about introducing the data instance selection mechanism based on data correlation pre-filtering to the message propagation imputation network (MPIN) [15] can benefit the imputation task when the accuracy and efficiency is relatively better.

In summary, the contributions of our work are as follows:

- Pre-filtering data instances to be involved in the MPIN continuous missing data imputation framework by selecting the most correlation data and removing data bias.
- Based on the filtered values, we report on extensive experiments showing that our proposed method can give a better results compared to the original MPIN at data imputation and that the continuous imputation framework is effectively and efficiently improved.

2   Related Work

In the context of missing data imputation, methods can be simply categorized into several kinds, including deletion methods, neighbor-based methods, constraint-based methods, regression-based methods, statistical-based methods, Matrix Factorization (MF) based methods, Expectation-Maximization (EM) based methods, Multi-Layer Perceptron (MLP) based methods and Deep Learning (DL) based methods [8].

With simple methods, including deletion or neighbor-based, constraint-based and statistical-based methods, they show their disadvantages. For example, through the use of the mean of the K neighbours, KNN-based imputation replaces the missing values in a data instance by locating its K nearest neighbours in a stream. On sparse data, however, these straightforward averaging methods are useless. Therefore, in order to increase efficacy, some studies with advanced, complicated methods such as deep learning have also been conducted, e.g., the integration of an RNN-based architecture with a generative adversarial network (GAN) [16,17,22]. Nevertheless, this combination may increase the training cost and cause unstable imputation results because GANs have never been easy to train [18]. The similarity graph on which the suggestion operates in [15] is advantageous to data stream imputation as it features a positive relational bias and allows for the recording of correlation [6]. The network allows an instance to relate to only its most similar neighbours.

The method in [9] was considered as a mediator between applications and communication interfaces. The relationship between data sources can be mined to deduce new knowledge. According to [27] three methods for the development of imputation models are available: a white box model, for example, in [10], physical relations are defined as mathematical equations because all relations are expected to be known; a black box model [26], for instance, neural networks if the self-learned model is purely based on the data; and a grey model [27] if correlations between various data are assumed. Nevertheless, the true inner relationship of data is not considered in those approaches when doing imputation. The author in [2] added label distribution on top of the standard GAIN, called Conditional Generative Adversarial Imputation Network (CGAIN) to make the estimation better, but the solution is more likely working with classification problems only. A method mentioned in [3] was created with the purpose of solving an optimization problem. The author wanted to reduce the number of physical sensors used in an indoor environment by determining the best subset of sensors that are worth keeping in a given room and replacing the unnecessary physical devices. After that, their proposed model is used to impute unobserved values.

In the concept of virtual sensors to recover missing values, numerous approaches have been proposed in different contexts. The project in [12] introduced a virtual sensor technique as an independent estimator trained through machine learning algorithms such as ANN, LR, SVR using historical data and data from neighboring sensors. As it comes out, the estimator can only predict one single missing data point for a faulty sensor at a time. Similarly, the virtual sensor in [21] was also created in the same manner to keep an indoor tracking system operating in case one physical sensor stops working. The authors in [26] proposed a way in which a virtual sensor was developed by using other available parameters obtained to produce completely new data. This virtual one joins with physical elements to implement a physical-analytical redundant system that is robust to a single fault of the physical sensors. However, there is no constraint to guarantee that the chosen parameters and values are suitable for the imputation. Those approaches are to deploy virtual sensors as a missing data recovery solution to compensate for the failure of a physical sensor. The authors in [23] also based on GAN model to propose an imputation technique working under a circumstance where a physical sensor is faulty. Although this research already takes data correlations into account, it cannot work with data streams.

Overall, the imputation models above suffer from several significant drawbacks. Firstly, the past events, phenomena, or data characteristics cannot be exploited properly. Secondly, most of the approaches, therefore, often ignore the correlation between data points, which is deemed important in preserving the distribution and variability of data so as to recover incomplete values more accurately. Finally, although a similarity graph is built based on data instance correlations, it cannot ensure enough coefficient information to be exploited in a time window. Furthermore, it may take time to search and calculate correlation weights among data instances, especially when many participating sensors increase. It is for this reason that we propose our method to fill this major gap.

3   Research Problem Formulation

Consider the space where sensors are placed and establish a network with a d-dimensional space $\mathbb{S} = S_1 \text{ x } ... \text{ x } S_d$. Let $\mathbf{X} = (X_1, ..., X_d)$ is an observed variable of sensor $\mathcal{S}$ taking values in $\mathbb{S}$, whose distribution we will denote $P(\mathbf{X})$. Obviously, a sensor data stream is an unlimited time series of sensor data instances. Therefore, we can express an observation stream at time t^{th} with $\mathbf{X^t} = (X_1^t, ..., X_d^t)$. Let $M^t = (M_1^t, ..., M_d^t)$ be a random variable named mask vector taking values in $\{0, 1\}^d$ derived from the X^t.

For each i $\in \{1, ... , d\}$, we define a new space $\tilde{\mathbb{S}}_i = \mathbb{S}_i \cup \{*\}$ where $*$ is simply a point not in any $\mathbb{S}_i$, representing a missing value. Let $\tilde{\mathbb{S}} = \tilde{\mathbb{S}}_1 \text{ x } ... \text{ x } \tilde{\mathbb{S}}_d$. Similarly, at time t^{th}, we can define a new random variable $\tilde{X}^t - (\tilde{X}_1^t, ..., \tilde{X}_d^t)$ $\in \tilde{\mathbb{S}}$ in the following way, expressed in Eq. (1):

$$\tilde{X}_i^t = \begin{cases} X_i^t & \text{if } M_i^t = 1 \\ * & \text{otherwise} \end{cases} \tag{1}$$

so that M^t indicates the observed and missing values of X^t at time t^{th}.

3.1   Data Instance Selection Mechanism Based on Correlation

Correlation metrics provide information about the direction and intensity of a link between two variables. The variables' degree of relationship is indicated by their strength and direction, which also show whether the relationship is trending in a good or negative way. To measure the correlation between two continuous or ordinal variables, there are many metrics, e.g., Pearson correlation coefficient, Spearman rank correlation coefficient, Kendall correlation coefficient, or a custom metric proposed in [3] etc. As long as we calculate the correlation with a proper metric, we are able to measure the similarity between two variables.

In terms of sensor data stream, we can arrange sensor data instances in order below based on the degree of data correlation at time t^{th} as follows, expressed in Eq. (2):

$$X^t = \begin{bmatrix} x^t_{s_1} & x^t_{p1_1} & x^t_{p2_1} & x^t_{p3_1} & \cdots & x^t_{p_{d_1}} \\ x^t_{s_2} & x^t_{p1_2} & x^t_{p2_2} & x^t_{p3_2} & \cdots & x^t_{p_{d_2}} \\ x^t_{s_3} & x^t_{p1_3} & x^t_{p2_3} & x^t_{p3_3} & \cdots & x^t_{p_{d_3}} \\ \cdots & \cdots & \cdots & \cdots & \cdots & \cdots \\ x^t_{s_n} & x^t_{p1_n} & x^t_{p2_n} & x^t_{p3_n} & \cdots & x^t_{p_{d_n}} \end{bmatrix} \qquad (2)$$

where $x^t_{s_i}$ are observed values of sensor $\mathcal{S}$, $x^t_{pi_i}$ are the values of correlated sensors at time t^{th} respectively, that are arranged left to right corresponding to the degree of correlation. By calculating the correlation, sensors that have the result below a certain defined threshold are considered "noise" or "bias" and should be ignored in the process of making data imputation.

The whole process of selecting the most correlated variables can be seen in Fig. (2) as follows:

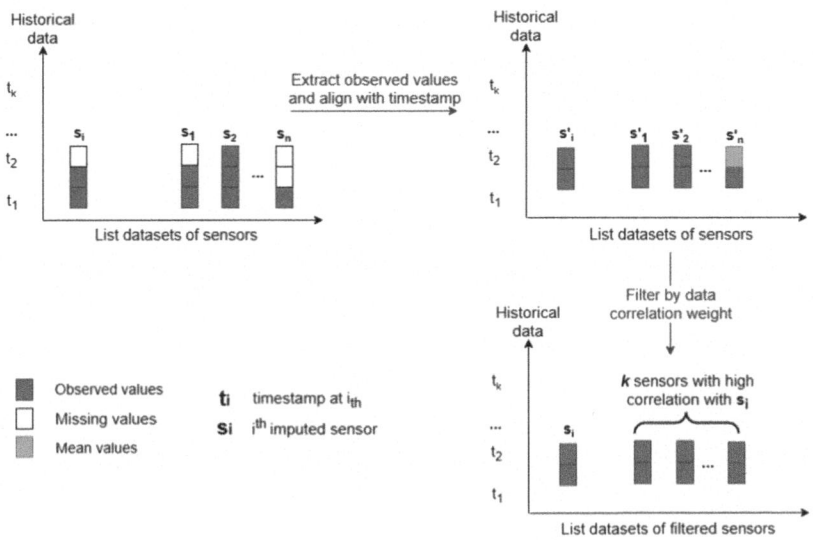

Fig. 2. Sensor data stream instances filtering mechanism.

After that k most correlated sensors are selected to be involved in the continuous imputation process. The similarity graph can not only be established with data instance correlation but also capture the distribution and variability of all strong correlated sensor data (Fig. 3).

3.2   Baseline Results

In order to setup a baseline results, we run the continuous imputation framework using MPIN with solar power dataset whose 21 sensors were deployed to

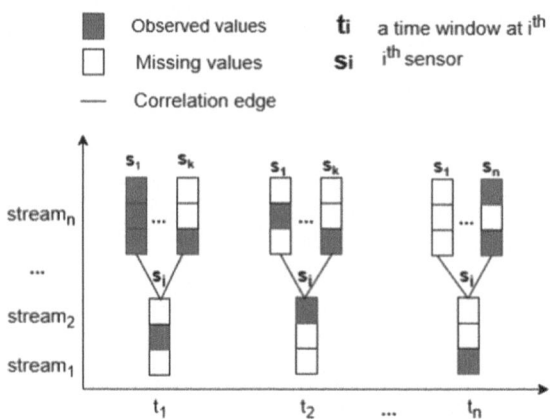

Fig. 3. Similarity graph on filtered correlated data instances.

continuously measure the power output of the plants in Watt. Details of solar power data set are described in Table 1.

Table 1. Solar dataset description

Attributes	Value
Samples	24000
Mean	36126
STD	52914
Minimum	0
Maximum	307891
25%	144
50%	10758
75%	51630

The algorithm of the whole process, including sensor data selection with data correlation, see Algorithm 1, proceeds in rounds among sensor data. Initially, historical observations of sensors is extracted to get complete data. After that, the extracted values are aligned by timestamp among observations. Next, lists of correlated sensors and their weights are calculated with the predefined metric. Finally, the correlation list consisting of data and correlation weights is fed into the continuous imputation network MPIN to recover missing values for each stream in a time window. The process is repeated for several rounds, after which the final MAPE errors of all data instances are reported.

We also evaluate the accuracy of our work by following up on the ratios of streams at intervals of one order of magnitude, ranging from 10%, 30%, 50% to 100% mentioned in the work [15] on the solar power dataset.

Algorithm 1. Continuous imputation with data correlation

1: **Input:** Number of sensors' historical data $i \in \{1, 2, \ldots, d\}$, number of rounds
    $r \in \{1, 2, \ldots, R\}$, number of epochs $e \in \{1, 2, \ldots, E\}$, correlation metric m
2: **Output:** Imputed values and MAPE errors of imputation
3: Initialize a correlation candidate list arr
4: **Correlation calculation:**
5: **for** each sensor i **do**
6:    Extract historical complete data s_i
7:    Align data by timestamp with remaining sensors' data $s_{remaining}$
8:    Calculate correlation between s_i with $s_{remaining}$ by metric m
9:    $arr \leftarrow cw_i$ (cw: correlation weight)
10: **end for**
11: **Continuous imputation:**
12: **for** each sensor i **do**
13:    **for** each round $r = 1, 2, \ldots, R$ **do**
14:        Get data instances of s_i at time t_{th}
15:        Continuously train MPIN model with input arr_i at time t^{th}
16:        Impute missing data of s_i at time t^{th}
17:        Calculate $MAPE_i$
18:        $MAPE_{array}$.push($MAPE_i$)
19:    **end for**
20:    Calculate average MAPE of sensor s_i
21: **end for**
22: Report MAPE errors and imputed values

3.3   Experimental Results

We conducted a series of experiments to evaluate the accuracy of the proposed approach, and the results are comparative. The selected correlation metric is Pearson because we first evaluate the performance of our work on the solar power dataset, which includes continuous time series data. We define our correlation degrees to determine if two historical data instances have relationships. Let w be the calculated weight, the degree of correlation is defined as follows:

- $0.8 \leq w \leq 1$: a strong positive correlation
- $0.6 \leq w < 0.8$: a medium positive correlation
- $0 < w < 0.6$: a weak positive correlation
- $-1 \leq w \leq -0.8$: a strong negative correlation
- $-0.8 < w \geq -0.6$: a medium negative correlation
- $-0.6 < w < 0$: a weak negative correlation
- $w = 0$: no correlation

We experimented our proposed approach on the solar power data with the positive defined thresholds. At first, we select only candidates having high correlation scores, and if the number of strong correlation ones is not sufficient, medium positive ones will be chosen. We define a threshold, which is the minimum number of sensors participating in each round of imputation tasks, is 12.

Besides, our configuration consists of 200 epochs, 4 time windows, and removed observation stream ratios $\in [0.1, 0.3, 0.5, 1.0]$. Each experiment was repeated for all data streams from all sensors, and the average accuracy scores proved by MAPE errors are presented in Table 2.

The experimental results revealed several important observations. Firstly, the test performance remained stable for most of the sensors participating in the process at all plants. This stability is crucial for maintaining accurate and reliable imputed outcomes, especially when the number of sensor data instances becomes larger. Secondly, as the number of data dimensions is reduced with only high correlation weights, the execution time needed for training and evaluating the continuous data stream imputation tasks is significantly improved. This can be explained because the amount of time taken to create the similarity graph is smaller when it only focuses on the high correlation sets.

Another significant finding is that the coefficient metric can be replaced depending on the characteristics of the data, whether it is continuous or ordinal values, and if it has a normal distribution and variability. This flexibility supports researchers and practitioners to explore different datasets, allowing for adapta-

Table 2. Report of accuracy scores of experimental usecases.

On sensor		Without data correlation		With data correlation	
		MAPE	Time	MAPE	Time
1st	0.1	0.6117 ± 0.2824	0.0451 ± 0.0027	$\mathbf{0.5477 \pm 0.2294}$	$\mathbf{0.0431 \pm 0.0015}$
	0.3	0.6724 ± 0.2658	0.0442 ± 0.0023	$\mathbf{0.6260 \pm 0.2254}$	$\mathbf{0.0435 \pm 0.0018}$
	0.5	0.7208 ± 0.2322	0.0442 ± 0.0020	$\mathbf{0.7045 \pm 0.2200}$	0.0745 ± 0.0031
	1.0	0.1955 ± 0.0048	0.0371 ± 0.0026	0.1964 ± 0.0040	$\mathbf{0.0354 \pm 0.0026}$
2nd	0.1	0.6080 ± 0.2760	0.0427 ± 0.0021	$\mathbf{0.5780 \pm 0.2711}$	0.0427 ± 0.0017
	0.3	0.6680 ± 0.2640	0.0427 ± 0.0023	$\mathbf{0.6506 \pm 0.2604}$	$\mathbf{0.4183 \pm 0.0017}$
	0.5	0.7211 ± 0.2474	0.0450 ± 0.0031	$\mathbf{0.7159 \pm 0.2416}$	0.0715 ± 0.0027
	1.0	0.1955 ± 0.0048	0.0370 ± 0.0023	$\mathbf{0.1955 \pm 0.0046}$	$\mathbf{0.0368 \pm 0.0026}$
3rd	0.1	0.6140 ± 0.2818	0.0410 ± 0.0030	$\mathbf{0.5946 \pm 0.2896}$	0.0451 ± 0.0037
	0.3	0.6693 ± 0.2661	0.0432 ± 0.0021	$\mathbf{0.6568 \pm 0.2681}$	$\mathbf{0.3933 \pm 0.0023}$
	0.5	0.7224 ± 0.2513	0.0416 ± 0.0028	$\mathbf{0.7160 \pm 0.2521}$	0.0661 ± 0.0028
	1.0	0.1955 ± 0.0048	0.0344 ± 0.0023	$\mathbf{0.1955 \pm 0.0046}$	0.0368 ± 0.0030
4th	0.1	0.6163 ± 0.2832	0.0428 ± 0.0030	$\mathbf{0.5956 \pm 0.2783}$	0.0431 ± 0.0020
	0.3	0.6717 ± 0.2680	0.0428 ± 0.0024	$\mathbf{0.6655 \pm 0.2574}$	$\mathbf{0.0408 \pm 0.0020}$
	0.5	0.7215 ± 0.2524	0.0402 ± 0.0038	$\mathbf{0.7205 \pm 0.2500}$	0.0765 ± 0.0030
	1.0	0.1955 ± 0.0048	0.0358 ± 0.0042	$\mathbf{0.1955 \pm 0.0047}$	$\mathbf{0.0345 \pm 0.0012}$
5th	0.1	0.6203 ± 0.2854	0.0640 ± 0.0023	$\mathbf{0.5894 \pm 0.2729}$	$\mathbf{0.0622 \pm 0.0021}$
	0.3	0.6752 ± 0.2700	0.0672 ± 0.0014	$\mathbf{0.6600 \pm 0.2600}$	$\mathbf{0.0624 \pm 0.0020}$
	0.5	0.7234 ± 0.2550	0.0688 ± 0.0024	$\mathbf{0.7189 \pm 0.2421}$	0.1004 ± 0.0038
	1.0	0.1955 ± 0.0048	0.0560 ± 0.0020	$\mathbf{0.1955 \pm 0.0044}$	$\mathbf{0.0526 \pm 0.0027}$

tion to specific contexts with their own metrics. By leveraging the experimental results, the accuracy of applying data correlation can be proved to effectively impute missing data. The stability of test performance across different stream ratios demonstrates the reliability of the approach.

We extracted the results of 5 sensors with the evaluation stream ratios mentioned earlier, including 0.1, 0.3, 0.5, and 1.0, to show the significant improvement of our proposed approach compared to the original framework. Obviously, the accuracy, which is illustrated through the highlighted mean absolute percentage error (MAPE) values in the 2 is better in most of the experiment scenarios. Furthermore, in some cases, the training and execution time are also reduced because the dimensions of the data are smaller when applying the proposed data correlation filtering mechanism.

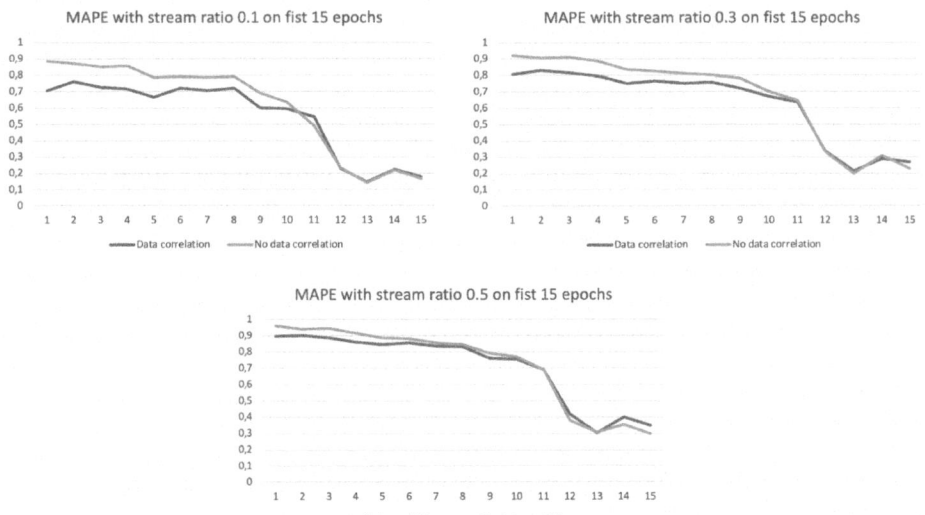

Fig. 4. Mean Absolute Percentage Error (MAPE) comparison between with data correlation and without data correlation application.

In order to visualize the trend as well as the distance between MAPE values of our proposal and the original framework, we select one experiment to draw a line graph illustrated in Fig. 4. Clearly, having the proposed data correlation filtering mechanism outperforms its former solution in most of the epochs, which is fully reflected in the final values in 2.

4   Conclusion

The integration of data correlations and the state-of-the-art continuous missing data imputation framework MPIN for data streams presents a promising approach to addressing the major problems of streaming data measured by physical sensors.

The research presented in this paper highlights the practical deployment of the solution in the sensor data stream project, demonstrating the feasibility and effectiveness of this approach in real-world scenarios. The experimental results validate the capability of the solution to maintain high levels of accuracy, even as the number of participating sensors with high correlations increases, showcasing its reliability and robustness.

The approach provides a useful solution to mediate the failure of physical sensors and guarantee the continuous operation of applications that rely on the sensor data stream. This technique for imputation can obviously have transformative impacts in the era of IoT, as missing data is an unavoidable problem. Thus, this promising approach can be widely used in different areas where the need for complete data is strictly required. It can be targeted to real-time observation systems where any single failure in data provision is not tolerated, including medical services, meteorology, transportation, agriculture, and energy. Besides, the approach is also suitable with ordinal data as long as the appropriate correlation metric is used properly.

Future research should aim to enhance the capabilities of the approach, ensuring that they can adapt to the other window types used in stream processing, e.g., sliding windows, while maintaining stability and reliability. Moreover, it is interesting to explore data imputation on dissimilar or strong negative correlation data. Besides, it is of interest to deploy the proposed techniques in a real sensor data streaming system - Smart Village project [11].

Data Availibility Statement. https://github.com/thanhquanse/DC-MPIN

References

1. Abadi, D.J., et al.: Aurora: a new model and architecture for data stream management. VLDB J. **12**, 120–139 (2003)
2. Awan, S.E., Bennamoun, M., Sohel, F., Sanfilippo, F., Dwivedi, G.: Imputation of missing data with class imbalance using conditional generative adversarial networks. Neurocomputing **453**, 164–171 (2021)
3. Brunello, A., Urgolo, A., Pittino, F., Montvay, A., Montanari, A.: Virtual sensing and sensors selection for efficient temperature monitoring in indoor environments. Sensors **21**(8), 2728 (2021)
4. Che, Z., Purushotham, S., Cho, K., Sontag, D., Liu, Y.: Recurrent neural networks for multivariate time series with missing values. Sci. Rep. **8**(1), 6085 (2018)
5. Chen, Y., Dong, G., Han, J., Wah, B.W., Wang, J.: Multi-dimensional regression analysis of time-series data streams. In: VLDB 2002: Proceedings of the 28th International Conference on Very Large Databases, pp. 323–334. Elsevier (2002)
6. Cini, A., Marisca, I., Alippi, C.: Multivariate time series imputation by graph neural networks. corr abs/2108.00298 (2021). arXiv preprint arXiv:2108.00298 (2021)
7. Digital, I.: Solar power panel dataset at open data DK. https://www.opendata.dk/city-of-aarhus/solcelleanlaeg
8. Fang, C., Wang, C.: Time series data imputation: a survey on deep learning approaches. arXiv preprint arXiv:2011.11347 (2020)

9. Furdik, K., Lukac, G., Sabol, T., Kostelnik, P.: The network architecture designed for an adaptable IoT-based smart office solution. Int. J. Comput. Netw. Commun. Secur. **1**(6), 216–224 (2013)
10. Guzmán, C.H.: Implementation of virtual sensors for monitoring temperature in greenhouses using CFD and control. Sensors **19**(1), 60 (2018)
11. HPCC: Smart village - IoT big data analytics. https://hpcc.vn/projects-2/
12. Ilyas, E.B., Fischer, M., Iggena, T., Tönjes, R.: Virtual sensor creation to replace faulty sensors using automated machine learning techniques. In: 2020 Global Internet of Things Summit (GIoTS), pp. 1–6. IEEE (2020)
13. IoT, T.: IoT prediction report 2024 (2024). https://iot.telenor.com/wp-content/uploads/2024/01/Telenor-IoT-Prediction-Report-2024.pdf
14. Kwak, S.K., Kim, J.H.: Statistical data preparation: management of missing values and outliers. Korean J. Anesthesiol. **70**(4), 407–411 (2017)
15. Li, X., Li, H., Lu, H., Jensen, C.S., Pandey, V., Markl, V.: Missing value imputation for multi-attribute sensor data streams via message propagation (extended version). arXiv preprint arXiv:2311.07344 (2023)
16. Liu, Y., Yu, R., Zheng, S., Zhan, E., Yue, Y.: Naomi: Non-autoregressive multiresolution sequence imputation. In: Advances in Neural Information Processing Systems, vol. 32 (2019)
17. Luo, Y., Cai, X., Zhang, Y., Xu, J., et al.: Multivariate time series imputation with generative adversarial networks. In: Advances in Neural Information Processing Systems, vol. 31 (2018)
18. Mescheder, L., Geiger, A., Nowozin, S.: Which training methods for GANs do actually converge? In: International Conference on Machine Learning, pp. 3481–3490. PMLR (2018)
19. Mesquita, D.P., Gomes, J.P., Junior, A., Nobre, J.S.: Euclidean distance estimation in incomplete datasets. Neurocomputing **248**, 11–18 (2017)
20. Mirylenka, K., Cormode, G., Palpanas, T., Srivastava, D.: Conditional heavy hitters: detecting interesting correlations in data streams. VLDB J. **24**(3), 395–414 (2015). https://doi.org/10.1007/s00778-015-0382-5
21. Pedrollo, G., Konzen, A.A., de Morais, W.O., Pignaton de Freitas, E.: Using smart virtual-sensor nodes to improve the robustness of indoor localization systems. Sensors **21**(11), 3912 (2021)
22. Qin, R., Wang, Y.: ImputeGAN: generative adversarial network for multivariate time series imputation. Entropy **25**(1), 137 (2023)
23. Quan, N.T., Hung, N.Q., Thoai, N.: Virtual sensor data imputation using generative adversarial imputation nets and pearson correlation. In: Yang, XS., Sherratt, R.S., Dey, N., Joshi, A. (eds.) International Congress on Information and Communication Technology, pp. 507–516. Springer (2023). https://doi.org/10.1007/978-981-99-3236-8_40
24. Sharaf, M.A., Beaver, J., Labrinidis, A., Chrysanthis, P.K.: Balancing energy efficiency and quality of aggregate data in sensor networks. VLDB J. **13**, 384–403 (2004)
25. Tran, T.T., Peng, L., Diao, Y., McGregor, A., Liu, A.: CLARO: modeling and processing uncertain data streams. VLDB J. **21**, 651–676 (2012)
26. Vitale, A., Corraro, F., Genito, N., Garbarino, L., Verde, L.: An innovative angle of attack virtual sensor for physical-analytical redundant measurement system applicable to commercial aircraft. Adv. Sci. Technol. Eng. Syst. J **6**, 698–709 (2021)

27. Yoon, S., Choi, Y., Koo, J., Hong, Y., Kim, R., Kim, J.: Virtual sensors for estimating district heating energy consumption under sensor absences in a residential building. Energies **13**(22), 6013 (2020)
28. Yoon, S., Lee, J.G., Lee, B.S.: NETS: extremely fast outlier detection from a data stream via set-based processing. Proc. VLDB Endow. **12**(11), 1303–1315 (2019)

Analyzing Social Networks Using Graph Neural Networks with Advanced Hyperparameter Optimization Techniques

Thuy Thi Tran[1]($\boxtimes$) (ID) and Nghia Quoc Phan[2] (ID)

[1] Network Management Center, University of Cuu Long,
Vinh Long 85000, Vietnam
`tranthithuy.dhcl@gmail.com`
[2] Assessment Office, Tra Vinh University, Tra Vinh 87000, Vietnam
`nghiatvnt@tvu.edu.vn`

Abstract. The exponential increase in social network data necessitates the development of advanced analytical techniques to better understand user interactions. This paper presents a robust framework that employs Graph Neural Networks (GNNs) for relationship prediction, enhanced by a variety of hyperparameter optimization methods, including Grid Search, Random Search, Bayesian Optimization, Evolutionary Optimization, and Neural Architecture Search (NAS). We also integrate the Louvain method for community detection, which uncovers the underlying structures within the network.Our comprehensive evaluation reveals the considerable impact of these methodologies on model performance, with Bayesian Optimization yielding the best results. Furthermore, the community detection analysis provides valuable insights that inform targeted engagement strategies by distinguishing between influential and non-influential users. This study significantly advances both theoretical understanding and practical applications in social network analysis, offering pathways for future research aimed at refining GNN architectures and incorporating additional features. Such enhancements could further improve the model's predictive power, ultimately fostering more meaningful interactions and community growth within social platforms.

Keywords: Graph Neural Networks · Hyperparameter Optimization · Community Detection · Social Network Analysis

1 Introduction

Social networks like Facebook, Twitter, and Instagram are central to human interaction, communication, and behavior, generating vast amounts of data. Traditional statistical methods struggle to analyze the complexity of these high-dimensional data, leading to the use of more advanced techniques like Graph Neural Networks (GNNs). GNNs model social network interactions by treating users as nodes and their relationships as edges, capturing both local and global patterns in the network to predict user behavior and relationships more accurately.

© ICST Institute for Computer Sciences, Social Informatics and Telecommunications Engineering 2025
Published by Springer Nature Switzerland AG 2025. All Rights Reserved
H. X. Huynh et al. (Eds.): GOODTECHS 2024, LNICST 648, pp. 173–187, 2025.
https://doi.org/10.1007/978-3-032-01472-6_14

However, GNN performance is highly dependent on hyperparameter selection, such as learning rates and network architecture. Optimizing these hyperparameters is crucial for model convergence and generalization. Techniques like Grid Search and Random Search are commonly used, but more advanced methods like Bayesian Optimization, Evolutionary Optimization, and Neural Architecture Search (NAS) are emerging as more efficient alternatives [4].

Additionally, community detection plays a key role in understanding the structure of social networks, revealing group dynamics and user behavior. Traditional methods like the Louvain algorithm help identify clusters within networks, offering insights into collective behavior.

This paper proposes combining GNNs with hyperparameter optimization and community detection techniques to create a robust framework for analyzing social networks. The goal is to improve relationship prediction accuracy and uncover meaningful community structures, contributing valuable insights for user engagement and network growth. By evaluating different hyperparameter optimization methods, the study aims to enhance the performance of GNNs and provide a comprehensive tool for understanding complex social networks.

This paper is structured as follows Section 2 presents the related work. Section 3 describes the proposed method. Section 4 provides the experimental results. Section 5 discusses the main findings. Section 6 concludes the paper.

2 Related Works

The integration of Graph Neural Networks (GNNs) in social network analysis has gained significant attention due to their ability to model and capture the complex relationships in social interactions. A key development in this area was the introduction of Graph Convolutional Networks (GCNs) by [1], which established a foundation for semi-supervised learning on graph-structured data, enabling effective node classification and link prediction. GCNs utilize localized graph convolutions, allowing the model to learn representations based on both node features and the graph's topology. Later studies have expanded on this by addressing scalability issues and enhancing interpretability, an important aspect for understanding the decisions made by GNN models [2, 10, 11].

Parallel to this, hyperparameter optimization has become a crucial area of research, influencing the performance of GNNs and other machine learning models. Bergstra and Bengio [3] highlighted the advantages of Random Search over traditional Grid Search, especially in high-dimensional spaces, where Random Search often outperforms Grid Search with fewer evaluations. Building on this, Snoek et al. [5] introduced Bayesian Optimization, a model-based probabilistic approach that efficiently navigates the hyperparameter space, providing superior results with fewer computational resources.

Evolutionary algorithms have also emerged as an effective method for hyperparameter tuning. Loshchilov and Hutter [6] demonstrated their use in machine learning, showing that evolutionary algorithms can evolve optimal configurations over generations, making them highly effective in complex search spaces where traditional methods may falter. Their adaptability allows for a balanced exploration-exploitation strategy, adding a valuable dimension to hyperparameter optimization.

Community detection is another vital aspect in social network analysis. The Louvain method, proposed by Blondel et al. [8], has become a benchmark for identifying community structures in large networks due to its efficiency and effectiveness. Recent studies have combined community detection techniques with GNNs, enhancing the analysis of user behavior by uncovering hidden structures in social networks [2]. This integration enables deeper insights into user interactions, helping to create more targeted interventions and improve user engagement strategies.

In conclusion, the convergence of GNNs, hyperparameter optimization, and community detection presents an exciting and promising area of research that can greatly improve our understanding of social networks. This study aims to contribute to this field by exploring the combined impact of these methodologies on relationship prediction and community identification in social network analysis.

3 Methodology

3.1 Graph Neural Network

The proposed Graph Neural Network model is specifically designed to analyze social network data by utilizing a multi-layer structure of Graph Convolutional Networks. This architecture effectively captures the complex interdependencies between users, leveraging both the topology of the graph and the features of the nodes. The model's flexibility allows for a customizable number of GCN layers; by default, it uses two layers, but this can be adjusted depending on the complexity of the dataset.

Each GCN layer includes a specified number of hidden units, set to 16 in this implementation, determining the dimensionality of the node representations at each stage. To prevent overfitting, a dropout layer with a rate of 0.5 is included as a regularization technique. During training, this layer randomly deactivates a subset of neurons, enhancing the model's ability to generalize to unseen data.

The model's architecture is structured into several functional layers. The input consists of a feature matrix representing the nodes in the graph. In the context of social networks, each node (representing a user) typically starts with a uniform feature set, often initialized to one. This simple initialization allows the model to learn more meaningful features directly from the graph structure itself [1].

The first GCN layer transforms the input features into a higher-dimensional space, enabling the model to learn more complex representations. Subsequent GCN layers perform similar transformations, capturing increasingly sophisticated node representations and incorporating information from neighboring nodes across multiple hops. After each GCN layer, the resulting feature matrix passes through a ReLU activation function, followed by a dropout operation. This sequence ensures non-linear transformations while reducing overfitting by ensuring that the model does not overly rely on any single feature [13].

The final GCN layer reduces the output dimension to match the number of target classes, which is two for relationship prediction. The logits from this layer are passed through a softmax function to produce class probabilities, facilitating the classification of relationships among users based on the learned representations [14].

The forward pass of the model follows a series of steps. Each node's features are processed through the layers of GCNs, learning rich node representations that encapsulate both local and global structural information. After each convolution, the features undergo a ReLU activation to introduce non-linearity, which is essential for capturing complex patterns. Dropout is applied after each convolution to promote robustness and prevent overfitting. Finally, the output of the last GCN layer is transformed into probabilities using the softmax function, yielding predictions about the likelihood of relationships between nodes.

This GNN architecture effectively uses multiple GCN layers to model and analyze the intricate relationships in social network data. Its flexible design allows for adaptation to various datasets, while the dropout mechanism improves generalization. Future improvements could include experimenting with alternative activation functions, exploring different graph convolution techniques, or integrating attention mechanisms to further enhance the model's ability to capture user interactions. This architecture represents a significant advancement in applying GNNs to social network analysis, paving the way for deeper insights into user behavior and relationship dynamics (Fig. 1).

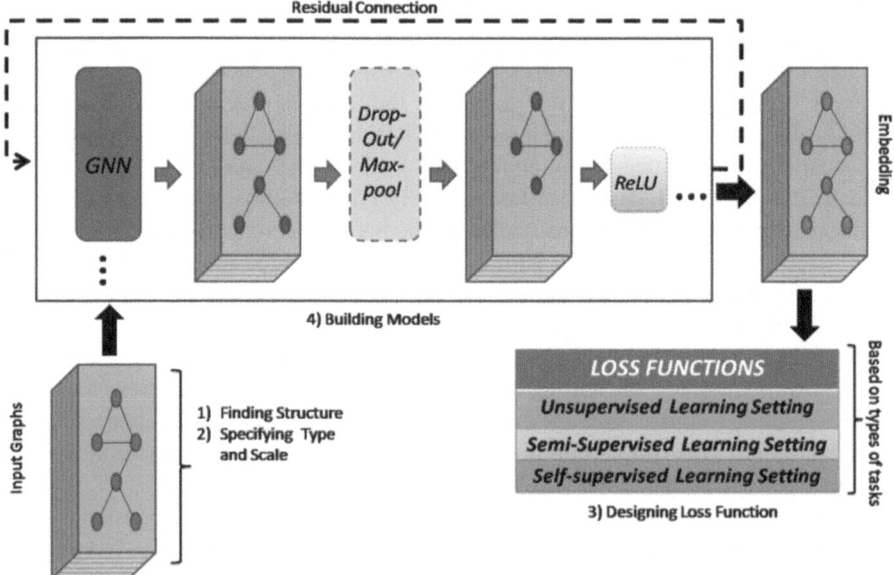

Fig. 1. GNN Architecture [15]

3.2   Hyperparameter Optimization

The model is trained using the AdamW optimizer along with a cross-entropy loss function (Eq. (1)), which is well-suited for classification tasks, particularly in multi-class settings. This combination ensures efficient optimization and effective learning of the model parameters, facilitating improved performance on the task of relationship prediction within the social network data.

$$L(y, \hat{y}) = -\sum_{i=1}^{C} y_i \log(\hat{y}_i) \tag{1}$$

where y is the true label, $\hat{y}$ is the predicted probability, and C is the number of classes. This combination ensures efficient optimization and effective learning of model parameters, leading to improved performance in predicting user relationships.

To enhance the model's performance further, various hyperparameter optimization techniques are employed. One of the primary methods used is Grid Search. This systematic approach involves exploring a predefined set of hyperparameter values in a structured manner. While Grid Search is thorough and can yield optimal results, it is often computationally expensive due to the exhaustive nature of evaluating all combinations within the specified ranges.

$$Total\ Evaluations = \prod_{j=1}^{N} k_j \tag{2}$$

where N is the number of hyperparameters and k_j is the number of values for each hyperparameter j.

Another effective method is Random Search, which selects hyperparameter combinations randomly from the predefined ranges. This technique allows for broader exploration of the hyperparameter space while often requiring fewer trials than Grid Search. Bergstra and Bengio [3] highlighted the advantages of Random Search, demonstrating its efficiency in identifying promising configurations without the exhaustive computational burden associated with Grid Search.

Bayesian Optimization is another advanced technique employed for hyperparameter tuning. This method builds a probabilistic model $P(f|x)$ of the objective function f based on previous evaluations of hyperparameter sets. By selecting promising hyperparameter combinations informed by past performance, Bayesian Optimization typically requires fewer iterations to converge on an optimal set of hyperparameters. This approach, as detailed by Snoek et al. [5], enhances the efficiency of the optimization process. The acquisition function $A(x)$ guides the search for optimal hyperparameters by balancing exploration and exploitation:

$$x_{next} = \arg\max_{x} A(x) \tag{3}$$

Evolutionary Optimization simulates natural selection principles to evolve a population of hyperparameter sets over generations. By evaluating the performance of various configurations and iteratively selecting and combining the most successful ones. This method leverages performance feedback to guide the search for optimal hyperparameters. Loshchilov and Hutter [6] demonstrated the effectiveness of this approach in the context of machine learning, highlighting its adaptability and robustness.

Lastly, Neural Architecture Search (NAS) represents a cutting-edge approach that automates the design of neural network architectures. NAS simultaneously optimizes both the architecture and hyperparameters, enabling the discovery of configurations that maximize model performance. This method, explored by Zoph and Le [7], has shown significant promise in generating efficient and effective architectures tailored to specific tasks.

3.3 Relationship Prediction

The prediction process begins by setting the model to evaluation mode, which adjusts its behavior to ensure that certain layers, such as dropout and batch normalization, operate correctly during inference. This step is crucial as it prevents the introduction of randomness into the predictions, allowing for more reliable outputs [16].

Next, the model enters a context where gradient calculations are disabled. This is essential during inference, as it reduces memory usage and enhances performance by not tracking gradients that are unnecessary at this stage. By disabling gradients, the model's parameters remain unchanged, ensuring stability in the predictions.

The model then processes the input data to generate output logits, which indicate the likelihood of relationships between pairs of nodes. The prediction mechanism identifies the class label associated with the highest probability for each input sample [14]. This step effectively determines the predicted relationship for each node pair based on the computed scores.

Finally, the predicted labels are formatted into a list, making it easier to handle and interpret the output for further analysis or reporting. This streamlined process encapsulates the essential steps required to derive relationship predictions from the trained model and input data, contributing to effective social network analysis.

3.4 Community Detection

Community detection is a crucial aspect of network analysis, aimed at identifying clusters of densely connected nodes within a graph. In this study, we implement community detection using the Louvain method, which has gained prominence due to its effectiveness in large networks and its ability to reveal underlying social structures [8, 9, 12].

The Louvain method operates through a two-phase process that optimizes modularity, a measure of the strength of division of a network into communities [8]. The modularity Q is defined as:

$$Q = \frac{1}{2m} \sum_{i=1}^{N} \sum_{j=1}^{N} \left(A_{ij} - \frac{k_i k_j}{2m} \right) \delta(c_i, c_j) \tag{4}$$

where, A is the adjacency matrix of the graph, m is the total number of edges, k_i and k_j are the degrees of nodes i and j, c_i and c_j are the communities of nodes i and j, $\delta(c_i, c_j)$ is 1 if $c_i = c_j$ and 0 otherwise.

In the first phase, the algorithm assigns each node to its own community and iteratively merges communities to maximize the modularity score Q. This phase continues until no further improvements can be made. In the second phase, the method constructs a new network where each community is represented as a single node, and the process is repeated on this simplified network.

One of the key advantages of the Louvain method is its computational efficiency, which allows it to handle networks with millions of nodes and edges. This makes it particularly suitable for social networks, where the interactions among users can create complex structures. By applying this method, we gain valuable insights into the social interactions and relationships that characterize the network, helping to uncover patterns of connectivity and community formation among users.

Furthermore, the output of the Louvain method not only identifies the communities but also quantifies the strength of the connections within and between these communities. This information can be leveraged to analyze user behaviors, detect influential nodes, and better understand the dynamics of social interactions.

Overall, the Louvain method serves as a robust tool in our analysis framework, enabling us to elucidate the intricate community structures inherent in social networks, thus enhancing our understanding of user relationships and interactions.

3.5 Measurements

This section provides a comprehensive overview of various metrics employed in network analysis, with a particular emphasis on centrality measures.

Degree centrality quantifies the number of direct connections a node has. Nodes with high degree centrality are often considered influential within the network [17].

$$C_D(v) = deg(v) \tag{5}$$

where $C_D(v)$ is the degree centrality of node v and $degdeg(v)$ is the degree of node v.

Betweenness centrality measures the extent to which a node lies on the shortest paths between other nodes, indicating its role as a connector in the network [17].

$$C_B(v) = \sum_{s \neq v \neq t} \frac{\sigma_{st}(v)}{\sigma_{st}} \tag{6}$$

where, σ_{st} is the total number of shortest paths from node s to node t, $\sigma_{st}(v)$ is the number of those paths that pass through node v.

Closeness centrality assesses how quickly a node can access all other nodes in the network, highlighting its efficiency in communication [18].

$$C_C(v) = \frac{1}{\sum_{u \in G} d(v, u)} \tag{7}$$

where $d(v, u)$ is the shortest path distance between nodes v and u.

4 Experiments

4.1 Data Used

The Facebook Combined dataset is a widely recognized resource in social network analysis, particularly valuable for evaluating algorithms in graph-based learning. Extracted from the Facebook platform, this dataset provides a detailed representation of friendships and interactions among users, making it an essential tool for research in graph theory, social networks, and machine learning applications [19]. Its accessibility for academic purposes has led to extensive use as a benchmark for various algorithms, allowing researchers to test and validate methodologies within a real-world social context.

Typically provided in a text file format, the dataset's structure is straightforward: each line represents an edge in the graph, connecting two nodes corresponding to individual users. Each edge is defined by two integers, separated by a space, which represent the IDs of the two users who are friends. This simple representation facilitates the construction of an undirected graph, where connections are bidirectional [20]. Such a format is conducive to various analyses, including community detection and link prediction.

In terms of key features, the dataset comprises 4,039 unique nodes, each representing an individual user, along with 88,234 edges that illustrate the friendship connections between users (Fig. 2). These edges signify direct relationships, allowing researchers to analyze the density and clustering of friendships, as well as the overall connectivity of the network. The Facebook Combined dataset is invaluable for research applications, such as community detection, where the goal is to identify groups of users that interact more frequently, and link prediction, which seeks to forecast potential future friendships based on existing structures [8, 21]. By leveraging this dataset, researchers can gain insights into social dynamics and user interactions, contributing to a deeper understanding of social networks.

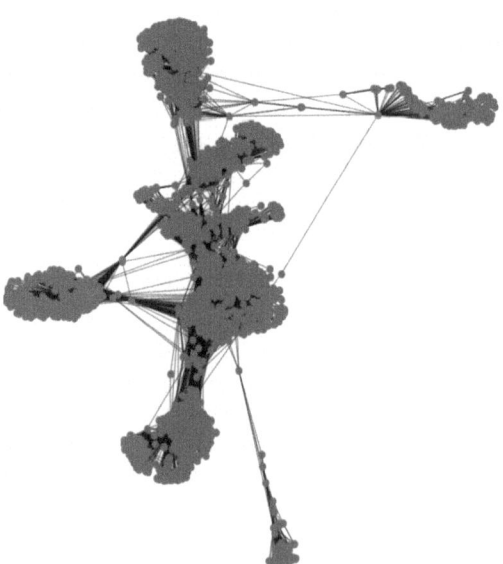

Fig. 2. Graph visualization of Social Network

4.2 Data Preprocessing

The initial step involves loading the data from a text file formatted as an edge list. Each line in this file represents a connection (or edge) between two nodes (users) in the social network. The data is read into a structured format, with columns labeled as source and target to clearly denote the relationships between the two nodes.

After loading the data, the next step is to identify unique nodes within the dataset. This is achieved by combining the source and target columns to form a comprehensive list of nodes and then extracting unique values. Each unique node is assigned a corresponding index through a mapping process, where each node ID serves as a key and its index as the value.

The edges defined in the dataset are then transformed into a numerical representation. Each node ID in the edges is replaced with its corresponding index from the unique node mapping. This transformation creates a tensor that represents the connections in the graph, facilitating the subsequent processing steps.

Each node in the graph is initialized with features, which serve as input for the model. In this implementation, each node is assigned a simple feature value of 1. This uniform feature initialization allows the model to learn more complex features directly from the graph's structure during training.

The final step involves encapsulating the processed information into a structured data object specifically designed for graph-based analysis. This object includes the node features, edge indices, and the total count of unique nodes. This structured format is essential for efficient manipulation and training of machine learning models in later stages.

4.3 Hyperparameter Optimization

The hyperparameter space configuration for Random Search and Grid Search defines a discrete set of values for each hyperparameter to be explored during the optimization process. For the learning rate, a list of values such as [0.001, 0.01, 0.1] is used to control the step size during model training. The weight decay is represented by a list of values [1e-4, 5e-4, 1e-3], which indicates the regularization strength aimed at preventing overfitting. Lastly, the dropout rate is defined by a list of values [0.3, 0.5, 0.7], determining the fraction of neurons to drop during training as a form of regularization. Both Random Search and Grid Search utilize these predefined values to systematically explore the hyperparameter space, allowing for a comprehensive evaluation of model performance.

```
param_grid = {
    'learning_rate': [0.001, 0.01, 0.1],
    'weight_decay': [1e-4, 5e-4, 1e-3],
    'dropout_rate': [0.3, 0.5, 0.7]
}
```

The Bayesian Space Configuration utilizes continuous ranges for hyperparameters, allowing for sampling during the optimization process. For the learning rate, the range spans from 1e-4 to 1e-1, enabling a flexible step size during model training. The weight decay is defined within a continuous range of 1e-4 to 1e-3, which helps regulate model complexity and prevent overfitting. Lastly, the dropout rate is specified within a continuous range from 0.3 to 0.7, determining the fraction of neurons to be dropped during training for regularization purposes. This continuous approach allows for a more nuanced exploration of the hyperparameter space, facilitating improved model performance.

```
space = [
    Real(1e-4, 1e-1, name='learning_rate'),
    Real(1e-4, 1e-3, name='weight_decay'),
    Real(0.3, 0.7, name='dropout_rate')
]
```

The Evolutionary Optimization Hyperparameter Space Configuration specifies tuples that represent the bounds for each hyperparameter, facilitating a structured exploration during optimization. The learning rate is defined within a range from 1e-4 to 1e-1, allowing for the investigation of various step sizes during model training. The weight decay is set within a range of 1e-4 to 1e-2, aiding in the control of overfitting through effective regularization. Additionally, the dropout rate is specified within a range of 0.3 to 0.7, providing variability in regularization techniques to enhance model robustness. This configuration enables a comprehensive assessment of hyperparameter interactions, ultimately contributing to improved model performance.

```
param_bounds = [
    (1e-4, 1e-1),  # learning_rate
    (1e-4, 1e-2),  # weight_decay
    (0.3, 0.7)     # dropout_rate
]
```

The Neural Architecture Search (NAS) Parameter Space Configuration involves sampling not only hyperparameters but also architecture parameters, offering significant flexibility in model design. The number of layers is randomly chosen between 1 and 5, allowing for variations in model depth. The hidden units are also randomly selected within a range of 8 to 64, which defines the complexity of each layer. Additionally, the learning rate is a continuous value randomly chosen between 1e-4 and 1e-1, enabling a flexible step size during training. The weight decay is similarly a continuous value randomly selected between 1e-4 and 1e-2, aimed at preventing overfitting. Lastly, the dropout rate is randomly chosen from a continuous range between 0.3 and 0.7, determining the fraction of neurons to drop during training for regularization. This comprehensive sampling strategy enhances the ability to discover optimal model architectures and hyperparameter configurations.

```
# Randomly sample architecture parameters
num_layers = random.randint(1, 5)
hidden_units = random.randint(8, 64)
learning_rate = random.uniform(1e-4, 1e-1)
weight_decay = random.uniform(1e-4, 1e-2)
dropout_rate = random.uniform(0.3, 0.7)
```

5 Results

5.1 Hyperparameter Optimization

Bayesian Optimization stands out as the best method in this evaluation, achieving the lowest final loss of 0.6916, indicating its superior performance in hyperparameter tuning. In comparison, Grid Search and Evolutionary Optimization also delivered competitive results, with best losses of 0.6925 and 0.6924, respectively. Both methods outperformed Random Search, which recorded a final loss of 0.6926, underscoring the benefits of systematic exploration in finding optimal parameter configurations. Additionally, Neural Architecture Search (NAS) produced a best loss of 0.6926 while exploring innovative architecture parameters. However, its performance highlights the significance of hyperparameter tuning and search space considerations, as it did not surpass the results of Bayesian Optimization or other methods. Random Search remains a viable option for quicker explorations, achieving competitive results with minimal computational overhead (Table 1). Overall, Bayesian Optimization is recommended for comprehensive tuning due to its capability to minimize loss effectively, thereby optimizing model performance compared to other strategies.

Table 1. Experimental results of machine learning model training parameters and loss values

	learning_rate	weight_decay	dropout_rate	Loss
GNN	-	-	-	0.6927
RS	0.01	0.0001	0.3	0.6926
GR	0.01	0.001	0.5	0.6925
BO	0.0098	0.6995	0.0086	0.6916
EO	0.0056	0.0051	0.3549	0.6924
NAS	0.0103	0.0037	0.4247	0.6926

NAS: 'num_layers': 4, 'hidden_units': 16,

5.2 Relationship Predictions

The results reveal a total of 2730 instances classified under label 0, which corresponds to non-influential users-typically characterized as new users or individuals exhibiting minimal interaction. In contrast, label 1 encompasses 1309 instances, representing influential users who possess a substantial number of followers and engage in frequent interactions. This distinction underscores the model's capability to differentiate between varying levels of user influence within the platform.

5.3 Most Influential User

To identify the most influential user in a social network, start by loading the network data into a suitable format, such as an adjacency list or edge list. Next, use a library like NetworkX to create a graph from this data. After establishing the graph, calculate centrality metrics to assess user influence, focusing on key measures such as degree centrality, which indicates the number of direct connections a node has; betweenness centrality, which shows how often a node appears on the shortest paths between others; closeness centrality, measuring how quickly a node can access other nodes; and eigenvector centrality, which considers both the quantity and quality of connections. Once you have calculated these metrics, rank the users based on their centrality scores to identify the most influential ones. Finally, visualize the results with appropriate tools to effectively present your findings, illustrating the influential nodes within the network.

Node 107 demonstrates significant prominence within the network, characterized by a degree of 1045, indicating strong connectivity with numerous other nodes. This high degree underscores its crucial role in facilitating interactions and information flow. Its betweenness score of 0.4805 highlights Node 107's importance as an intermediary in communication pathways, allowing it to control and influence the flow of information effectively. Additionally, with a closeness score of 0.4597, the node can reach others quickly, enhancing its capacity for rapid communication. Lastly, the maximum influence score of 1045.94 further emphasizes its strategic importance in affecting other nodes, collectively illustrating Node 107's critical role in shaping the network's dynamics (Table 2).

Table 2. Node Centrality Metrics

Node	Degree	Betweenness	Closeness	Max_Influence_Score
107	1045	0.4805180786	0.4596994536	1045.940218

5.4 Community Detection

The community detection process identifies distinct user groups, enhancing our understanding of network dynamics and informing targeted engagement strategies. The distribution of nodes across these communities reveals significant variation in size: Community 1 contains 983 nodes (24.3%), Community 2 has 815 nodes (10.2%), and Community 3 consists of 548 nodes (13.6%). Additional communities include Community 4 with 543 nodes (13.4%), Community 5 with 372 nodes (9.2%), and smaller groups such as Community 6 (219 nodes, 5.4%), Community 7 (208 nodes, 5.1%), and Community 8 (206 nodes, 5.1%). The smaller communities, including Community 9 (59 nodes, 1.5%), Community 10 (37 nodes, 0.9%), Community 11 (25 nodes, 0.6%), Community 12 (18 nodes, 0.4%), and Community 13 (6 nodes, 0.1%), further illustrate the diversity of user interactions (Table 3). This nuanced distribution can be leveraged to develop tailored communication strategies within the network. Figure 3 presents a community visualization of a social network, highlighting distinct user groups identified through the community detection process. This analysis enhances our understanding of network dynamics and informs targeted engagement strategies.

Table 3. Communication Network Node Distribution

Communication	No nodes	Proportion (%)
1	983	24.3
2	815	10.2
3	548	13.6
4	543	13.4
5	372	9.2
6	219	5.4
7	208	5.1
8	206	5.1
9	59	1.5
10	37	0.9
11	25	0.6
12	18	0.4
13	6	0.1

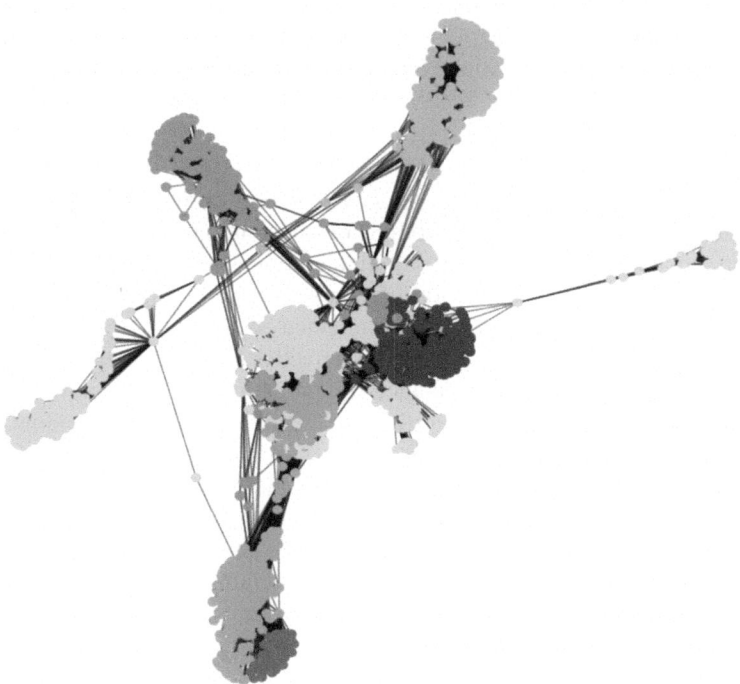

Fig. 3. CommunityVisualization of Social Network

6 Discussion

The findings of this study highlight the effectiveness of employing Graph Neural Networks (GNNs) for relationship prediction in social networks, particularly when combined with advanced hyperparameter optimization techniques. The superior performance of Bayesian Optimization (final loss of 0.6916) demonstrates its capability to explore the hyperparameter space more efficiently than traditional methods like Grid Search and Random Search. This suggests that systematic approaches to hyperparameter tuning can significantly enhance model accuracy, which is crucial in the context of social networks where user interactions are complex and multifaceted.

The community detection analysis, facilitated by the Louvain method, revealed distinct user groups within the network. Understanding these communities is vital for developing targeted engagement strategies, as it allows for customization of communication approaches based on the varying characteristics and sizes of these groups. For instance, the largest community (Community 1) can serve as a focal point for outreach efforts, while smaller communities may require more personalized strategies to enhance interaction and integration.

Moreover, the classification of users into non-influential and influential categories provides deeper insights into user behavior. The significant differentiation between these groups underscores the model's ability to identify key influencers who can drive interactions and information dissemination. The prominence of Node 107 as a highly connected and influential node further emphasizes the strategic importance of identifying and leveraging such nodes to facilitate effective communication within the network.

7 Conclusion

In conclusion, this study demonstrates the powerful application of Graph Neural Networks combined with hyperparameter optimization techniques in analyzing user interactions within social networks. The successful integration of community detection allows for a nuanced understanding of network dynamics, while the differentiation between influential and non-influential users informs targeted engagement strategies.

Bayesian Optimization emerges as the most effective hyperparameter tuning method, significantly improving model performance compared to other strategies. The insights gained from this research not only contribute to the theoretical understanding of social network dynamics but also provide practical implications for practitioners seeking to optimize user engagement and interaction on social platforms.

Future research could explore further refinements to the GNN architecture and the integration of additional features, such as temporal dynamics or content-based attributes, to enhance the predictive power of the model. By continuing to advance our understanding of social network behavior, we can better inform strategies that promote meaningful interactions and foster community growth.

References

1. Kipf, T.N., Welling, M.: Semi-supervised classification with graph convolutional networks. arXiv preprint arXiv:1609.02907 (2016)

2. Wu, Z., Pan, S., Chen, F., et al.: A comprehensive survey on community detection with deep learning. IEEE Trans. Neural Netw. Learn. Syst. **31**(7), 2472–2488 (2020)

3. Bergstra, J., Bengio, Y.: Random search for hyper-parameter optimization. J. Mach. Learn. Res. **13**, 281–305 (2012)

4. Feurer, M., Klein, A., Hutter, F.: Auto-sklearn 2.0: hands-free AutoML via meta-learning. In: Proceedings of the 18th Python in Science Conference (2019)

5. Snoek, J., Larochelle, H., Adams, R.P.: Practical Bayesian optimization of machine learning algorithms. Adv. Neural. Inf. Process. Syst. **25**, 2951–2959 (2012)

6. Loshchilov, I., Hutter, F.: CMA-ES for hyperparameter optimization. In: Proceedings of the 5th International Conference on Learning Representations (ICLR) (2016)

7. Zoph, B., Le, Q.V.: Neural architecture search with reinforcement learning. arXiv preprint arXiv:1611.01578 (2017)

8. Blondel, V.D., Guillaume, J.L., Lambiotte, R., Lefebvre, E.: Fast unfolding of communities in large networks. J. Stat. Mech. Theory Exp. **2008**(10), P10008 (2008)

9. Rossetti, G., et al.: Community detection in dynamic networks. ACM Comput. Surv. **53**(5), 1–38 (2020)

10. Zhang, H., et al.: Graph neural networks for social network analysis: a review. IEEE Trans. Knowl. Data Eng. **34**(4), 1502–1515 (2020)

11. Hamilton, W., Ying, R., Leskovec, J.: Inductive representation learning on large graphs. In: Advances in Neural Information Processing Systems (NeurIPS), 1024–1034 (2017)

12. Wu, L., et al.: A survey on community detection with graph neural networks. arXiv preprint arXiv:1906.05383 (2019)

13. Hochreiter, S., Schmidhuber, J.: Long short-term memory. Neural Comput. **9**(8), 1735–1780 (1997)

14. Goodfellow, I., Bengio, Y., Courville, A.: Deep Learning. MIT Press (2016)

15. Waikhom, L., Patgiri, R.: Graph neural networks: methods, applications, and opportunities. https://doi.org/10.48550/arXiv.2108.10733 (2021)

16. Srivastava, N., Hinton, G., Krizhevsky, A., Sutskever, I., Salakhutdinov, R.: Dropout: a simple way to prevent overfitting in neural networks. J. Mach. Learn. Res. **15**(1), 1929–1958 (2014)

17. Freeman, L.C.: Centrality in social networks: conceptual clarification. Soc. Netw. **1**(3), 215–239 (1979)

18. Bavelas, A.: Communication patterns in task-oriented groups. J. Acoust. Soc. Am. **22**(6), 725–730 (1950)

19. Leskovec, J., Lang, K.J., Lee, J., Dasgupta, A.: Community structure in large networks: natural cluster sizes and the absence of large well-defined clusters. Internet Netw. Econ. **2007**, 666–676 (2007)

20. Hernández, L.A., et al.: Analyzing social network data: a comprehensive review. Soc. Netw. Anal. Min. **10**(1), 1–20 (2020)

21. Liben-Nowell, D., Kleinberg, J.: The link prediction problem for social networks. In: Proceedings of the 12th International Conference on Information and Knowledge Management, pp. 556–559 (2007)

Automatic Recognition and Scoring System in Military Training Applies Modern Deep Learning Techniques

Minh-Trieu Truong[1], Van-Dung Hoang[1(✉)], and Cong-Hieu Le[2]

[1] HCMC University of Technology and Education, No. 1 Vo Van Ngan, Thu Duc, Ho Chi Minh City 720000, Vietnam
`dunghv@hcmute.edu.vn`
[2] Electric Power Department, Dong Ha, Quang Tri Province 520000, Vietnam

Abstract. The development of intelligent systems is making a significant impact on various aspects of life, especially in the military. However, in Vietnam, research of intelligent systems that utilize deep learning (DL) in the military domain remains limited. In this work, we will propose an intelligent system for military applications that utilizes modern deep learning technologies. This system is designed to address the task of automatic recognition and scoring in military training, consisting of two main modules: the action recognition module and the scoring module. Our contribution consists in the implementation of a comprehensive pipeline for the action recognition module with a skeleton-based approach, proposing a method to evaluate training video quality by calculating the distance between joint movement vectors in reference videos and trainee videos; presenting a complete experiment that integrates both modules on the dataset of military training videos. The construction of a military training video dataset is also part of the work we have undertaken. Experimental results demonstrate that the system based on our proposed method is feasible and has great potential for practical applications. With an accuracy of up to 95% for the action recognition module, while the scoring module can analyze and assess the differences and execution quality of the actions between the reference videos performed by experts and the training videos performed by trainees, based on various distance metrics.

Keywords: Intelligent system · military training · action recognition · automatic scoring system

1 Introduction

In recent years, the rapid advancement of technologies related to Artificial Intelligence (AI) and Deep Learning (DL) has significantly influenced various aspects of life, particularly in the military sector. Despite these advancements, research and implementation of intelligent systems that leverage AI and DL within the

H. X. Huynh et al. (Eds.): GOODTECHS 2024, LNICST 648, pp. 188–203, 2025.
https://doi.org/10.1007/978-3-032-01472-6_15

military domain in Vietnam remain relatively limited. This paper focuses on exploring and developing intelligent systems specifically designed for military applications, particularly for automatic recognition and scoring in military training.

The field of action recognition has gained considerable attention, aiming to construct algorithms, models, and systems capable of automatically understanding and classifying human actions from real-world surveillance videos. At its core, Human Action Recognition (HAR) involves analyzing and processing videos containing human actions, extracting relevant features from the frames—such as RGB (Red, Green, Blue), RGB-D (Red, Green, Blue, Depth), optical flows, and human skeleton data. These features are then utilized to build and train models that learn to predict the labels of actions present in any given video. This task is inherently complex within the domain of computer vision.

Most existing approaches primarily focus on the entire context of the video frames by employing Convolutional Neural Network (CNN) models for feature extraction. However, these models often suffer from limitations in accuracy and generalizability when applied in practice. As a response to these challenges, our research proposes a novel solution that integrates modern deep learning techniques, specifically skeleton-based methods, to enhance the effectiveness of action recognition and scoring in military training contexts.

This paper presents a comprehensive overview of our proposed solution for an automatic recognition and scoring system in military training, which applies modern deep learning techniques and consists of two main modules: an action recognition module and a scoring module. The action recognition module focuses on accurately identifying and classifying military training actions using advanced algorithms that analyze video data. By leveraging skeleton-based methods, this module is designed to improve recognition accuracy even in complex and variable training scenarios. The scoring module will be processed after the recognition process by automatically evaluating the quality of the recognized actions against established standards. This module incorporates various metrics to assess the performance and execution quality of military training actions, providing detailed feedback on areas of improvement. By combining action recognition with automatic quality assessment, our approach offers valuable insights into the effectiveness of military training protocols. Our contributions not only address the technical challenges in the field of action recognition but also aim to provide a practical application for intelligent systems in military training, ultimately serving as a foundation for future research in this area. In addition, a special feature of this research is the system's high generalization capability, as it can be widely applied not only in military training but also in areas such as hazardous action training or medical training, our solution is designed to work effectively across different domains, provided that there are benchmark datasets available for evaluation.

2 Related Works

In this domain, action recognition tasks have become a popular research direction, achieving numerous achievements in recent years. The continuous publication of articles and studies in the fields of Action Recognition and Action Classification has demonstrated the significant influence of this research area, particularly recent studies such as [1–8], which have presented various approaches including the use of graph networks, graph convolutional networks, skeleton-based methods, and more modern transformers models. As for automated systems assessing action quality, they are still relatively new but have garnered significant interest from researchers in this field due to their powerful application potential and their large impact on various aspects of life. Research combining action recognition with automatic action quality assessment solutions aimed at building automatic action recognition and scoring systems in military training is highly meaningful and provides many benefits. However, this research direction also faces many challenges and difficulties, especially when intelligent systems applied to the military require high accuracy, considerable complexity, and specific data characteristics.

As mentioned, the approaches for action recognition tasks are indeed very diverse. In the early stages of this research direction, most methods were based on local features such as HOG (Histogram of Oriented Gradient), HMB (Histogram of Motion Boundary), and HOF (Histogram of Optical Flow) [9–12]. Subsequently, there were methods based on analyzing information and features of images, specifically color images such as RGB and RGB-D in frames and images [13,14]. In addition to these approaches, another direction involves hybrid methods using machine learning technologies like SVM and k-NN [15]. Initially, these solutions worked quite effectively as they addressed the posed problem, but as larger datasets emerged and data became more complex, the limitations of these solutions became apparent. In recent years, thanks to the robust development of deep learning networks, new research based on applying complex deep learning techniques has begun to emerge, demonstrating superior effectiveness for action recognition and action classification tasks, with some notable studies such as [16–19]. An overview of the main development directions in the deep learning era for action recognition tasks shows that, firstly, there are studies on Human action recognition based on CNNs, followed by methods using RNN-LSTMs and hybrid models combining CNNs and RNN-LSTMs. In the past two years, as Transformer models have developed significantly, Human action recognition solutions based on Transformers and Vision Transformers have started to become the predominant research direction [20–26].

A prominent trend in the deep learning era for action recognition is the skeleton-based approach [27–29]. These methods represent body movement through frames by tracking the positions of joints and limbs. This representation can be displayed as 2D or 3D graphs or as heat maps in space, time, or both. The general idea of these approaches is to use pose estimation models such as Open-Pose [30], DensePose [31], AlphaPose [32], or MediaPipe Pose [33] to estimate human poses in frames or images. The output of these models will be a sequence of skeleton frames corresponding to the individuals present in the frame. From these skeleton sequences, features can be extracted or used as input to train deep learning models with the goal of action classification. Skeleton-based approaches for action recognition tasks demonstrate superior accuracy because they capture detailed human movement in videos effectively by monitoring and tracking the motion of individual joints, which greatly influences the identification of human actions in tasks related to human action recognition.

For evaluation systems and performance assessment applications in the military, there are still relatively few studies focusing on tasks related to this research direction. Most of the previous evaluation systems were developed based on expert assessments. However, thanks to advances in modern deep learning technologies, some systems have the capability to automatically assess performance by comparing reference actions that need to be evaluated with actions performed correctly by experts based on various vector distances. In this research, we will focus on investigating and studying the construction of a system to assess the quality of actions performed during military training by comparing the movement trajectories of individual human joints between standard videos and videos recorded during military training. The measures we will investigate and study to evaluate the similarity between the movement vectors include Euclidean Distance [34] and Cosine Distance [35].

3   Proposed Method

3.1   Action Recognition

Overall Idea

As presented earlier, in this research, we survey and present an approach to recognition of human action in the real world based on skeleton structures. This is a prominent research direction with many promising results in the field of action recognition in recent years. In the scope of this research, for the action recognition module, we build on some of the outstanding previous research in this area and make several adjustments to improve performance as well as optimize the system's computational resources. The overall idea of this approach consists of two main parts: First, we utilize pose estimate models for skeleton extraction from videos in the dataset. After extracting the skeleton, we perform several pre-processing steps, including data normalization and noise removal, to clean up unnecessary data. This skeleton data are then further adjusted to serve as input for two different tasks: one for action classification and the other for quality assessment and action scoring. After building the skeleton dataset, we proceed with the second stage of the action recognition module, which is action classification. From the extracted skeleton data, we restructure and merge the skeleton data of actions under the same label. After pre-processing, we encode the action classes using one-hot encoding and proceed to construct several deep learning models for action classifier. These models are based on a standard architecture with different parameters and layer counts, and we train them on the skeleton dataset that we have extracted. During the model training process, we make several adjustments to improve model accuracy and identify the best hyper-parameter set. After training, we obtain the inference model with the best performance on our dataset.

3.1.1 Skeleton Extraction

Pose estimate models are deep learning-based models tasked with estimating human poses, with outputs represented in various forms such as 2D poses, 3D poses, or heatmaps, etc. In recent years, the research direction focusing on the development and improvement of pose estimate models has attracted significant attention from the research community due to the diverse applications and the importance of this task in intelligent systems, especially in human-related intelligent systems such as human-robot interaction, robotic arms, healthcare, and notably, human action recognition. The three main types of pose estimate models are Kinematic Models [36], Planar Models [36], and Volumetric Models [36]. In this research, we focus on Kinematic Models, a skeleton-based model.

Skeleton extraction is a process of applying pose estimate models to estimate and predict the position of human joints or keypoints in frames or images. These models are essentially a collection of deep learning models and techniques trained on large datasets. They take in frames or images containing humans as input and output the coordinates of joints and limb orientations representing the human body structure. In our research, the input for the skeleton extraction process is a sequence of frames from videos in the dataset, and the output is a set of joint coordinates for each person in the frame.

We use MediaPipe Pose for our experiments. Among the many pose estimate models developed in recent years with different performances and features, MediaPipe Pose stands out as one of the top-performing models. Developed and maintained by Google, MediaPipe Pose is one of the leading models in the field of pose estimation and is classified as a Kinematic model. For each pose, MediaPipe Pose predicts a total of 33 joints. For each joint, the model predicts 4 values: x-coordinate, y-coordinate, z-coordinate, and a confidence score s. Thus, we have a vector of length $33 \times 4 = 132$ values for each pose, represented as $[x_0, y_0, z_0, s_0, \ldots, x_n, y_n, z_n, s_n]$ where n is the depth of the skeleton feature vector (here $n = 32$). From the videos in the original dataset, we separate them into sequences of frames and pass each frame through the MediaPipe Pose model for skeleton extraction. After processing all frames, we obtain a matrix of size $m \times n$, where m is the number of frames in the video, n is the depth of the skeleton feature vector.

3.1.2 Action Classification

After the skeleton extraction process, we obtained a skeleton dataset from the original dataset. This will be the dataset used to train the action classification model for this stage. First, we perform data restructuring, such as removing unnecessary data columns like frame IDs and data indices, and concatenating skeleton data of actions under the same label. Then, we encode the labels using one-hot encoding and split the dataset into two subsets for *training* and *testing* with a ratio of 80/20. After completing the pre-processing and preparing the data for training, we design and construct a deep learning architecture based on Long Short-Term Memory (LSTM) to train on the skeleton data we have built.

Long Short-Term Memory (LSTM) is a family of deep learning architectures derived from Recurrent Neural Networks (RNNs), designed to handle sequential information tasks such as sequence/time-series data. RNNs were initially developed to solve tasks involving sequential data, something that traditional Convolutional Neural Networks (CNNs) architectures struggled with. Initially, RNNs showed superior effectiveness, as there were few models capable of handling sequential data at the time. However, the major drawback of RNNs is the vanishing gradient problem, meaning that while RNNs carry information from previous layers to subsequent layers, this information only lasts for a limited number of states before it gradually fades away due to the vanishing gradient. This essentially means that RNNs can only learn from a few states close to them, and as more layers are added, they lose more information from earlier layers.

LSTM is designed as an enhancement of RNNs to learn long-term dependencies in sequential data or more specifically to overcome the vanishing gradient problem of RNNs. The architecture of LSTM consists of three primary gates: the input gate i, the forget gate f, and the output gate o, along with the cell state C.

Input Gate i: This gate determines how much of the incoming information will affect the new state. It is computed using the formula:

$$i_t = \sigma(W_i \cdot [h_{t-1}, x_t] + b_i)$$

where *sigma* is the sigmoid function, and the output ranges from $[0, 1]$.

Forget Gate f: This gate decides how much information from the previous state will be discarded, calculated as:

$$f_t = \sigma(W_f \cdot [h_{t-1}, x_t] + b_f)$$

Output Gate o: This gate regulates the amount of information that will be output from the cell. It is determined by:

$$o_t = \sigma(W_o \cdot [h_{t-1}, x_t] + b_o)$$

Cell State C: The cell state acts as the internal memory of the LSTM model, updated through the equation:

$$C_t = f_t \cdot C_{t-1} + i_t \cdot \tilde{C}_t$$

where $\tilde{C}_t$ represents the new information calculated from the current input.

Output: Finally, the output of the LSTM at time step t is computed as:

$$h_t = o_t \cdot \tanh(C_t)$$

With its special design consisting of different information gates, this architecture allows LSTM to effectively store and manage important information over long sequences, addressing the vanishing gradient problem commonly encountered in traditional RNNs.

In this research, to perform action classification, we design and build several models based on the standard LSTM architecture but with different parameters and customizations, including the parameter set $[unit, dropout, return\_sequences, number\_of\_layers]$. These parameters are adjusted during training to find the best hyper-parameter set and architecture configuration. Our training input consists of two vectors, X and y, representing the skeleton dataset we built, where X is the skeleton feature vector with a size of $[m \times n \times k]$ and y is the action label vector encoded using one-hot encoding with a size of $[m \times h]$, where m is the number of samples in the skeleton dataset, n is the time steps, k is the depth of the skeleton feature vector, and h is the number of action labels in the dataset. After training, we obtain the inference model with the best performance on our dataset.

3.2   Action Evaluation and Scoring

The proposed method for the action evaluation and scoring module is shown in Fig. 1. In this module, our objective is to evaluate and score the actions performed by military trainees during training by comparing two types of videos: reference videos and training videos. The reference videos consist of recordings of standard movements performed by experts, which are used as a benchmark for evaluating the training videos, which capture the actions performed by the trainees. This is an important stage and a key contribution to our research. This phase is carried out through a series of processing steps, and below are the detailed processes of the action evaluation and scoring module, which involves analyzing the movement or posture in each video by working with skeleton matrices.

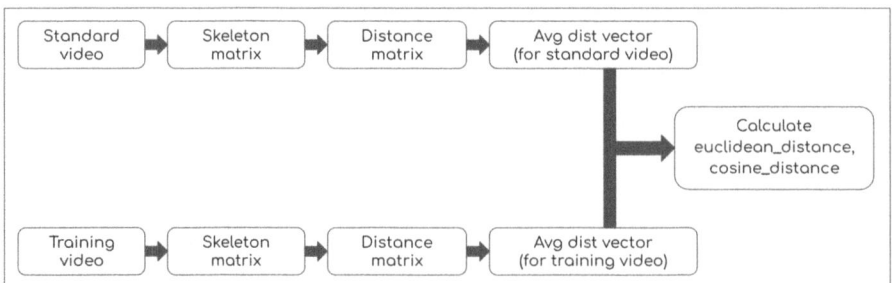

Fig. 1. The proposed method for the action evaluation and scoring module.

Skeleton Extraction
First is the skeleton extraction process. In this phase, we utilize a pose estimate model, specifically MediaPipe Pose, to extract the coordinates of the joints

for each pose in the frames, as previously described in the skeleton extraction section. After this process, we obtain a skeleton dataset represented as a matrix, referred to as *skeletons_matrix*, where each frame contains the coordinates of the joints in three-dimensional (3D) space and the corresponding confidence score for each joint. Specifically, each joint j at frame i consists of four values: x_{ij}, y_{ij}, z_{ij} representing the 3D coordinates, and s_{ij} is the confidence score for that joint. This representation allows us to accurately track the movement of the joints across different frames.

The skeleton matrix *skeletons_matrix* has a size of $m \times n$, where m is the number of frames and n is the number of predicted joints multiplied by 4 (representing the x, y, z, and s values for each joint). This matrix is represented as follows:

$$skeletons\_matrix = \begin{pmatrix} (x_{11}, y_{11}, z_{11}, s_{11}) & (x_{12}, y_{12}, z_{12}, s_{12}) & \cdots & (x_{1k}, y_{1k}, z_{1k}, s_{1k}) \\ (x_{21}, y_{21}, z_{21}, s_{21}) & (x_{22}, y_{22}, z_{22}, s_{22}) & \cdots & (x_{2k}, y_{2k}, z_{2k}, s_{2k}) \\ \vdots & \vdots & \ddots & \vdots \\ (x_{m1}, y_{m1}, z_{m1}, s_{m1}) & (x_{m2}, y_{m2}, z_{m2}, s_{m2}) & \cdots & (x_{mk}, y_{mk}, z_{mk}, s_{mk}) \end{pmatrix}$$

where each element $(x_{ij}, y_{ij}, z_{ij}, s_{ij})$ represents the position coordinates x, y, z, and the confidence score s of joint j at frame i.

Distance Matrix Calculation

After obtaining the skeleton matrix, we compute the distance matrix, denoted as *distance_matrix*, to measure the changes in joint positions between consecutive frames. The distance between the position of joint j at frame i and frame $i-1$ is determined based on the changes of joint k at time t:

Changes of joint k at time t

$$\Delta x_t^{(k)} = x_{t+1}^{(k)} - x_t^{(k)}$$
$$\Delta y_t^{(k)} = y_{t+1}^{(k)} - y_t^{(k)}$$
$$\Delta z_t^{(k)} = z_{t+1}^{(k)} - z_t^{(k)}$$

$$d_{ij} = \left(\Delta x_t^{(k)}, \Delta y_t^{(k)}, \Delta z_t^{(k)} \right)$$

The distance matrix *distance_matrix* has a size of $(m-1) \times n$, where each element d_{ij} represents the change in position of joint j between the two consecutive frames i and $i-1$.

This matrix takes the form:

$$D = \begin{pmatrix} d_{11} & d_{12} & \cdots & d_{1k} \\ d_{21} & d_{22} & \cdots & d_{2k} \\ \vdots & \vdots & \ddots & \vdots \\ d_{(m-1)1} & d_{(m-1)2} & \cdots & d_{(m-1)k} \end{pmatrix}$$

The values in the *distance_matrix* reflect the degree of joint movement over time.

Average Distance Vector Calculation

After obtaining the distance matrix, to provide a general representation of joint movement throughout the video, we compute the average distance vector for each joint. This value is determined by averaging the distances of joint j between consecutive frames. The formula for calculating the average distance vector for joint j is:

$$\text{avg\_dist\_vector}(j) = \frac{1}{m-1} \sum_{i=1}^{m-1} d_{ij}$$

The average distance vector will have the form:

$$\text{avg\_dist\_vector} = (\text{avg}(d_1),\ \text{avg}(d_2),\ \dots\ \text{avg}(d_k))$$

This vector describes the average movement level of each joint across frames and has a size of $1 \times n$. This vector is used for comparisons between different videos.

Euclidean Distance Calculation

After calculating the average distance vector for each video, we can evaluate the similarity between two videos by computing the Euclidean distance between these vectors. The Euclidean distance between the average vectors $\mathbf{u}$ (standard video) and $\mathbf{v}$ (training video) is calculated using the formula:

$$\text{Euclidean distance} = \sqrt{\sum_{i=1}^{n} (u_i - v_i)^2}$$

In our context the Euclidean distance is calculated using the formula:

$$d_{\text{euclidean}}\left(\mathbf{V}_{\text{standard}}, \mathbf{V}_{\text{training}}\right) = \sqrt{\sum_{k=1}^{N} \left(\mathbf{V}_{\text{standard}}^{(k)} - \mathbf{V}_{\text{training}}^{(k)}\right)^2} \times 100$$

This distance reflects the difference in joint movement levels between the two videos, with smaller values indicating greater similarity.

Cosine Distance Calculation

In addition to Euclidean distance, to evaluate the similarity in the direction of joint movements, we use Cosine distance, this distance measures the angle between two vectors. The Cosine distance between the average vectors $\mathbf{u}$ (standard video) and $\mathbf{v}$ (training video) is calculated using the formula:

$$\text{Cosine similarity} = \frac{\mathbf{u} \cdot \mathbf{v}}{\|\mathbf{u}\| \|\mathbf{v}\|}$$

$$\text{Cosine distance} = 1 - \text{Cosine similarity}$$

$$\text{Cosine distance} = 1 - \frac{\mathbf{u} \cdot \mathbf{v}}{\|\mathbf{u}\| \|\mathbf{v}\|}$$

In our context the Cosine distance is calculated using the formula:

$$d_{\text{cosine}} \left(\mathbf{V}_{\text{standard}}, \mathbf{V}_{\text{training}} \right) = 1 - \frac{\mathbf{V}_{\text{standard}} \cdot \mathbf{V}_{\text{training}}}{\|\mathbf{V}_{\text{standard}}\| \, \|\mathbf{V}_{\text{training}}\|}$$

where $\mathbf{u} \cdot \mathbf{v}$ is the dot product of the two vectors, and $\|\mathbf{u}\|$ and $\|\mathbf{v}\|$ are their magnitudes. Cosine distance reflects the similarity in movement direction, with smaller values indicating greater similarity between the two videos in terms of movement direction.

4 Experimental Evaluation and Analysis

4.1 Experimental Material

In this research, the construction of a dataset related to military training activities is also considered a crucial part of our effort. To experiment and evaluate the proposed method, we constructed a video dataset with the support of experts, military soldiers, and cadets. The proposed system consists of two main modules: the action recognition module and the action evaluation and scoring module. Therefore, two sub-datasets were built according to different requirements and methods. All videos in the datasets we developed are entirely from real-world military training activities in Vietnam. The detailed description and structure of each sub-dataset for each module will be presented later.

For the Action Recognition Module
Our sub-dataset consists of all videos capturing actions performed during the training process of cadets and soldiers. This sub-dataset will include four action classes: [$chao, quay\_phai, quay\_sau, quay\_trai$], and all videos will be labeled accordingly. This sub-dataset is then processed by splitting all videos into sequences of sequential frames, with the sample size described in detail in Table 1. The sequences of frames after being split from the original dataset are divided into training and testing sets in an 80/20 ratio. The action classes are encoded using one-hot encoding, which will be used as input to train the action classification model.

Table 1. Detailed description and sample size (frame) of both dataset built for the action recognition module.

action	label	training_set	validation_set	total
chao	[1, 0, 0, 0]	2484	621	3105
quay_phai	[0, 1, 0, 0]	909	227	1136
quay_sau	[0, 0, 1, 0]	1101	275	1376
quay_trai	[0, 0, 0, 1]	960	240	1200

For the Action Evaluation and Scoring Module
This is the main module and plays a crucial role in the entire proposed method, so the dataset will be collected and processed in a more complex manner. First, videos capturing actions performed during the training of cadets and soldiers will be collected according to the same four action classes: [*chao, quay_phai, quay_sau, quay_trai*], as in the action recognition module. However, in this sub-dataset, the videos will be built with two distinguishable quality levels. Specifically, the first sub-dataset will consist of videos demonstrating standard actions performed by military soldiers and experts, and this will be considered the benchmark dataset for evaluating actions. The second sub-dataset will be built by recording the actions performed by cadets during field training. This sub-dataset will be considered the training video set, used to test and evaluate the quality of the proposed solution. In real-world deployment, the second sub-dataset will be the training video dataset to be evaluated, recorded by capturing military trainee performances, while the first sub-dataset is used as the benchmark to assess these training videos. Detailed descriptions of both sub-datasets built for the action evaluation and scoring module are presented in Table 2.

Table 2. Detailed description and sample size (frame) of both sub-datasets built for the action evaluation and scoring module.

sub-dataset	chao	quay_phai	quay_sau	quay_trai
training	4813	1812	3552	1889
standard	1127	767	445	374

4.2   Experimental Results

For the Action Recognition Module

Table 3. The Accuracy and Loss of prediction results for action recognition module

	Loss(%)	Accuracy(%)
Training	0.1640	92.25
Validation	0.1430	94.02

Our dataset, MediaPipe Pose Landmark model, LSTM model

To experiment and evaluate the action recognition module, we trained the action classification model for a total of 64 epochs. The learning process of the model demonstrated improvements in both accuracy and loss on both the training and validation sets. The model initially had an accuracy of around 52% at the beginning of training. Throughout the first 40 epochs, the model showed significant improvement, and after completing 64 epochs, it achieved an accuracy of 92.25% on the training set, with a corresponding loss of 0.1640. The accuracy on the validation set also showed stable progress, approaching 96% in the final epochs.

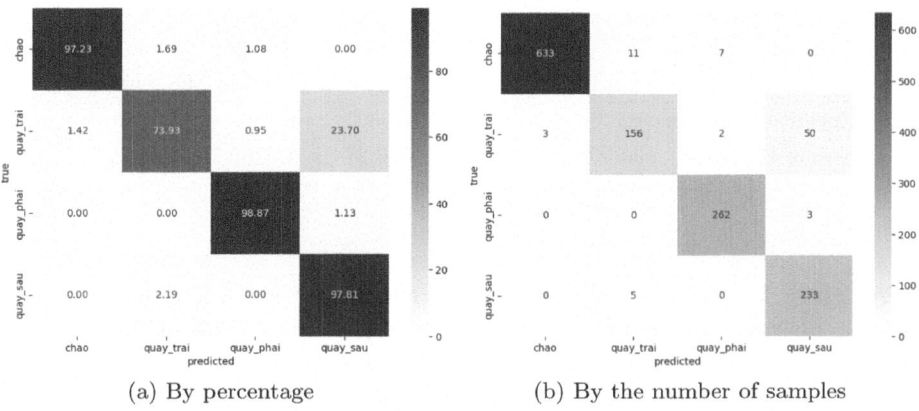

(a) By percentage   (b) By the number of samples

Fig. 2. Confusion matrix of action prediction results.

The training results indicate that, although there were some minor fluctuations during the learning process, particularly in the early phase between the 15-th and 35-th epochs, the model still exhibited fairly stable overall performance with minimal signs of over-fitting. All of this suggests that our proposed solution for the action recognition module has good learning capacity and effective generalization, as evidenced by the narrowing gap between training and validation accuracy. Additionally, the high results on the validation set further confirm the feasibility of applying our action recognition solution in practical settings. Some details of experimental results are demonstrated in Fig. 2a, Fig. 2b and Table 3.

For the Action Evaluation and Scoring Module

For the action evaluation and scoring module, the proposed method demonstrated its effectiveness in evaluating the quality of actions. For each data sample to be evaluated, our solution computed both Euclidean and Cosine distances between vectors representing the average displacement of joint coordinates across frames, constructed based on the movement of joints throughout the action. These movements were compared between a reference video (used as a benchmark) and training videos performed by military trainees, which needed quality assessment. Specifically, the results shown in Table 4 and Table 5 indicate that videos capturing actions of high quality (those most similar to the reference video) had smaller Euclidean distances and higher Cosine similarity values, reflecting greater motion similarity. Conversely, for actions that did not meet quality standards, the Euclidean distances were larger, and Cosine similarity values were lower, indicating more significant differences in movement.

Table 4. Results of distance analysis from the action videos of military trainees.

	Sample 1	Sample 2	Sample 3	Sample 4	Sample 5
Euclidean Distance	0.6453	2.4133	1.6523	2.5812	1.5500
Cosine Distance	0.0071	1.6445	0.4139	1.6253	0.3068
	Sample 6	Sample 7	Sample 8	Sample 9	Sample 10
Euclidean Distance	2.4926	1.5962	2.3899	1.6598	2.5845
Cosine Distance	1.6714	0.3409	1.6495	0.3526	1.6337
	Sample 11	Sample 12	Sample 13	Sample 14	Sample 15
Euclidean Distance	1.7289	2.5869	1.6505	2.6833	1.6730
Cosine Distance	0.5051	1.5302	0.3527	1.6460	0.4362

Each sample is a video recording of an action performed by military trainees.

All these findings suggest that our proposed method not only accurately reflects differences in motion patterns but also provides a clear deviation index for assessing action quality. This enhances the value of our solution, as it offers strong generalizability and can be applied across various contexts in different domains, not just limited to military training.

Table 5. Distance analysis results of additional samples.

	Sample 1	Sample 2	Sample 3	Sample 4	Sample 5
Euclidean Distance	0.2019	1.0654	0.8652	0.9923	0.9706
Cosine Distance	0.0040	0.4881	0.1992	0.3346	0.2999
	Sample 6	Sample 7	Sample 8	Sample 9	
Euclidean Distance	0.9628	0.9558	0.9269	0.9466	
Cosine Distance	0.2725	0.2860	0.2898	0.2961	

Each sample is a video recording of an action performed by military trainees.

5   Conclusions

In summary, through the experimental results of our research, we have demonstrated that our proposed methods for the evaluation and action recognition modules are highly effective and applicable in assessing military training activities. This research can serve as a foundation for further studies on applying AI and DL technologies in military training or can be used as a basis for building automatic recognition and scoring systems for evaluating the quality of training activities across various domains.

For future research, several key directions can be developed to enhance the effectiveness and applicability of the system. First, there is potential for deeper experimental research with various pose estimation models, particularly those that output heat maps. This would allow the system to capture more detailed movements and improve action recognition accuracy. Second, applying weights to each joint during motion analysis could be beneficial, as different joints hold varying levels of importance for specific actions. This weighted approach may provide deeper insights into the dynamics of movement. Finally, implementing our proposed solution in real-world scenarios involving more complex actions during military training would be advantageous. By addressing these issues, we believe that our system can be significantly improved, paving the way for broader applications of AI and DL across various fields of life.

References

1. Wanyan, Y., Yang, X., Dong, W., Xu, C.: A comprehensive review of few-shot action recognition (2024). https://arxiv.org/abs/2407.14744
2. Shafizadegan, F., Naghsh-Nilchi, A.R., Shabaninia, E.: Multimodal vision-based human action recognition using deep learning: a review. Artif. Intell. Rev. **57**, 178 (2024). https://doi.org/10.1007/s10462-024-10730-5
3. Nguyen, T.T., Kawanishi, Y., Komamizu, T., Ide, I.: Action selection learning for multi-label multi-view action recognition (2024). https://api.semanticscholar.org/CorpusID:273163203
4. Cavallo, A., Gao, Z., Isufi, E.: Sparse covariance neural networks (2024). https://arxiv.org/abs/2410.01669
5. Liu, M., Liu, H., Guo, T.: Cross-model cross-stream learning for self-supervised human action recognition (2024). https://arxiv.org/abs/2307.07791
6. Xiao, S., Li, Y., Kim, Y., Lee, D., Panda, P.: ReSpike: residual frames-based hybrid spiking neural networks for efficient action recognition (2024). https://arxiv.org/abs/2409.01564
7. Abdelkawy, A., Ali, A., Farag, A.: EPAM-Net: An efficient pose-driven attention-guided multimodal network for video action recognition (2024). https://arxiv.org/abs/2408.05421
8. Wang, J., Bergeret, E., Falih, I.: Skeleton-based action recognition with spatial-structural graph convolution (2024). https://arxiv.org/abs/2407.21525
9. Wang, H., Klaser, A., Schmid, C., Liu, C.-L.: Action recognition by dense trajectories. In: 2011 IEEE Conference on Computer Vision and Pattern Recognition (CVPR), pp. 3169–3176. IEEE (2011)
10. Dalal, N., Triggs, B., Schmid, C.: Human detection using oriented histograms of flow and appearance. In: Leonardis, A., Bischof, H., Pinz, A. (eds.) ECCV 2006. LNCS, vol. 3952, pp. 428–441. Springer, Heidelberg (2006). https://doi.org/10.1007/11744047_33
11. Patel, C.I., Labana, D., Pandya, S., Modi, K., Ghayvat, H., Awais, M.: Histogram of oriented gradient-based fusion of features for human action recognition in action video sequences. Sensors **20**(24), 7299 (2020). https://doi.org/10.3390/s20247299
12. Sun, S., Kuang, Z., Ouyang, W., Sheng, L., Zhang, W.: Optical flow guided feature: a fast and robust motion representation for video action recognition (2018). https://arxiv.org/abs/1711.11152
13. Kong, Y., Fu, Y.: Discriminative relational representation learning for RGB-D action recognition. IEEE Trans. Image Process. **25**(6), 2856–2865 (2016)

14. Zhang, J., Li, W., Ogunbona, P.O., Wang, P., Tang, C.: RGB-D-based action recognition datasets: a survey. Pattern Recogn. **60**, 86–105 (2016)
15. Vishwakarma, D.K., Kapoor, R.: Hybrid classifier based human activity recognition using the silhouette and cells. Expert Syst. Appl. **42**(20), 6957–6965 (2015)
16. Dash, S., Mishra, S.R., Srujan Raju, K., Narasimha Prasad, L.V.: Human action recognition using a hybrid deep learning heuristic. Soft. Comput. **25**(20), 13079–13092 (2021). https://doi.org/10.1007/s00500-021-06149-7
17. Pham, H.H., Khoudour, L., Crouzil, A., Zegers, P., Velastin, S.A.: Video-based human action recognition using deep learning: a review (2022). https://arxiv.org/abs/2208.03775
18. Tasnim, N., Baek, J.-H.: Deep learning-based human action recognition with keyframes sampling using ranking methods. Appl. Sci. **12**(9), 4165 (2022). https://doi.org/10.3390/app12094165
19. López-Lozada, E., Sossa, H., Rubio-Espino, E., Montiel-Pérez, J.Y.: Action recognition in videos through a transfer-learning-based technique. Mathematics **12**(32), 3245 (2024). https://doi.org/10.3390/math12203245
20. Raj, R., Kos, A.: An improved human activity recognition technique based on convolutional neural network. Sci. Rep. **13**(1) (2023). https://doi.org/10.1038/s41598-023-49739-1
21. Shaikh, M.B., Chai, D., Islam, S., Akhtar, N.: From CNNs to transformers in multimodal human action recognition: a survey. ACM Trans. Multimed. Comput. Commun. Appl. **20**(8), 1–24 (2024). https://doi.org/10.1145/3664815
22. Alomar, K., Aysel, H.I., Cai, X.: RNNs, CNNs and transformers in human action recognition: a survey and a hybrid model (2024). https://arxiv.org/abs/2407.06162
23. Shi, J., Zhang, Y., Wang, W., Xing, B., Hu, D., Chen, L.: A novel two-stream transformer-based framework for multi-modality human action recognition. Appl. Sci. **13**(2058), (2023). https://doi.org/10.3390/app13042058
24. Cao, K., Wang, M.: Human behavior recognition based on sparse transformer with channel attention mechanism. Front. Physiol. **14**, 1239453 (2023). https://doi.org/10.3389/fphys.2023.1239453
25. Chen, T., Mo, L.: Swin-fusion: Swin-transformer with feature fusion for human action recognition. Neural Process. Lett. **55**, 11109–11130 (2023). https://doi.org/10.1007/s11063-023-11367-1
26. Ulhaq, A., Akhtar, N., Pogrebna, G., Mian, A.: Vision transformers for action recognition: a survey (2022). https://arxiv.org/abs/2209.05700
27. Duan, H., Zhao, Y., Chen, K., Lin, D., Dai, B.: Revisiting skeleton-based action recognition (2022). https://arxiv.org/abs/2104.13586
28. Yan, S., Xiong, Y., Lin, D.: Spatial temporal graph convolutional networks for skeleton-based action recognition (2018). https://arxiv.org/abs/1801.07455
29. Duan, H., Wang, J., Chen, K., Lin, D.: PYSKL: towards good practices for skeleton action recognition (2022). https://arxiv.org/abs/2205.09443
30. Cao, Z., Hidalgo, G., Simon, T., Wei, S.-E., Sheikh, Y.: OpenPose: realtime multi-person 2D pose estimation using part affinity fields (2019). https://arxiv.org/abs/1812.08008
31. Güler, R.A., Neverova, N., Kokkinos, I.: DensePose: dense human pose estimation in the wild (2018). https://arxiv.org/abs/1802.00434
32. Fang, H.-S., et al.: AlphaPose: whole-body regional multi-person pose estimation and tracking in real-time (2022). https://arxiv.org/abs/2211.03375
33. Kim, J.-W., Choi, J.-Y., Ha, E.-J., Choi, J.-H.: Human pose estimation using mediapipe pose and optimization method based on a humanoid model. Appl. Sci. **13**(2700) (2023). https://doi.org/10.3390/app13042700

34. Dokmanic, I., Parhizkar, R., Ranieri, J., Vetterli, M.: Euclidean distance matrices: essential theory, algorithms, and applications. IEEE Signal Process. Mag. **32**(6), 12–30 (2015). https://doi.org/10.1109/msp.2015.2398954

35. Steck, H., Ekanadham, C., Kallus, N.: Is cosine-similarity of embeddings really about similarity? In: Companion Proceedings of the ACM Web Conference 2024, vol. 201, pp. 887–890 (2024). https://doi.org/10.1145/3589335.3651526

36. Zheng, C., et al.: Deep learning-based human pose estimation: a survey (2023). https://arxiv.org/abs/2012.13392

Enhancing Transformer-Based Object Detection Model for Aerial Images

Dung Nguyen[1]📷, Van-Dung Hoang[3]📷, and Van-Tuong-Lan Le[2]([✉])

[1] University of Sciences, Hue University, Hue city, Vietnam
`nguyendung@hueuni.edu.vn`
[2] Hue University, Hue city, Vietnam
`lvtlan@hueuni.edu.vn`
[3] HCMC University of Technology and Education, Ho Chi Minh city, Vietnam
`dunghv@hcmute.edu.vn`

Abstract. The object detection models with transformers have pioneered a new direction in object detection by utilizing the transformer architecture. However, there are still limitations in performance, particularly when processing objects in aerial images. In this paper, the object detection model is proposed to enhance the efficiency of aerial object detection based on the detection transformers (DETR) technique. The CrossEntropy loss function is replaced with the Focal Loss to mitigate the impact of class imbalance and improve classification performance for small objects. Additionally, the model's backbone is replaced with Swin Transformer, a more robust architecture for capturing multi-scale image features. Finally, static object queries are replaced with Dynamic Object Queries, enabling the model to initialize and automatically adjust bounding box information during training. The model is trained and evaluated on the VisDrone dataset, showing significant improvements in accuracy and convergence speed compared to the original version. Specifically, the improved model achieves an mAP of 34.7 at an IoU threshold of 0.5, a 50% increase, and significantly reduces the number of training epochs compared to the original DETR model. These results demonstrate that these improvements not only enhance detection efficiency but also pave the way for new applications of DETR in aerial image object detection tasks.

Keywords: Aerial Image · Transformer · Swin Transformer · Object detection · Computer Vision

1 Introduction

In recent years, object detection in aerial images has become a crucial research field in computer vision, with widespread applications in various areas such as military [1,2], surveillance, autonomous vehicle [3–7], agriculture [8], and environmental protection [9]. The rapid development of drone and satellite imaging

ⓒ ICST Institute for Computer Sciences, Social Informatics and Telecommunications Engineering 2025
Published by Springer Nature Switzerland AG 2025. All Rights Reserved
H. X. Huynh et al. (Eds.): GOODTECHS 2024, LNICST 648, pp. 204–217, 2025.
https://doi.org/10.1007/978-3-032-01472-6_16

technology has generated massive amounts of data, creating an urgent need for the development of highly accurate and efficient object detection models.

The DETR model [10], introduced by Carion et al. in 2020, revolutionized object detection methods by applying the Transformer architecture [11], replacing traditional CNN-based approaches [12]. With its ability to effectively handle spatial relationships in images, DETR has achieved promising results in object detection tasks. However, this model still faces limitations when dealing with small objects and environments with high object overlap, particularly in aerial images.

To address these limitations, this paper proposes an improved version of the DETR model, focusing on enhancing the efficiency of object detection in aerial images. Specifically, we replace the CrossEntropy loss function with Focal Loss to mitigate the impact of class imbalance during training and replace the backbone with Swin Transformer to improve multi-scale image feature extraction. Additionally, we replace static object queries with Dynamic Object Queries, making the model more flexible in predicting bounding boxes for objects.

Our study was conducted on the VisDrone dataset [13], with the aim of demonstrating that these improvements will result in higher efficiency in object detection from aerial images. Experimental results show that the improved model achieved a mAP at the IoU threshold of 0.5, a 50% increase compared to the original DETR model. These results not only confirm the potential of new techniques in improving object detection accuracy, but also pave the way for further development in applying DETR to aerial image object detection tasks.

The paper is organized as follows: Sect. 1 introduces the research background, current challenges in object detection from aerial images, along with an overview of the DETR model and its limitations that require improvement. Section 2 presents related works to provide an overview of object detection methods and the development of the DETR model. Section 3 details the proposed improved model. Section 4 outlines the implementation process, including the dataset, data augmentation techniques, feature extraction, and experimental model details. Section 5 reports the experimental results and analyzes the model's performance. Finally, Sect. 6 summarizes the key findings and proposes directions for future research.

2   Related Works

Traditional CNN-Based Object Detection Models: Before the advent of Transformer-based models, convolutional neural network (CNN)-based object detection methods dominated the field. Models like Faster R-CNN [14], YOLO [15–17], and SSD [18] achieved significant success in object detection from natural images. These models utilize CNN architectures to extract image features and grid-based methods for object localization.

However, when applied to aerial images, these methods face several limitations. Aerial images often contain small objects with high variability in scale and irregular distribution. Grid-based methods such as YOLO and SSD struggle to accurately detect small objects, while Faster R-CNN requires a multi-step process, increasing computational complexity. The high resolution and complex details in aerial images demand more robust models capable of handling diverse object scales and complex spatial structures.

These challenges highlight the need for new approaches that can better capture spatial representations and simplify object detection workflows, particularly for aerial imagery.

Transformer-Based Object Detection Models: The introduction of DETR marked a paradigm shift in object detection by applying Transformer architecture to this task. Unlike traditional CNN models, DETR eliminates the need for grids and anchor boxes, relying instead on a self-attention mechanism to directly learn global spatial relationships from the entire image. This results in a simpler and more efficient detection pipeline.

However, DETR also exhibits limitations, particularly in detecting small objects and its slow convergence rate, which are exacerbated in the context of aerial images. To address these issues, several improvements have been proposed. Deformable DETR [19] introduces a deformable attention mechanism that focuses on important regions of the image, enhancing small object detection and speeding up convergence. Conditional DETR [20] improves training efficiency by introducing conditional attention, which clarifies the relationship between queries and object locations, leading to faster convergence. DAB-DETR [21] further enhances object localization by incorporating dynamic anchor boxes into object queries, allowing the model to better predict both the position and scale of objects. These improvements make DETR-based models more suitable for detecting small and densely packed objects in high-resolution aerial imagery.

3   Proposed Method

The structure of the proposed model, illustrated in Fig. 1, consists of three main parts: the Backbone, Dynamic Object Queries, and the Transformer module.

The model pipeline begins with preprocessing the data to prepare for the training process. The image data is augmented to improve the training quality. Next, the input images are passed through the Swin Transformer, where image features are extracted. After feature extraction, the model generates Dynamic Anchor Boxes based on the image features to adjust the size and shape of the anchor boxes, tailored to the objects in the specific context. Finally, the features and object queries are fed into the Transformer module, where the attention mechanisms learn the relationships between objects. The output from the Transformer module is used to detect and classify objects in the images, utilizing Focal Loss to optimize the loss function, thereby enhancing accuracy for imbalanced object classes.

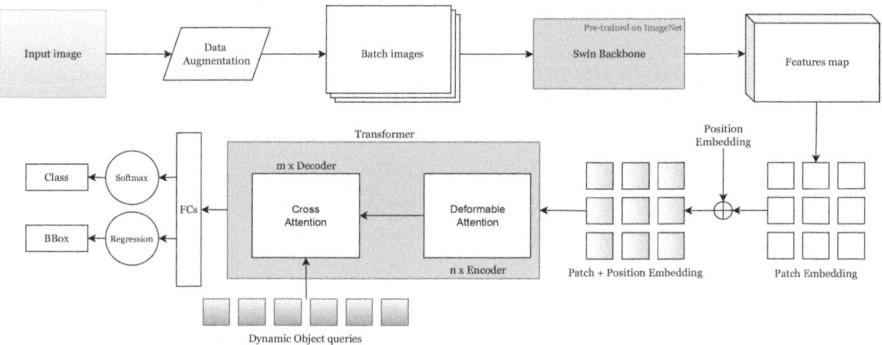

Fig. 1. Transformer-based the proposed DSwin model.

3.1 Feature Extraction

In the context of object detection, feature extraction plays a crucial role in accurately identifying and locating objects within images. The Swin Transformer operates by first receiving a high-resolution input image, which is then divided into fixed-size patches, typically measuring 4 × 4 or 7 × 7 pixels. These patches are transformed into input vectors that are embedded into a higher-dimensional space using embedding layers, allowing the model to effectively capture the image's features. The Swin Transformer employs a multi-layer architecture for feature extraction, with each layer consisting of Swin Transformer Blocks that leverage window-based self-attention techniques. This innovative approach enables the model to concentrate on specific regions of the image while significantly reducing computational costs compared to global attention methods. By utilizing moving windows, the Swin Transformer analyzes pixel relationships within localized regions while retaining global spatial information through its Shifted Windowing mechanism.

When utilized as the backbone in deep learning models, the Swin Transformer acts as a primary feature extractor, enhancing the model's learning capabilities. Its advanced architecture not only captures intricate features from the input image but also facilitates effective processing of multi-scale information. In the realm of object detection, employing the Swin Transformer as a backbone markedly improves accuracy in both classifying and locating objects. The features extracted provide rich insights into the shapes, sizes, and spatial relationships among objects, which assist subsequent layers, such as classification and regression layers, in making more precise predictions. Ultimately, the outputs from the Transformer layers are concatenated and passed through a Multi-Layer Perceptron (MLP) to generate final features for various tasks, including image classification, object detection, and segmentation. With its ability to preserve spatial information and handle diverse processing demands, the Swin Transformer stands out as an ideal choice for applications that require high accuracy in detecting objects within complex images.

3.2 Transformer

The Transformer block in the proposed model consists of three main components: the feature map from the Backbone Swin Transformer with Positional Encoding (PE), an Encoder utilizing Deformable Attention, and a Decoder combined with Dynamic Object Query through Cross Attention. Each component plays a crucial role in processing the feature map and helps the model focus on objects in the image, optimizing detection and recognition efficiency.

First, the Swin Transformer Backbone is responsible for generating the feature map from the input image. Swin Transformer divides the image into small patches and applies the attention mechanism within local windows, reducing computational complexity while maintaining the ability to capture spatial and channel information from the image. Then, Positional Encoding (PE) is added to the feature map to provide positional information of the patches, helping the model recognize the relative positions of different parts of the image.

Next, the feature map from the Backbone is fed into the Encoder, where Deformable Attention is applied. Deformable Attention is an enhanced version of Self-Attention, allowing the model to focus only on important regions within the feature map instead of calculating attention for all pairs. This improves processing efficiency, especially in tasks related to detecting small objects or objects with significant spatial transformations. The "sampling points" in Deformable Attention are automatically adjusted to select the most relevant and important regions corresponding to the objects in the image.

Afterward, the Decoder takes the input from the Encoder and performs Cross Attention between the features from the Encoder and Dynamic Object Query, which represents the objects to be detected. Dynamic Object Query is a crucial component because these queries are not fixed but are dynamically adjusted based on the input, making the model more flexible in detecting objects of varying shapes, sizes, and positions. Cross Attention enables the model to learn how to link the features from the Encoder with the object queries, accurately identifying the objects in the image.

Finally, the combination of Dynamic Object Query and Cross Attention in the Decoder allows the model to make precise predictions about the key attributes of the objects, such as bounding boxes, object classification, and other relevant information. The dynamic nature of the Object Queries allows the model to not only effectively predict existing objects but also expand its recognition capabilities for previously unknown objects.

3.3 Dynamic Object Queries

Dynamic object queries are a significant improvement over traditional object detection models. Instead of using static object queries, the model implements Dynamic object queries, allowing it to automatically adjust the size and shape of the object queries based on the characteristics of the objects and the surrounding context. The pseudocode for this process can be found in Algorithm 1. This not only minimizes the effort required for manual optimization but also enhances the accuracy of object detection within images. In this context, the following functions are key to the implementation:

– Function *AnalyzeObjectSizes*: Analyzes the sizes of objects in the dataset;
– Function *CreateDynamicObjectQueries*: Creates dynamic anchor boxes based on object sizes and aspect ratios;
– Function *GenerateDynamicObjectQueries*: Combines predictions from the model with anchor box creation for each image.

Algorithm 1. Dynamic Object Queries Creation

1: **Input:** Dataset $D = \{I_1, I_2, \ldots, I_N\}$, Model M, Aspect Ratios $R = \{r_1, r_2, \ldots, r_K\}$
2: **Output:** Dynamic Object Queries $A = \{A_1, A_2, \ldots, A_N\}$
3:
4: **Function 1:** `AnalyzeObjectSizes`(D)
5: object_sizes $\leftarrow []$
6: **for** each image I in D **do**
7:     **for** each object o in $I.objects$ **do**
8:         size $\leftarrow$ `GetSize`(o)
9:         object_sizes.append(size)
10:     **end for**
11: **end for**
12: **return** object_sizes
13:
14: **Function 2:** `CreateDynamicObjectQueries`(object_sizes, R)
15: object_queries $\leftarrow []$
16: **for** each size in object_sizes **do**
17:     **for** each ratio in R **do**
18:         width $\leftarrow$ size $\times$ ratio
19:         height $\leftarrow$ size $\div$ ratio
20:         object_queries.append((width, height))
21:     **end for**
22: **end for**
23: **return** object_queries
24:
25: **Function 3:** `GenerateDynamicObjectQueries`(I, M)
26: object_sizes $\leftarrow$ M.Predict(I)
27: $A \leftarrow$ `CreateDynamicObjectQueries`(object_sizes, R)
28: **return** A

3.4   Loss Function

In the proposed model, the overall loss function is structured to include Focal Loss, L1 Loss, and IoU Loss to optimize the training process. Here is a detailed description of each component of the loss function:

Focal Loss: As previously mentioned, Focal Loss helps mitigate the impact of easily classifiable samples, especially in object detection tasks with class imbalance. The structure of the Focal Loss function is:

$$FL(p_t) = -\alpha_t(1 - p_t)^\gamma \log(p_t) \tag{1}$$

where:

- p_t: Represents the predicted probability of the true class.
- α_t: Balances the importance of positive and negative samples, helping to focus more on hard-to-classify examples.
- γ: A focusing parameter that adjusts the rate at which easy examples are down-weighted. A higher value of γ puts more focus on misclassified examples.

L1 Loss: L1 Loss is used to measure the accuracy of the predicted bounding box locations. L1 Loss calculates the difference between the predicted coordinates and the actual coordinates of the bounding boxes:

$$L_1(y, \hat{y}) = \sum_{i=1}^{N} |y_i - \hat{y}_i| \tag{2}$$

where:

- y represents the actual coordinates.
- $\hat{y}$ represents the predicted coordinates.
- N is the number of bounding boxes.

IoU Loss: IoU (Intersection over Union) Loss measures the accuracy of the predicted bounding box compared to the actual bounding box. IoU is calculated as follows:

$$IoU = \frac{Area\ of\ Overlap}{Area\ of\ Union} \tag{3}$$

- The *Area of Overlap* is the area of the intersection between the predicted bounding box and the ground truth bounding box.
- The *Area of Union* is the total area covered by both the predicted and ground truth bounding boxes.

IoU Loss can be defined as:

$$L_{IoU} = 1 - IoU \tag{4}$$

Overall Loss Function: The overall loss function of the proposed model can be expressed as:

$$L_{total} = FL + L1 + L_{IoU} \tag{5}$$

In which each component can be multiplied by different weights (λ_1, λ_2, λ_3) to adjust their importance during training:

$$L_{total} = \lambda_1 \cdot FL + \lambda_2 \cdot L1 + \lambda_3 \cdot L_{IoU} \tag{6}$$

By combining these components, the proposed model can optimize object detection performance, improving accuracy in locating and classifying objects within images.

4 Experiments And Results

4.1 Dataset

The VisDrone dataset is an important resource for research and development in the field of object detection from drone footage. First published in 2018, this dataset includes approximately 7,019 images and videos, with millions of frames captured in diverse environments such as urban areas, rural settings, and various weather conditions. The high-resolution images, typically ranging from 720p to 1080p, provide sharp details, enhancing accuracy in object detection and classification.

The dataset contains 10 object classes, including people, vehicles, and other items, all labeled with bounding boxes. The number of images in the training set is 6,471, and in the validation set is 548. Objects are often depicted under challenging conditions, including occlusions, varying lighting, multiple scales, and complex backgrounds. These challenges make the VisDrone dataset a robust benchmark for evaluating the performance of deep learning models in real-world scenarios.

Additionally, the dataset is divided into two main parts: a training set and a validation set, allowing for rigorous model evaluation. Statistics on the number of objects in both sets illustrate the distribution of objects across different categories. This provides an overview of the data's balance, which is essential for training and validating object detection models. The VisDrone dataset is described in Fig. 2. With its richness and diversity, this dataset opens up many opportunities for improving deep learning models and applying them across various fields.

4.2 Data Augmentation

Data augmentation is an important technique for improving the accuracy and generalization of deep learning models, particularly in object detection tasks. The main goal of data augmentation is to create new versions of the training dataset by applying various transformations to the original images, thereby enriching the input data that the model can learn from. Below are some data augmentation methods commonly used:

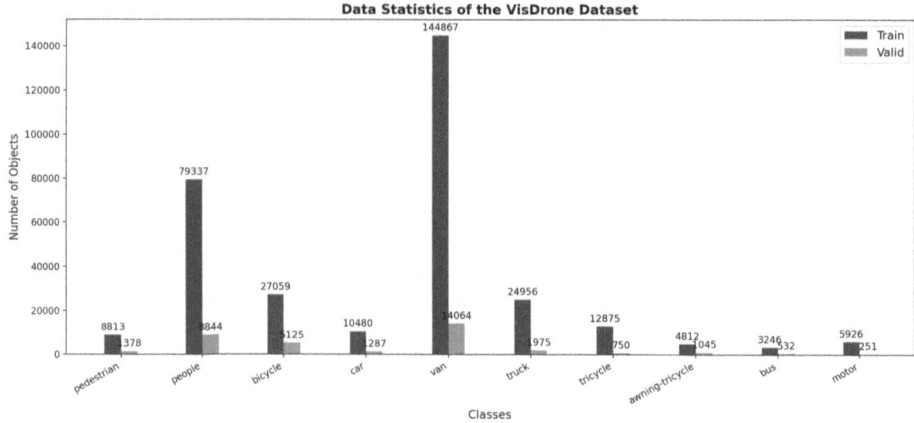

Fig. 2. Data Statistics of the VisDrone Dataset.

- **Rotation and Flipping:** Rotating images by a certain angle and flipping them horizontally or vertically to create different versions of the same object. This helps the model learn the flexibility of the object in different positions and perspectives.
- **Adjusting Brightness and Contrast:** Modifying the brightness, contrast, and saturation of images can help the model become familiar with different lighting conditions, thereby improving its ability to recognize objects in various environments.
- **Cropping and Zooming:** Cropping parts of images or zooming in to create objects at different sizes. This method helps the model identify objects of varying sizes in real-world situations.
- **Aspect Ratio Modification:** Changing the aspect ratio of images to simulate different variations of the object. This is particularly useful in object detection tasks, where objects can have many different shapes and sizes.

4.3   Training Techniques and Parameters

The model is trained using the AdamW optimizer with a learning rate scheduler to adjust the learning rate appropriately throughout the training phases. Additionally, we employ various data augmentation techniques, including rotation, translation, zooming, and brightness adjustments, to improve the model's generalization capabilities and prevent overfitting. These augmentations help the model to perform well on unseen data by simulating various real-world conditions. Details of the experimental parameters and configurations are provided in Table 1 for a comprehensive overview of the training environment and settings.

Table 1. Experimental parameters and environment

Parameter	Value
Epochs	50
Optimizer	AdamW
Learning rate	0.00001
Batch size	1
Numbers of Encoder	8
Numbers of Decoder	8
Heads of Attention	4
Attention of Encoder	Deformable Attention
Attention of Decoder	Cross Attention
Framework	Pytorch 1.10
Platform	CUDA 11.1
GPU	Quadro RTX

4.4 Evaluation Metrics

To evaluate the performance of the model, we use the following evaluation metrics:

Precision: Precision is the ratio of correctly predicted positive detection (True positives) to the total number of predicted positives (True positives + False positives). It answers the question: *Out of all the detected objects, how many were correct?*

$$Precision = \frac{TP}{TP + FP} \qquad (7)$$

where:

- TP (True Positives): Correctly predicted positive cases.
- FP (False Positives): Incorrectly predicted positive cases.

High precision means that most of the positive predictions are correct.

Recall. Recall is the ratio of correctly predicted positive detection (True positives) to the total number of actual positives (True positives + False negatives). It answers the question: *Out of all the actual objects, how many were correctly detected?*

$$Recall = \frac{TP}{TP + FN} \qquad (8)$$

where:

- TP (True Positives): Correctly predicted positive cases.
- FN (False Negatives): Actual positives that were missed by the model.

High recall means that the model correctly detects most of the actual objects.

mAP (Mean Average Precision): mAP is the mean of the Average Precision (AP) values for all classes in a dataset. It is commonly used to evaluate the performance of object detection models.

- mAP is then calculated by averaging the AP values across all classes:

$$mAP = \frac{1}{|C|} \sum_{c \in C} AP_c \qquad (9)$$

where:

- C is the set of all classes,
- $|C|$ is the number of classes.
- AP_c is the Average Precision for class c

$$AP = \int_0^1 P(R)\, dR \qquad (10)$$

where:

- $P(R)$ is the precision at a given recall level.

mAP provides a single score that summarizes how well a model performs across all object categories.

4.5   Experimental Results

We conducted experiments with three different versions of the model. The configurations of the experimental versions are described in Table 2.

Table 2. Configurations of Swin Transformer Versions

Component	Swin-Tiny	Swin-Small	Swin-Base
Number of Layers	[2, 2, 6, 2]	[2, 2, 18, 2]	[2, 2, 18, 2]
Number of Heads	[3, 6, 12, 24]	[3, 6, 12, 24]	[4, 8, 16, 32]
Input Size	224 × 224	224 × 224	224 × 224
Embedding Size	96	96	128
Patch Size	4 × 4	4 × 4	4 × 4
Number of Channels	768	768	1024
Window Size	7	7	7

The experimental results of the model are presented in Table 3. The experimental results demonstrate that the DSwin model exhibits superior performance in detecting large and medium-sized objects. Among the three versions of DSwin, the $DSwin^{base}$ version achieved the highest mAP score of 18.0%, surpassing other models such as Def-DETR (17.2%) and DAB-DETR (16.1%). This indicates the model's strong capability in identifying and detecting objects within images.

The $mAP^{0.5}$ scores further highlight the superiority of DSwin, with the $DSwin^{base}$ version reaching 34.7%, higher than many models such as DAB-DETR (30.6%) and Con-DETR (29.6%). This demonstrates that the model not only performs well in detecting large objects but also maintains efficiency when assessing the similarity of objects using the IoU metric.

While Def-DETR excels in detecting small objects with an mAP^s of 9.5%, DSwin also demonstrates competitive performance with an mAP^s of 9.0%. This indicates that DSwin not only focuses on large objects but also effectively detects small objects, thereby expanding its applicability in real-world scenarios.

The combination of Dynamic Object Query and Cross Attention in the various versions of DSwin provides an effective approach for detecting and classifying objects. The high mAP^m and mAP^l scores indicate that the model can adapt flexibly to different object sizes, thereby optimizing detection performance in various real-world situations.

Table 3. Experimental results on several models

Model	Epochs	Params	GFlops	mAP	mAP@0.5
DETR [10]	150	41M	96G	11.8	23.1
Def-DETR [19]	150	40M	193G	17.2	29.8
DAB-DETR [21]	150	44M	102G	16.1	30.6
Con-DETR [20]	150	44M	101G	15.8	29.6
$DSwin^{tiny}$	50	47M	22G	15.4	30.2
$DSwin^{small}$	50	66M	22G	16.3	31.6
$DSwin^{base}$	50	107M	25G	**18.0**	**34.7**

5   Conclusions

An enhanced version of the DETR model based on Transformer is presented in this study, aimed at optimizing aerial object detection capabilities and addressing the limitations of the original architecture. The Focal Loss function is implemented to effectively mitigate the effects of class imbalance, resulting in a significant enhancement in the model's performance, particularly for small objects. The Swin Transformer backbone is integrated to facilitate superior multi-scale feature extraction, thereby improving the overall robustness of the model.

Furthermore, the introduction of Dynamic Object Queries is noted, enabling the model to flexibly initialize and adjust bounding box predictions throughout the training process. When evaluated on the VisDrone dataset, a 50%

increase in mAP is observed at an IoU threshold of 0.5 compared to the original DETR model. Additionally, improvements in mAP, mAP^s, mAP^m, and mAP^l are achieved, demonstrating better performance across various scales of objects. Specifically, the model shows enhanced accuracy in detecting small objects (mAP^s), medium objects (mAP^m), and large objects (mAP^l), while a significant reduction in training epochs is also noted.

These findings underscore the effectiveness of the enhancements made in improving detection accuracy and convergence speed, highlighting the potential for the improved DETR model to be deployed in various aerial imaging applications. Overall, the advancements made in this paper represent a meaningful step forward in utilizing Transformer architectures for real-world object detection tasks.

Acknowledgements. This research is funded by Hue University under the grant number DHH2025-01-226. We sincerely thank Hue University for supporting this research.

References

1. Ouyang, Y., Wang, X., Ruizhe, H., Honghui, X., Shao, F.: Military vehicle object detection based on hierarchical feature representation and refined localization. IEEE Access **10**, 99897–99908 (2022)
2. Janakiramaiah, B., Kalyani, G., Karuna, A., Prasad, L.N., Krishna, M.: Military object detection in defense using multi-level capsule networks. Soft Comput. **27**(2), 1045–1059 (2023)
3. Arunnehru, J., et al.: Deep learning-based real-world object detection and improved anomaly detection for surveillance videos. Mater. Today Proc. **80**, 2911–2916 (2023)
4. Zhou, W., Cai, C., Zheng, L., Li, C., Zeng, D.: ASSD-YOLO: a small object detection method based on improved YOLOv7 for airport surface surveillance. Multimedia Tools Appl. **83**(18), 55527–55548 (2024)
5. Gupta, A., Anpalagan, A., Guan, L., Khwaja, A.S.: Deep learning for object detection and scene perception in self-driving cars: survey, challenges, and open issues. Array **10**, 100057 (2021)
6. Lee, D.-H., Chen, K.-L., Liou, K.-H., Liu, C.-L., Liu, J.-L.: Deep learning and control algorithms of direct perception for autonomous driving. Appl. Intell. **51**(1), 237–247 (2021)
7. Ni, J., Shen, K., Chen, Y., Cao, W., Yang, S.X.: An improved deep network-based scene classification method for self-driving cars. IEEE Trans. Instrum. Measur. **71**, 1–14 (2022)
8. Singh, P., Krishnamurthi, R.: IoT-based real-time object detection system for crop protection and agriculture field security. J. Real-Time Image Proc. **21**(4), 106 (2024)
9. Dou, Z., et al.: An improved YOLOv5s fire detection model. Fire Technol. **60**(1), 135–166 (2024)
10. Carion, N., et al.: End-to-end object detection with transformers. In: European Conference on Computer Vision, pp. 213–229. Springer (2020)
11. Vaswani, A.: Attention is all you need. Advances in Neural Information Processing Systems (2017)

12. LeCun, Y., Bottou, L., Bengio, Y., Haffner, P.: Gradient-based learning applied to document recognition. Proc. IEEE **86**(11), 2278–2324 (1998)
13. Zhu, P., et al.: Detection and tracking meet drones challenge. IEEE Trans. Pattern Anal. Mach. Intell., 1 (2021)
14. Ren, S., He, K., Girshick, R., Sun, J.: Faster r-CNN: towards real-time object detection with region proposal networks. IEEE Trans. Pattern Anal. Mach. Intell. **39**(06), 1137–1149 (2017)
15. Redmon, J., Divvala, S., Girshick, R., Farhadi, A.: You only look once: unified, real-time object detection. In: 2016 IEEE Conference on Computer Vision and Pattern Recognition (CVPR), pp. 779–788 (2016)
16. Redmon, J., Farhadi, A.: YOLO9000: better, faster, stronger. In: 2017 IEEE Conference on Computer Vision and Pattern Recognition (CVPR), pp. 6517–6525 (2017)
17. Wang, C.-Y., Bochkovskiy, A., Yuan, H., Liao, M.: YOLOv7: trainable bag-of-freebies sets new state-of-the-art for real-time object detectors. In: 2023 IEEE/CVF Conference on Computer Vision and Pattern Recognition (CVPR), pp. 7464–7475 (2023)
18. Liu, W., et al.: SSD: single shot multibox detector. In: Leibe, B., Matas, J., Sebe, N., Welling, M. (eds.) ECCV 2016. LNCS, vol. 9905, pp. 21–37. Springer, Cham (2016). https://doi.org/10.1007/978-3-319-46448-0_2
19. Zhu, X., Su, W., Lu, L., Li, B., Wang, X., Dai, J.: Deformable DETR: deformable transformers for end-to-end object detection. arXiv preprint arXiv:2010.04159 (2020)
20. Meng, D., et al.: Conditional DETR for fast training convergence. In: Proceedings of the IEEE/CVF International Conference on Computer Vision, pp. 3651–3660 (2021)
21. Liu, S., et al.: DAB-DETR: dynamic anchor boxes are better queries for DETR. arXiv preprint arXiv:2201.12329 (2022)

Water Quality Inspection System for Mariners Using EKI's Continuous Learning Algorithms

Ngo-Ho Anh-Khoi[1]([✉]), Tran Thanh-Nam[1] [iD], Nguyen Van-Linh[1],
and Nguyen Anh-Duy[2]

[1] Nam Can Tho University, Can Tho, Vietnam
{nhakhoi,ttnam,nguyenvanlinh}@nctu.edu.vn
[2] Adhightech Ltd., Ho Chi Minh City, Vietnam
nguyenanhduy@adhigtechn.com

Abstract. The article addresses the issue of clean water inspection for sailors at sea, highlighting two main limitations: the current clean water dataset is limited, and the classification of clean water is underdeveloped. Public datasets mostly categorize water into two levels—drinkable and non-drinkable—without providing more detailed classifications (different levels of water quality). Developing a more comprehensive dataset will take time, as data will need to be added gradually. Additionally, the dataset outputs will need to be more diverse, with multiple layers and sub-classifications to better represent water quality. To tackle this problem, the article proposes using EKI *(Evolving with Klinkenberg's Idea)* algorithms, which belong to the family of incremental learning methods. These algorithms can be applied to the existing datasets despite their limitations, and with EKI's incremental learning capabilities, the system can adapt to new requirements without needing a complete redesign, such as modifying class structures or adding more classes and sub-classes of water quality levels and categories. The article also compares four different EKI algorithms through experiments and identifies the most effective one, achieving a high level of accuracy in clean water inspection. The system will be converted to an IoT format to establish an electronic circuit for forming a water quality inspection device in the future.

Keywords: Water quality · water quality assessment · mariner tools · EKI Algorithms · water quality classification

1 Introduction

Humans cannot live without clean water; it is not only essential for daily life but also crucial for preventing diseases related to bacterial infections and dehydration. Therefore, ensuring a safe and sustainable water supply is a top priority, requiring innovative solutions and effective management. Currently, water storage systems on ships are complex and pose potential risks to sailors, passengers, and fishermen. Especially during offshore fishing expeditions, the health of fishermen plays a key role in the success and safety of each journey. One of the greatest challenges fishermen face is securing and maintaining clean water throughout their time at sea.

© ICST Institute for Computer Sciences, Social Informatics and Telecommunications Engineering 2025
Published by Springer Nature Switzerland AG 2025. All Rights Reserved
H. X. Huynh et al. (Eds.): GOODTECHS 2024, LNICST 648, pp. 218–230, 2025.
https://doi.org/10.1007/978-3-032-01472-6_17

Many articles have highlighted various risks concerning unclean water quality on ships. These writings also discuss common causes of water contamination. In [1], the following common causes are mentioned: drinking water systems located near hazardous materials such as wastewater and heat sources. Water production processes on ships, like desalination or reverse osmosis, can pose health risks due to pipe corrosion. Since the clean water production and management systems still present many risks, ships that travel extensively and spend long periods at sea often lack specific equipment to automatically and accurately test water quality, leading to potential health hazards. Various methods have been suggested to detect contaminated water, such as observing the color or appearance of the water (cloudy water, foamy water, milky water, etc.), floating particles, crystals, or white sediment. However, some methods, such as tasting and smelling, are still not safe [3].

Today, thanks to continuous technological advancement, artificial intelligence (AI) has become a focal point in science and technology. Some AI integrated solutions and measurement devices are being tested and developed. One project in Quang Nam, Vietnam, researched underground water quality in Hoi An City, aiming to apply machine learning models to forecast and monitor groundwater quality, aiding in effective pollution management. The research used machine learning models such as linear regression (LR), random forests (RF), support vector machines (SVM), k-Nearest Neighbors (KNN), and Cubist to predict groundwater quality. The project's final results were highly successful, with the Cubist model achieving impressive reliability, with R2 scores of 98.8% and 96%, respectively [5]. A creative solution from the Clean Water AI research team helps inspect water quality, released in 2018 to detect dangerous bacteria and harmful particles in water [2]. This method utilizes deep learning with convolutional neural networks (CNN) through the Caffe framework. The dataset used in the study, as mentioned by the research group, includes data files related to fungi and bacteria, which are used to extract images for training and classification to detect bacteria in water sources. Additionally, another notable AI method involves the use of sensor devices to extract water images. This is the research of Akula Rajitha and colleagues [4], combining IoT sensor technology to extract real-time, high-frequency data, which is then processed using integrated AI systems.

The issue of clean water is currently constrained by two main factors: first, the overall dataset for clean water remains limited, and the current goals for clean water quality are still underdeveloped. Specifically, publicly available clean water datasets primarily classify water into two levels (drinkable and non-drinkable) instead of offering more detailed gradations. A more detailed dataset has yet to be developed and may take considerable time to establish, with data being incrementally added step by step. Furthermore, the output of such datasets must inevitably be diversified with additional layers and subcategories. This particular issue in AI is classified as incremental learning and evolving learning. However, all the aforementioned methods are static, meaning they only learn once. This contrasts with the approach discussed in this paper, which focuses on continuous learning, wherein new data is continuously utilized to improve the model.

The paper proposes a solution that applies algorithms based on the EKI *(Evolving with Klinkenberg's Idea)* technique to existing and commonly used datasets, despite certain limitations previously noted. Klinkenberg's EKI method emphasizes using a single parameter 'n', to determine the size of data batches, thereby minimizing the loss of critical information caused by generalization techniques in evolving learning methods.

With EKI and its incremental learning capabilities, the system can seamlessly transition to a new system without requiring redesign (e.g., adjusting class semantics, adding classes, and subcategories). The paper conducts experiments and compares four EKI algorithms, identifying the best-performing algorithm for this issue, achieving high accuracy. The project also aims to develop an automated measuring device, enabling sailors and fishermen to easily carry and test water quality on-site automatically. The goal is to mitigate risks during long sea voyages where access to clean water is extremely limited. This study provides decision-making tools to ensure optimal water quality testing, enhancing health outcomes for sailors in the maritime industry and fishermen on distant fishing expeditions.

2   Research Method

From the perspective of practical application, creating the necessary dataset for the learning and prediction process in the experimental environment of Vietnam, while starting with a reference dataset currently in circulation, poses a challenge. Although the water quality in the common dataset, measured in other countries, may be similar to that in Vietnam, differences may still exist in specific cases. In Vietnam, due to the lack of relevant databases, an immediate predictive system cannot be established. Creating the dataset for this study, which will enable learning and building a prediction system, requires considerable resources, which could take years or even decades to complete.

At present, this solution remains challenging to implement. A more costeffective approach that has been applied in similar cases is the use of continuous learning models. Instead of waiting for a sufficient amount of data to conduct the learning process and build the predictive system, we can use a small amount of data to improve a similar or closely related model. This is done by continuously adjusting its conceptual content through the addition of new, more relevant data, gradually shifting the initial conceptual content (based on the common dataset) towards the new conceptual content (based on Vietnam's dataset). In computer science, this process is called "concept drift", and the model is continuously improved through the addition of new, more accurate data (such as land and crop data from Vietnam). This method allows the predictive system to be used immediately and gradually improved over time, rather than waiting for a long period before an enhanced model becomes available. This study compares the balanced accuracy of four continuous learning algorithms enhanced with the EKI (*Evolving with Klinkenberg's Idea*) technique [12]: EKI-AdaBoost, EKI-GaussianNB, EKI-KNeighbors, and EKI-LDA. The goal is to select the optimal algorithm.

During the investigation of relevant datasets, several datasets were found and reviewed, including the following: Aditya Kadiwal's "Water Quality" dataset, which contains a significant amount of erroneous data (missing or incomplete data in certain rows/columns), negatively affecting future machine learning applications [8]; the "Indian Water Quality Data" by Anbarivan N.L. and Anjali Vasudevan, which contains textual information, making data normalization challenging and rendering it unsuitable for classification algorithms and, therefore, not applicable to the current study [6]; and finally, the "Water Quality" dataset by Mssmarty Pants, which contains 21 columns and over 8,000 rows of data. This dataset is relatively complete and has been widely used for scientific research, making it the chosen dataset for this study [7]. All of the listed datasets pertain to water quality prediction, but only one dataset meets the requirements of this research, as the other datasets present significant issues when applied to this project. The dataset needed to be numeric, with specific classifications and sufficient fields to yield objective results. Only the "Water Quality" dataset by Mssmarty Pants meets these criteria and was therefore selected for this research. The "Water Quality" dataset includes the following characteristics and descriptions:

Aluminium: Present in various sources such as food, water, and cooking utensils, aluminum is harmful to health in high doses, causing damage to bones and tissues. (Range in the dataset: 0 to 5.05).

Ammonia: A colorless gas with a pungent odor (NH3), ammonia is not highly toxic to humans but can transform into carcinogens in water at high concentrations. (Range in the dataset: 0 to 29.84).

Arsenic: A highly toxic compound, even small amounts of arsenic in water can be lethal. According to WHO data, arsenic levels higher than 0.01 mg/l can be deadly. (Range in the dataset: 0 to 1.05).

Barium: A pollutant found in some water treatment systems that remains under-researched for its environmental and health impacts. (Range in the dataset: 0 to 4.94).

Cadmium: One of the most dangerous metals for human health, frequent consumption of cadmiumcontaminated water increases cancer risks. (Range in the dataset: 0 to 0.13).

Chloramine: Known for its unpleasant odor, high chlorine residue levels in water can have adverse health effects. (Range in the dataset: 0 to 8.68).

Chromium: A heavy metal that can cause cancer if ingested in significant amounts. (Range in the dataset: 0 to 0.9).

Copper: Found in water, copper must be kept below 2 mg/l to prevent health issues such as neurological damage. (Range in the dataset: 0 to 2).

Fluorine: Excessive fluorine intake can affect bones and joints, increasing the risk of bone cancer and thyroid issues. (Range in the dataset: 0 to 1.5).

Bacteria: Microorganisms present in contaminated water can cause severe illnesses, such as diarrhea and fever. (Range in the dataset: 0 to 1).

Viruses: Similar to bacteria, but with potentially more dangerous health consequences. (Range in the dataset: 0 to 1).

Lead: Commonly found in water due to pipe corrosion or industrial waste, lead contamination must remain below 0.01 mg/l for safety. (Range in the dataset: 0 to 0.2).

Nitrates: High levels of nitrates in boiled water can form nitrosamines, which increase cancer risks. (Range in the dataset: 0 to 19.83).

Nitrites: Similar to nitrates, nitrites in boiled water pose a serious health risk. (Range in the dataset: 0 to 2.93).

Mercury: A small amount of mercury exposure can cause significant health problems, including developmental issues in infants and neurological damage. (Range in the dataset: 0 to 0.01).

Perchlorate: A strong oxidizer used in rocket fuel and fireworks, perchlorate contamination in water is a significant health concern. (Range in the dataset: 0 to 60.01).

Radium: Present in groundwater as radium226 and radium228, longterm ingestion can increase the risk of bone cancer. (Range in the dataset: 0 to 7.99).

Selenium: Essential in small amounts, excessive selenium intake can lead to toxicity, causing symptoms like hair loss and mood instability. (Range in the dataset: 0 to 0.1).

Silver: Silver nanoparticles can weaken the immune system and increase the risk of severe illnesses like Alzheimer's and cancer. (Range in the dataset: 0 to 0.5).

Uranium: Naturally occurring in groundwater, uranium contamination poses significant health risks due to its radioactive properties. (Range in the dataset: 0 to 0.09).

From a practical application perspective, one challenge is that the dataset used for learning and prediction will be a commonly circulated dataset. Although most water sources share similar characteristics, there will inevitably be slight variations in close cases. In Vietnam, there is currently no available database on this issue, making it impossible to implement a prediction system right away. Creating a dataset specifically for this topic would be very costly, not only in terms of effort and money but also in time, which could take several years or even decades. This solution is almost impossible at present. A more affordable alternative, which has been used in similar cases, is continuous learning [12]. Instead of waiting for a large enough dataset to perform learning and build the prediction system, small data packages can be used to incrementally improve the model by adjusting the concept's internal representation, gradually pushing the initial concept (from the common dataset) closer to the new concept (Vietnam's dataset) continuously, allowing the system to be used immediately without waiting. This transformation of the internal concept is known as "concept drift". The model will be continuously improved, or more accurately, continuously adjusted thanks to the addition of more accurate data (data from Vietnam's soil and crops). This idea allows the prediction system to be used right away and gradually improves from the small differences in the model, rather than having to wait a long time before the model can be fully utilized.

From a machine learning standpoint, a significant challenge with current datasets is that traditional data tends to remain static over time, requiring a complete retraining whenever new data is introduced. Classical algorithms require full retraining with every new dataset addition, which is inefficient in dynamic real-world environments, such as cases where real-world data has not yet arrived (data that shares characteristics with the current dataset), while the existing data is sufficient to perform the task. Instead of waiting for real-world data to accumulate fully, and considering that the current data is not significantly different from the real-world data, continuous learning algorithms can be employed to gradually improve the model in real-time as the real-world data arrives.

Modern practice demands continuous real-time training to update prediction models effectively, leading to extensive research in continuous learning methods, also known by similar terms like incremental learning and evolving learning. Continuous learning methods have been extensively studied and analyzed in [10]. One of the simplest methods is the sliding window technique, which has been applied to many classical algorithms to facilitate continuous learning [13]. This method continuously updates the model at each time step 't' by using the most recent training data within a predefined window size 's'. The window size 's' can be based on time or the number of data points and often overlaps with the previous window 'w'. In each iteration, a new model is trained, reflecting an updated set of classes. The basic model of the sliding window is illustrated below:

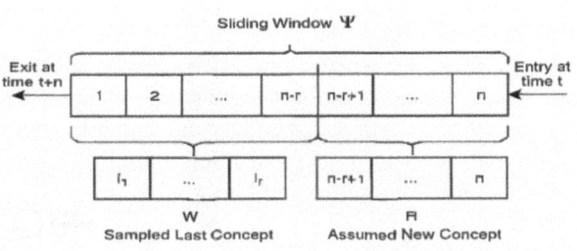

Fig. 1. The Operating Model of the Sliding Window Technique. Source: Adapted from Raab's research [16].

Choosing the optimal window size is critical, with some methods automatically determining the best size based on accuracy metrics [14, 15]. This study aims to explore methods for determining window size based on Klinkenberg's idea of finding the best window size 's' in different classical problems [11]. The core idea is to manage information loss by adjusting the learning data density within the optimally chosen window size. Implementing Klinkenberg's methods involves using a single parameter, 'n', to determine the batch size, thus controlling the loss of vital information from generalization techniques used in evolving learning methods. This research applied EKI- algorithms, so called Evolving with Klinkenberg's Idea (EKI) [12, 17]: EKI-AdaBoost, EKI-GaussianNB, EKI- Kneighbors, and EKI-LDA. These algorithms apply Klinkenberg's concept combined with the sliding window technique to enhance classical methods, transforming them into approaches capable of continuous learning.

3 Experimental Results

The dataset used in this experiment consists of two parts: a training dataset comprising 5,600 records (70% of the original data) and a test dataset containing 2,400 records (30% of the original data). The location of these records changes with each experiment, and the data is randomly shuffled each time, then reshuffled after training.

The experiment is conducted using an offline batch learning model (batch size = 699), meaning the system must perform 699 steps (Batch 699), with each step consisting of about 129 records. The model used in the experiment segments the dataset into smaller groups over 35 steps, meaning each data packet contains 129 records. This number is manageable for experimentation. At each step, the system calculates the balanced accuracy metrics for the results.

Traditional accuracy measures the ratio of correctly classified cases to the total, and while generally reliable, this metric can be misleading in cases of severe class imbalance, such as a 90:10 ratio. For instance, if 100 cases are tested, 99 of which are diseased and 1 healthy, the accuracy may appear high even if no meaningful model is present. Therefore, for imbalanced datasets, Balanced Accuracy (BA) is used.

The choice of evaluation metrics depends on the problem's objectives and the dataset's composition. In cases of significant class imbalance, where one class is under-represented, traditional accuracy becomes unreliable. Hence, metrics like the Area Under the ROC Curve (AUC) and BA are preferred. Metrics like balanced accuracy, sensitivity, and specificity are less effective for imbalanced data. For detecting consensus, metrics based on the true positive rate/false positive rate, such as balanced accuracy, sensitivity, and FScore, are appropriate. Conversely, for detecting dissent, metrics based on the true negative rate/false negative rate, such as specificity, are suitable, though less common in practice. Sensitivity, balanced accuracy, and FScore are criticized for ignoring the true negative cell of the confusion matrix and being prone to predictive bias [9]. BA, which includes both the true positive rate and the true negative rate, provides a balanced assessment, making it suitable for both consensus detection and imbalanced data scenarios [10]. BA is a crucial and simple metric for evaluating binary classifiers in class imbalance contexts, where one class is much more prevalent than the other. Balance Accuracy inherently adjusts weights to address imbalance, so there is no need to add additional weights. The formula for Balanced Accuracy (BA), providing a practical and optimal evaluation, is:

Balanced Accuracy (BA) $= \frac{1}{2}$ *(Specificity + Sensitivity)*.

By applying the four new continuous learning algorithms (EKI-AdaBoost, EKI-GaussianNB, EKI- KNeighbors, EKI- LDA) that incorporate Klinkenberg's idea and the sliding window technique, this method ensures fairness in the balanced accuracy of the data when comparing results from different algorithms. The average experimental results of these algorithms are shown in the graph below (Fig. 2).

Among the algorithms, the EKI-AdaBoost model demonstrated the highest average performance, with a BA rate of 82.96%. This shows that the EKI-AdaBoost model has good generalization capabilities. The EKI-LDA model ranked second with an average of 74.15%, which still performs well and stably, making it a viable option under suitable conditions. The other two models, EKI-GaussianNB, achieved an average performance of 66.72%, showing consistency but not superiority. Meanwhile, the EKI-Kneighbors model had the lowest average rate of 61.59%, indicating instability and unsuitability for the current dataset (Table 1).

When comparing the two highest-performing models, EKI-AdaBoost and EKI-LDA, the difference is insignificant, with a 10.76% advantage for EKI-AdaBoost. The EKI-AdaBoost model achieved a BA rate of 82.96%, outperforming EKI-LDA, which had a BA rate of 74.15%. Both models demonstrate high applicability potential, but EKI-AdaBoost still edges out in delivering more stable and better results. Therefore, although EKI-LDA is a viable option, EKI-AdaBoost remains the more optimal solution for this problem.

In terms of the final batch rate, EKI-AdaBoost stands out with a rate of 84.32%, surpassing EKI-LDA at 74.68%, creating a 9.64% difference. The other algorithms did

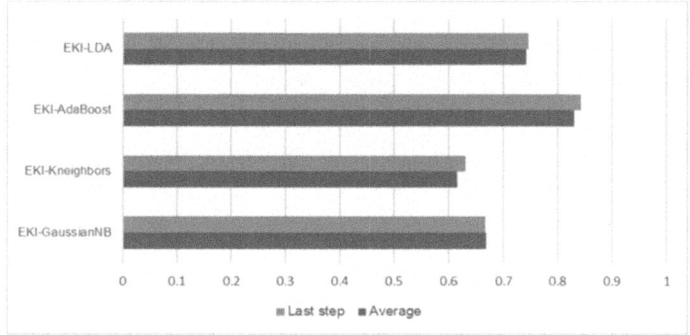

Fig. 2. Average Balanced Accuracy and Final Batch Balanced Accuracy of the EKI-Algorithms

Table 1. Average Balanced Accuracy and Last step's Balanced Accuracy of the EKI Algorithms

EKI- Algorithms	Average Balanced Accuracy (%)	Final Batch Balanced Accuracy (%)	Standard Deviation (%)
EKI- GaussianNB	66.72	66.68	0.76
EKI- LDA	74.15	74.68	1.79
EKI- Kneighbors	61.59	62.99	1.49
EKI- AdaBoost	82.96	84.32	4.08
EKI- GaussianNB	66.72	66.68	0.76

not show significant differences, with only small deviations between average results and final batch results. Notably, EKI-KNeighbors achieved 62.99% in the final batch, lower than EKI-GaussianNB, which had a rate of 66.68%, resulting in a 3.69% difference. In the final batch results, EKI-AdaBoost consistently demonstrated superior performance, affirming its top position for this task. Thus, when comparing final batch results, EKI-AdaBoost clearly emerges as the most effective algorithm, surpassing the others and proving its suitability for this specific application (See Fig. 1).

Besides averaging the algorithms' results, another approach is to compare the experimental model results according to 'n' to illustrate the progress in balanced accuracy. This method provides a more comprehensive and detailed overview, allowing for a more precise evaluation of the experimental model's outcomes. The results of the balanced accuracy progress are illustrated in the chart below.

Among the four algorithms compared by the incremental learning method, EKI-AdaBoost maintained the highest accuracy rate throughout the process, starting at a relatively high level and steadily increasing, reaching nearly 85% by the final stage. This demonstrates that EKI-AdaBoost is the most effective algorithm in the group. EKI-LDA, which started with a lower accuracy rate than AdaBoost but still outperformed the other algorithms, remained stable around 74% throughout, showing consistency and stable performance. Meanwhile, EKI-GaussianNB also maintained a steady accuracy rate of around 67% after an initial rapid increase, though it did not reach the levels of

AdaBoost or LDA, it still showed stability after the first few steps. In contrast, EKI-KNeighbors had the lowest accuracy rate in the group, hovering around 60%, reflecting weaker performance compared to the other algorithms. In summary, EKI-AdaBoost was the best-performing algorithm with the highest and steadily increasing accuracy over time. EKI-LDA also performed well, maintaining stability throughout, while EKI-KNeighbors had the lowest performance, and EKI-GaussianNB achieved an average but stable performance (Fig. 3).

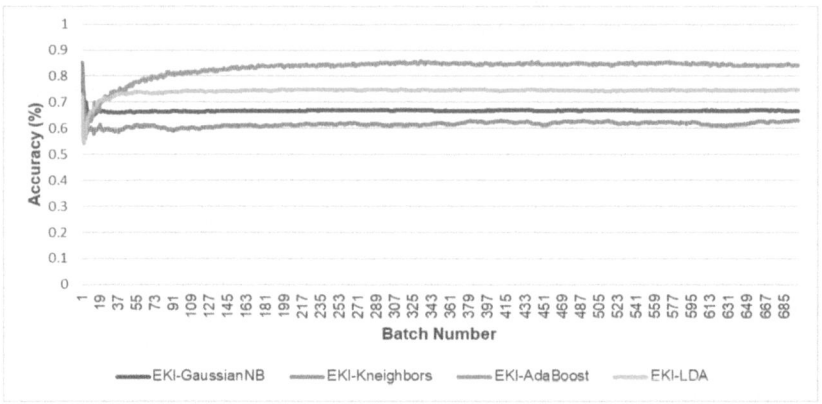

Fig. 3. Balanced Accuracy Progress Chart of the EKI-Algorithms

Based on the analysis results, EKI-AdaBoost outperforms the other algorithms in terms of performance, maintaining the highest and most stable accuracy over time. The AdaBoost algorithm offers several strengths when applied to classification problems, particularly in improving accuracy and model performance. One of EKI-AdaBoost's most notable advantages is its ability to combine multiple weak learners, typically simple decision trees, to form a strong learner. This enables the model to effectively learn from

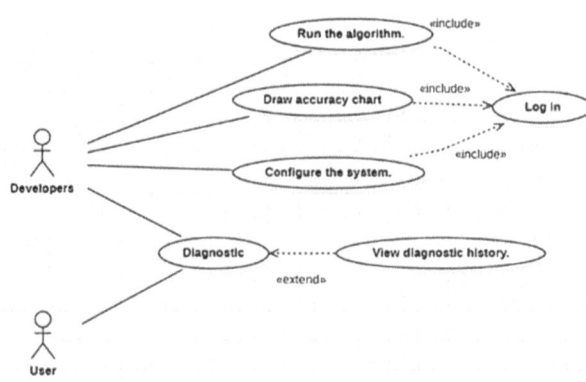

Fig. 4. Use-case Diagram of the System

complex or imbalanced datasets. Moreover, AdaBoost incorporates an automatic weight adjustment mechanism for data samples, focusing more on hard-to-classify samples in each iteration. As a result, the algorithm continuously improves its learning capability and reduces errors during training. With an increasing number of iterations, EKI-AdaBoost's performance gradually enhances, making it more robust and stable compared to other classification algorithms such as EKI-GaussianNB, EKI-KNeighbors, or EKI-LDA.

Table 2. Hardware Specifications for the Water Quality Testing Device

Specification	Details
CPU	Quad-core Cortex-A72 (64-bit) running at 1.5GHz
GPU	Supports H264 (1080p60 decode, 1080p30 encode), OpenGL ES 3.0 graphics, H.265 (4kp60 decode)
RAM	Supports up to 4GB
Operating Voltage	5V with a minimum current of 3A
GPIO Ports	28 I/O pins
LAN	Available
PoE	Supported
WIFI	Available
Bluetooth	Version 5.0
HDMI	2 HDMI ports supporting 4k displays (mini-HDMI)
Power Supply	Supports DC power jack or mini USB-C port
Expansion Connectivity	40 pins (supports SPI, I2C, LCD, UART, PWM, SDIO)
USB	2 USB 2.0 ports and 2 USB 3.0 ports
Camera	supported via CSI interface
Operating Temperature	From 0 to 50 degrees Celsius
Display	XPT2046 Touch Controller 480x320px

Additionally, EKI-AdaBoost has the advantage of requiring minimal parameter tuning and can adapt well to both binary and multiclass classification problems. Notably, this algorithm is less prone to overfitting when applied to large datasets due to the strong generalization capability of the combined model. With a small dataset, EKI-AdaBoost remains efficient and stable, ensuring high classification accuracy. These characteristics make EKI-AdaBoost an effective choice for classification problems that demand high accuracy and consistent results. Making it the preferred choice for tasks that require high accuracy and consistency during execution. This algorithm is also applied in the design of an automated water quality inspection system using artificial intelligence.

4   Conclusion

The study addressed the deployment challenges by adopting the *Continuous Machine Learning* model to tackle the issue of dataset creation for the environmental conditions in Vietnam. From a practical application perspective, building a specific dataset tailored to Vietnam's environment is crucial for training and prediction processes. However, starting with a reference dataset from shared global databases poses significant challenges. While there are similarities in the collected water quality data, differences may still exist in specific cases. In Vietnam, since there is no related dataset available, building a prediction system immediately is not feasible. Creating a dataset for this topic to conduct learning and build a prediction system requires considerable resources, including time and costs that could span several years or even decades. Currently, this solution is quite difficult to implement.

At present, a more efficient and cost-effective solution has been implemented by employing the continuous learning method. Instead of waiting for a large volume of data to develop and train the system, it is possible to start with a small dataset to gradually improve an existing and relatively suitable model. By continuously adding new and more relevant data, the system incrementally adjusts its initial conceptual framework (based on shared datasets) toward new concepts that align more closely with Vietnam's specific data. In computer science, this process is referred to as "concept drift", which allows the model to be continuously refined as it incorporates increasingly accurate data (e.g., soil and water quality data from Vietnam). This approach enables the prediction system to be utilized immediately while being iteratively improved over time through corrections of minor errors, rather than waiting for an extended period to develop a fully refined model.

Based on the results presented in the previous section, the final algorithm chosen to address the problem is the EKI-AdaBoost algorithm. The project will include functional nodes such as prediction functions, running classical algorithms, a list of processed models, system configuration, and login. It will be deployed in a website environment, divided into two main functions: an algorithm installer (administrator or developer) and a diagnostician (user), as shown in the Usecase diagram below (Fig. 4). The system will be converted to an IoT format to establish an electronic circuit for forming a water quality inspection device in the future.

To develop the system into an IoT device, a cost analysis of sensor devices, as mentioned in [19], has been conducted. It is evident that sensor devices can cost as much as $500.00. However, the cost and price can vary depending on the country and its stage of development. Currently, the market offers various options based on user needs. Below is a compiled list of devices currently available on the market for a cost-benefit analysis:

- Water quality tester meter AE86061 Dissolved oxygen PH nitrite ammonia nitrogen - $280
- Hanna HI98194 - 36,915,000đ ~ $1,456.45
- HORIBA WQ-310P-S - $1,644.92
- EUTECH Cyberscan PCD650 set - 95,158,800đ ~ $3,745.78
- Portable Water Quality Analyzer D.O Tester Fluorescent Dissolved Oxygen Meter - $705.00

The research team recognized that although advanced water quality measuring devices are available at prices reaching thousands of USD, this approach is not suitable for the goal of achieving cost-effective and feasible solutions for countries with middle and low incomes. Therefore, the research team conducted testing and filtering to select commonly available and reasonably priced devices, such as the Raspberry Pi board (only around 70–100 USD). To further clarify hardware requirements, technical specifications will be presented in Table 2.

The results of the research and implementation of artificial intelligence algorithms show that designing a handheld device using AI technology to assess clean water for seafarers is essential and highly applicable. Given the challenges sea-farers face in storing water over long voyages, which can lead to compromised water quality and health risks, the introduction of this device will significantly enhance water quality monitoring and ensure better health safety.

This study not only introduces the methods and data used but also clearly presents the experimental results and the application of the concept drift model alongside related algorithms. The application of AI for clean water inspection on ships is not just an advanced technological solution but also a crucial step toward protecting the health of seafarers under the harsh conditions of the sea.

References

1. S4S.: Ensuring drinking water quality on board. Official page of Safety For Sea (2018). https://safety4sea.com/cmensuringdrinkingwaterqualityonboard/
2. Peter, M., Shenk, J., Hong, S.A., Han, S.: Clean Water AI. Official page of Hackster (2018). https://www.hackster.io/cleanwaterai/cleanwateraie40806
3. Alameda County Water District: water quality self diagnostic tool (2024). https://www.acwd.org/167/WaterQualitySelfDiagnosticTool
4. Akula, R., et al.: Machine learning and AI driven water quality monitoring and treatment. E3S Web Conf. **505**, 03012 (2024). https://doi.org/10.1051/e3sconf/202450503012
5. Le, P.C., Ngo, V.T.: Application of machine learning models in underground water prediction: a case study in Hoian City, Quangnam Province. B2022DNA04 (2022)
6. Ramakrishnan, V.: India Water Quality Data (2016). https://www.kaggle.com/datasets/venkatramakrishnan/indiawaterqualitydata
7. MsSmartyPants: Water quality (2021). https://www.kaggle.com/datasets/mssmartypants/water-quality
8. Kadiwal, A.: Water Quality (2021). https://www.kaggle.com/datasets/adityakadiwal/water-potability
9. Powers, D.M.: Evaluation: from precision, recall and Fmeasure to ROC, informedness, markedness and correlation. arXiv preprint arXiv:2010.16061 (2020)
10. Ho, N., Khoi, A.: Méthodes de classifications dynamiques et incrémentales: application à la numérisation cognitive d'images de documents, Doctoral dissertation, Tours (2015)
11. Klinkenberg, R.: Learning drifting concepts: example selection vs. example weighting, special issue on incremental learning systems capable of dealing with concept drift. Intell. Data Anal. **8**(3), 281–300 (2004)
12. Ngo H.A.-K., Pham V.-T., Trinh T.-L., Tran, V.-T.: Evolving with Klinkenberg's idea (EKI) algorithms for automatic identification of Sa Huynh antique glass artifacts. In: The 13th Conference on Information Technology and Its Applications (CITA 2024) (2024)

13. Bifet A., Gavalda R.: Learning from TimeChanging data with adaptive windowing. SDM, 443–448 (2007)
14. Lazarescu, M., Venkatesh, S., Bui, H.: Using multiple windows to track concept drift. Intell. Data Anal. **8**(1), 29–59 (2003)
15. Last, M.: Online classification of nonstationary data streams. Intell. Data Anal. **6**(2), 129–147 (2002)
16. Raab, C., Heusinger, M., Schleif, F.M.: Reactive soft prototype computing for concept drift streams. Neurocomputing **416**, 340–351 (2020). https://doi.org/10.1016/j.neucom.2019.11.111
17. Ngo, H.A.-K., Vo, K.-D., Nguyen, A.-D., Ngo, H.A.K.: Optimizing botanical farm crop variety selection: integration of machine learning mechanisms for green technology and sustainable solutions. In: The 2nd Conference on Sustainability and Emerging Technology (CSET 2024), Vietnam (2024)
18. Ngo, H.A.K., Nguyen, V.-L., Vo, K.-D., Nguyen, A.-D.: Building an optimal crop variety system using continuous learning methods with Eki Technology. In: The 9th Information and Communication Technology Conference 2024 (ICT 2024), Vietnam (2024)
19. de Camargo, E.T., et al.: Low-cost water quality sensors for IoT: a systematic review. Sensors **23**(9), 4424 (2023). https://doi.org/10.3390/s23094424

Author Index

The manufacturer's authorised representative in the EU is Springer
Nature Customer Service Centre GmbH, Europaplatz 3, 69115 Heidelberg,
Germany. If you have any concerns regarding our products, please
contact ProductSafety@springernature.com

Printed and bound by CPI Group (UK) Ltd, Croydon, CR0 4YY
29/04/2026
02099461-0009